D0175913

THE
KNOT OF TIME

LINDSAY RIVER AND SALLY GILLESPIE

THE
KNOT OF TIME

ASTROLOGY AND THE FEMALE EXPERIENCE

ILLUSTRATED BY SARAH McDONAGH

PERENNIAL LIBRARY

Harper & Row, Publishers, New York
Cambridge, Philadelphia, San Francisco, London
Mexico City, São Paulo, Singapore, Sydney

A hardcover edition of this book was published in 1987 by Harper & Row, Publishers.

THE KNOT OF TIME. Copyright © 1987 by Lindsay River and Sally Gillespie. Illustrations copyright © 1987 by Sarah McDonagh. All rights reserved. Printed in the United States of America. No part of this book may be used or reproduced in any manner whatsoever without written permission except in the case of brief quotations embodied in critical articles and reviews. For information address Harper & Row, Publishers, Inc., 10 East 53rd Street, New York, N.Y. 10022. Published simultaneously in Canada by Fitzhenry & Whiteside Limited, Toronto.

First PERENNIAL LIBRARY edition published 1989.

Library of Congress Cataloging-in-Publication Data

River, Lindsay.
   The knot of time.

   "Perennial Library."

   Reprint. Originally published: London : Women's Press, 1987.
   Includes index.
   1. Astrology. 2. Women—Psychology—Miscellanea. I. Gillespie, Sally. II. Title.
BF1729.W64R58   1989   133.5'088042   87-45657
ISBN 0-06-091555-2 (pbk.)

89 90 91 92 93 FG 10 9 8 7 6 5 4 3 2 1

For Marie, who led me to the volcano,
for the woman who taught me the language of the birds,
for Poulaki, who showed me how they fly,
for Jenjoy, who put into my hand the golden thread that leads
to the knot of time . . .

LR

. . . and for Leonie and her heavenly questions.

SG

Contents

Authors' Note

This book has been written for women, and for men who honour womanhood and female experience. We have generally used the female pronoun to include both men and women, just as the child of each sex was once enclosed within the female form.

We have learned our astrology from the histories of many cultures, few of them Christian. The abbreviation BCE (Before the Christian Era) is used in this book instead of the more familiar BC (Before Christ) and CE (Christian Era) is used instead of AD (Anno Domini).

When writing about the ancient world in which astrology originated the choice of geographical terminology raises various difficulties. For greater accuracy we have used terms defined by archaeologists, such as Old Europe (an area far smaller than the continent of Europe, which includes most of modern Yugoslavia, Hungary, Rumania, Bulgaria and Greece) and the Ancient Near East (which includes, for our purposes, sites in Asia Minor, Mesopotamia, The Levant, The Aegean, Mediterranean Africa and Egypt). While it does not often seem appropriate to use modern geographical terms for the ancient world (for the present day national boundaries did not apply) the use of the archaeological terms can sometimes be confusing and serve to obscure the connections between ancient cultures and the people who live in the same areas today. Where we have felt that it made sense historically we have used more modern terms to emphasise these connections.

We have given examples of famous women to show how they have expressed the signs of the zodiac that are prominent in their charts. Sadly, our examples are necessarily drawn only from those women for whom we could find full birthdates, which biographers do not always record. Many women of achievement, born in obscurity, poverty,

slavery, or for whom we have only limited biographical material accessible, have had to be omitted.

When we speak of 'relationships' we do not automatically assume these to be between those of opposite sexes, or between those of the same sex; we do not assume them necessarily to be sexual relationships or non-sexual. We write for a time when the quality and depth of the interaction will define a relationship; we write for the Age of Aquarius.

At the knot of time where there is no time
where the strands of past present and future meet
at the hub of the wheel that encircles the universe
at the navel of the world, the Omphalos,
at the womb of the world, Delphi,
at Byblos,
Gizeh,
Jerusalem,
Mecca,
Chidambaram,
Benares,
Mount Meru,
Uluru,
Cuzco,
Black Mesa,
Uisnech,
Pumlumon,
Glastonbury,
Ife,
Kariba,
at the centre of the world
in the caves which are the dark cleft of the Mother
sit the old wisewomen
the sibyls
the grandmothers
who understand the oracle
who guard the wisdom
who bring it forth into day.

Prologue

In the beginning there was only one Being. Without name, without shape, without limits, without beginning or end, being the eternal substance and the eternal void. In time (although there was no time) she became aware of her self, and of vague patterns of light and dark. She conceived a desire to know her self, to see what she was.

She saw the vastness of space and galaxies forming and dying. She watched nebulae exploding; she felt the incandescence inside the stars; she was aware of dark absences in space. She saw stars that encircled each other, planets encircling stars, moons encircling planets. She saw meteorites, asteroids and comets moving through space. She saw one spiral galaxy, and on its outer arm she watched a particular star, encircled by planets.

She watched one planet as it cooled and she saw a Moon moving around it. She watched the Moon set and the Sun rise. She gazed at her self that was revealed in the light of the Sun. She saw mountains and valleys, rivers and seas, islands and continents. She listened and heard the sounds of water, of the wind, and of animals and birds moving about and calling to each other. She felt the heat of the desert and the cold of the glacier, the roughness of rock and the softness of moss. She smelled flowers, she smelled the sea and she smelled the sulphurous gas escaped from volcanoes. She tasted salt and honey and bitter herbs.

She wondered what she would do with this beauty and variety, and her wondering led into a long dream. She dreamed there was another with her, whose spirit matched hers and in whose eyes she saw reflected her own power and beauty. She cried out with love and recognition, and her cry was the sound of the first of her birth pains. With pain and with joy she gave birth to her first two children, a girl and a boy.

As she suckled her children she knew she must name them, and she looked to the sky around her. The Sun, the Moon and eight shining planets were gathered in the eastern part of the sky, and this would never happen again until the day of a new creation. The planet Mars was just rising and she dedicated her children to this planet and named them both by a name we cannot know, but which in our day we call *Aries*.

She kept the children with her while aeons passed and then she dreamed again.

She awoke with the great conjunction in *Taurus*, and her children *Taurus* were born under the planet Venus. This happened ten more times so that she bore twelve pairs of twins. Each pair was named for a part of the great star wheel that turned in the sky.

As they grew up in a fertile valley, the young girls naturally formed a circle together and the boys another. Their mother was not always with them, but she told them that each circle had important discoveries to make. As they grew older she was increasingly absent and only visited them once in a while.

The story of the boys has been written, but is incomplete. The story of the girls has been told, but has been forgotten. It is of their story that we will start to tell.

Each sister was equally beautiful and equally creative. When they were old enough to go where they would go and do what they would do, their mother called them together and asked them to make their choices.

'Earth is now full with other creatures,' she told them. 'There are people who look like you and your brothers, but their lives are much shorter. Unlike you they were born when the planets made complex patterns in the sky. Never again will it happen that a child is born all *Aries* or all *Pisces*. Yet each one has the ways of one or two signs strong within her or him, and so they remind me of you and your brothers. Now, I would like to know what your choices are, whether you will go out into the world or stay here in this valley, and what direction you would like your lives to take.'

Three of the young women stood up. They were *Aries*, *Leo* and *Sagittarius*. They said they would build a great fire that could be seen night and day, and that they would tend the fire and look at the shapes in its flames.

Aries said, 'I shall take fire to all who want it so that new life may

start for all creatures, because I love beginnings. I love to be active and to initiate. I have fallen in love with life itself. Again and again I shall leap from the dark into an unknown light. I shall confront whatever I meet on my path, for I love to express my vigour. My enthusiasm gives me the power to cut through all obstacles. I shall travel by the most direct path, for I am driven onward towards life by my inspiration.'

Leo said, 'I shall tend the great fire for I feel in my own heart a fire burning: it is the love I have for the world, and my joy in life. By the light of the great fire I shall tell stories; I shall dance and sing; I shall drum; I am exhilarated by creation. I shall send my creation into the furthest shadows of darkness like the pulse that follows the heartbeat, to drum the joy of the fire, to dance the heart, to sing life.'

Sagittarius said, 'I shall wander far and wide, considering the vastness, and rejoice in it. I shall wander over plains and steppes and I shall visit the fires that are lit all over the earth; I shall study the ways of the different peoples. I shall search for the wisdom that illuminates their customs, the flame behind the flame. I shall carry fire to brighten the darkness between, because I have the power to warm myself and others with my belief.'

The Fire sisters set off together, full of enthusiasm.

Three more stood up. They were *Taurus*, *Virgo* and *Capricorn*. 'We want to stay close to the land', they said, 'and experience through the senses the changes the Earth undergoes.'

Taurus said, 'I shall never tire of the valley. I shall find out what I love and what displeases me; I shall also know the value of everything that I contact. I shall be aware of my own body in every part, and of the body of the Earth. I shall wriggle my toes in the sticky clay and feel it squelch deliciously around my feet, then I shall feel the stream tingling over my toes as the clay dissolves. I shall collect clay and gather mosses, and by feeling their textures I shall start to create for myself the beauty that is in the Earth.'

Virgo said, 'I want to understand every flower, and to know the nature of every animal, every fish, every bird. I shall watch them so that I can learn how best we should eat, and how to heal ourselves when we are sick, for they know these things. I shall have practical help to give, a splint for the bird's broken wing, and I shall tie back the bush that overshadows the small plants. I shall be the friend of the nature spirits. I love the natural order of the created world which gives me clarity.'

Capricorn said, 'I have been touched by fascination for what's difficult. I shall go out into the desert and into the craggy heights of the wilderness. There I shall learn to build myself a shelter from the Sun's rays, for my teacher is the real and the necessary. I love to discover my strength, my patience and my endurance. And as hardship becomes my friend I shall always find another challenge ahead of me, for I am the creator of the means to survive.'

And so the Earth sisters committed themselves to keeping their feet on the ground they loved.

Three more sisters then stood up. They were *Gemini*, *Libra* and *Aquarius*. They said: 'We want to go where we can feel the breeze and the strong winds. We will go higher in the hills and live with the creatures of air.'

Gemini said, 'I shall fly like the bee and the butterfly to taste each flower, to drink the variety of their colours, for I rejoice in the ever-changing moment. On the hillside I shall seek a place where I can think most clearly in the sharp air of morning; I shall pursue my desire to know, for I am enchanted by ideas and exhilarated by the use of my mind. I love to make connections and to shape word-pictures; I shall tell my stories to the birds and learn from them to speak their language.'

Libra said, 'I shall build a temple on the mountain in the clear air. It will be perfectly beautiful and I shall place there everything that pleases me most. Yet it will not be overfull, for each object will be chosen after long thought. It will be a place where balance can be found, a place to find harmony. My body resonates with the sounds of stillness, of beauty, of perfection in form, and I want to share these with you. You may come to my temple to find peace with each other and to end disputes, for no discord will remain there. It will be a place for love.'

Aquarius said, 'I shall ponder the uniqueness and eccentricity of the mountain flowers, for I love the beauty of the strange and the rare. I shall delight in my own strangeness, my difference from my sisters, and I shall send my thoughts out to all the people of Earth who feel themselves outsiders, and I shall hold fast to our common experience, our equality. I shall watch the storm from a height and the lightning flash will light up for me possibilities as yet unknown. Because I love the future and I love to discover what is beyond our present imagination.'

And so the Air sisters went up the mountain where the air flowed freely about them.

Then the three Water sisters stood up. They said: 'We will go to the places where water flows and where there are depths.'

Cancer said, 'I will find a beach where the the tide is gentle and where there is sun and shade. Sometimes I shall venture forth on the tide, but I shall always return to my own harbour. I shall live in a cave and for me it will be a nurturing place. You may come there to give birth, or when you are sick, whenever you seek the safe darkness to lick your wounds. When I am in my boat I shall learn from the sea how to touch the past; I shall watch the Moon and learn sensitivity from the tide's response to her. Because I love the depth of imagination and I love to take care of all that is vulnerable and defenceless.'

Scorpio said, 'I shall walk along the cliffs and watch the rough surf; I shall delight in the high tide at full Moon. I shall feel that intensity and it will match my own. I shall follow the river to its underground source, and there I shall think long and deep about the mysteries of birth and death and the power of sexual love, of who we are and our meaning. Why do the plants grow up each year and later lose their leaves or die away? I shall wonder these things and I shall find my answers through my own experience. For there is nothing that I fear except myself, and that, too, I have the courage to face.'

Pisces said, 'I shall find a quiet pool in the forest and I shall be alone there often. I shall gaze into the deep, still water and that stillness will be in me. I shall sleep by my pool and dream, and I shall leave you messages in oracles and poems. Or you may dream with me (for you are as much myself as I am you and your dreams are also my dreams). You may join me and wait through the night till the animals come to drink. Then I will show you shape-changing and we will become the animals. My magic can heal, for it comes from the place where there is no separation and we are all one, where the water of the pool merges again and is lost in the ocean.'

And so the Water sisters went together to find the deep places they needed.

The sisters each followed their chosen paths and were happy in them. Those who travelled sometimes met their brothers, also on journeys of discovery; those who stayed at home saw them in the valley. They asked their mother why they had formed themselves into two circles instead of one large one.

'It is important', she said, 'that you discover how to make the complete circle yourselves, and for your brothers to discover it too. Were

you always together you might divide the circle in two, your brothers forming one half of it and you the other. All of you would lose by this division. But if you discover a true desire to work with your brothers and they with you, there is nothing that can stop you.'

They were satisfied with this answer, but asked her about humankind and the tension they had started to sense between the women and men of the Earth.

Their mother paused. 'I will not tell you everything I know. You can discover much by listening to each other. Trust me that human beings will not always stay as they are now. Their meeting with you and with your brothers will be one of the ways they will discover their true selves, though it will not be the only way. Now they are watching the sky at night. Soon they will find out that the planets move amongst the pattern of the stars. They will name the parts of the sky with different names according to the tongues they speak, for the discovery will come in many places and in many different ways. But whatever sound and whatever picture they choose they will be invoking your names. A new cycle of your relationship with humankind is beginning. You will not see me often but you can learn from me by listening to each other, and by remembering that the circle is whole and that no part is greater than another.'

1
Patterns of Possibility
Astrology as an Art of Self-Understanding

As Above, So Below

Astrology is the study of the planets and stars and their interrelationships with life on earth. As a science it evolved at a time when everything that happened was thought to be interconnected and significant. Life on earth was seen as a mirror of the order in the heavens: 'as above, so below'. This feeling of interconnectedness, however, has been lost by the majority of people living in industrialised societies.

Our planet faces a crisis that has come from the loss of that awareness, and from the specialisation of different branches of knowledge. It is a situation where the left hand does not know what the right hand is doing. The scientist, the manufacturer and the politician have increasingly pursued their objectives without being aware of the far-reaching effects of their work.

The word 'crisis' comes from the Greek and means 'a time for decision'.[1] As we make decisions about the ways we can best protect the Earth and her creatures, and ensure our own survival, it is useful to turn to the old philosophies that were based on a sense of interconnectedness.

Essentially, astrology is not only a science for the study of planetary movements but also an art of interpretation and a philosophy, a system of understanding both the cosmos and the individual self. Though ancient in origin, it has been reinterpreted and expanded in the light of contemporary psychology.

Central to astrology is the idea that to understand the cosmos we must also understand the self, that each person is a universe in miniature. It was the sixteenth-century philosopher-physician Paracelsus who expanded the ancient concept of 'as above, so below' to include

the idea that each person is a 'Sun and a Moon and a heaven filled with stars. . . . Imagination is creative power.'[2]

To understand ourselves we need to become aware of the interconnections we weave in and out of our environment. Astrology gives us a language for this, and this book is intended to be a guide to fluency in astrological concepts. It introduces the reader to the horoscope, the diagram astrologers draw up to examine the state of the solar system at one particular moment in time, and develops astrological ideas about the meanings we can derive from it.

The following chapter (Chapter 2) traces the origins and development of astrology from its earliest roots in the experience of wise women who watched the sky and noted the cycles of the Moon. In Chapter 3 the basic structure of the horoscope is explained and all its component parts introduced. Chapters 4 to 8 expand upon the meanings of each component, and ideas and imaginative associations are brought in from many world cultures to illustrate astrological themes. Chapter 9 shows how the many variable factors in the horoscope can be brought together and synthesised, and how we can understand the developments within our own lives as a movement towards personal wholeness. In Chapter 10 we look towards the future and consider how an astrological viewpoint can help us understand the current planetary crisis.

Natal Astrology

Astrology is the study of the subtle combinations of planetary cycles that make up one moment; *natal* astrology considers what it means to a person to have been born at one unrepeatable point in time, and in one particular part of the earth's surface.

The variations from horoscope to horoscope are complex, and any one birth moment is a single possibility out of an elaborate range of interrelationships of the planets whose number stretches out towards infinity. This is why one horoscope never recurs; the variables are too many.

When considering the personal horoscope (Chapters 3 to 9) we turn our attention to the planets, the relationships between them, the signs of the zodiac and the houses of the horoscope in which they appear.

The signs of the zodiac in the horoscope provide one factor within this complex system. It is unfortunate that the zodiac signs have been given an undue and overwhelming predominance over the rest of the chart in newspaper columns and magazines. This unbalanced astrology is believed by many to represent the whole of the art, and has come to be used as a way of dividing up people and of putting them into boxes labelled with the names of the twelve zodiac signs. 'Typing' people is far from true astrology, however. Knowing the whole horoscope (rather than just the characteristics of the sign in which the Sun appears at birth) shows that we all have similarities, for we all have the same planets featured in our charts. Each manifests a subtle and complex mixture of these different energies, however, according to the disposition and interaction of the planets in the horoscope.

Categorical statements, applied to individuals merely on account of their month of birth, are bad astrology. We need to learn the basic language of astrology by learning the characteristics of each sign, for we cannot integrate the components of the horoscope into one whole picture until we understand the parts we are dealing with. Chapter 6 explores very fully the approach to life typical of each zodiac sign. It must be clearly understood, however, that when an astrologer writes about Virgo, for instance, (not one Virgoan person, but the sign Virgo itself) she is talking about an abstraction, a totally unmixed manifestation of the sign's energy which can never actually occur in real life. The *Sunsign*, which comes from the month of birth, gives a major emphasis in the horoscope, but this will be modified by many other factors.

Horoscope Interpretation as a Path to Self-Understanding

The whole chart must be interpreted to analyse the person's potential, to show the resources she has, the skills she uses and those she could develop. It helps to validate qualities previously taken for granted but which the horoscope indicates are special talents.

The birth chart shows that qualities we thought we lacked are there within the psyche, though buried. For example, a timid person who wants to be assertive is looking for her own hidden courage, while a person remote from others who wants to have closer friendships seeks

to discover the quality of openness within herself. Astrology can help to make changes real by describing the parts of ourselves that are as yet unfamiliar, and suggesting the nature of the blocks we have to our own growth.

The authors of this book understand astrology to be a therapy which gives each person power gained from a clearer understanding of herself. Learning basic astrology provides the tools for a method of self-help, with the horoscope as the chart of the self to be explored. At first it will only be possible to grasp a small part of the horoscope's meanings, and however well we come to know the horoscope there will always be something we can learn – a new and perhaps surprising interpretation.

Astrology can show how periods of personal crisis are, in fact, testing times, which help us to discover ourselves. Its teaching leads us out of the debilitating confusion where we can only ask 'Why is this happening to me?' When we need to make decisions astrology can give us guidance in examining all the available options and in realising the deeper implications of each; in work situations, too, the chart can show where our strengths and weaknesses lie and can illuminate our interactions with workmates. In all relationships, in fact, astrology can help our understanding of the interaction between two people, whether friends, relatives, lovers or partners. The creative potential in the relationship can be examined, as well as the difficulties.

The Stars Incline – They do not Compel

Every birth chart is a map not only of the self as it is but of opportunity for development. Together with her horoscope each person inherits a social and physical environment which modifies the ways in which she is able to express her potential. Although we do not all have equal opportunities, nevertheless the horoscope always seems to suggest a way for each of us to take hold of more power in our lives.

The movements of the planets in the sky throughout a person's life can be related to her birth horoscope to indicate times of particular growth and change, when barriers to her full self-expression may be crossed.

Astrology has often been used fatalistically, the horoscope being

seen as a description of the person's inescapable destiny. However, every planetary configuration has both positive and negative potential. An ancient maxim is 'the stars incline, they do not compel'; our times of birth do not automatically doom or bless us, for we can determine *how* we will express the inclinations that the planets represent. Neither does the horoscope provide us with alibis. We can misuse astrology by believing, for instance, 'There is no point in struggling with this trait in my character, as I've got Moon square Mars; I can't help it.' No one need be complacent about the negative expression of any aspect in the chart, for she could find its more creative possibilities. All the difficulties in the horoscope can be transformed into strengths, if we so choose.

The true role of astrology is to outline the possibilities available and allow the individual to make choices based on a deeper understanding of her own needs and motivations. We are not passive victims of a predetermined destiny, and as the planets move through the heavens during our lives we can be active participants in their patterns of change and transformation.

Synchronicity

The understanding of astrology has been broadened by Jung's development of the idea of *synchronicity*.[3] This concept explains how events which happen at the same time (such as a child's birth and a particular pattern in the heavens) may be interrelated without one being the cause of the other. The planets do not *cause* events or determine character by having an effect on human life. Rather they are *indicators* of the particular energy of each moment.

The pattern of the planets gives us a reading of the current energies within the solar system, just as the pulses the acupuncturist reads tell her the state of the vital energy of the patient. Astrology provides a language so that we can read the patterns in the sky and know the energies available for each person at her birth.

'There was a star danced, and under that was I born,' wrote Shakespeare of Beatrice. So it is for each child, for at the moment of her birth we can see from the horoscope the dance of the Earth around the Sun, of the Moon around the Earth, the dance of each of the

planets with Sun and Moon, and with each other. Beyond our solar system each child is also part of the dance of our star, the Sun, with our galaxy, and our galaxy with the universe.

We are dancing not to someone else's tune, but to our own inner music. Astrology offers us a way to become more attuned to ourselves, to the pattern of the moment when we were born, and to a cosmic order beyond our individual experience. Our own pattern becomes clear over the years; we may intuitively respond to it rather than rationally understand it. The more attuned we become to our own pattern the more we are able to realise its potential in our lives.

Astrology and Female Experience

Astrology's beginnings were in a time when knowledge and power were guarded as much, or more, by women than men. If we use astrology creatively rather than fatalistically it can become a tool for both women and men to free themselves from past conditioning into fixed masculine and feminine roles. Much of the potential in a horoscope is wasted because we fulfil social expectations about our manner of personal self-expression. In fact, gender cannot be shown by the birth chart, and by discovering the full potential the horoscope outlines we can start to recover what has been lost. Astrology is one path back to wholeness; it is an art of healing.

Astrology originated from an awareness of women's cyclic experience, as the following chapter explores and details. Yet in the past few thousand years the art has moved too far away from its roots, and has been developed by theorists who have been more aware of men's, rather than women's, experience.

The cyclic understanding of the wisewomen of ancient times has survived within astrology, and it has recently re-entered the art in a more conscious way through the introduction of ideas from Jungian psychology which stress the value of women's traditions.

Many concepts, definitions and interpretations in the traditional astrology of the past two-and-a-half thousand years need to be re-examined and re-expressed so that they are more relevant to women's experience. Women astrologers today are actively engaged in reclaiming the past; as skywatchers and as wisewomen who know

how to interpret celestial patterns.[4] It is an exciting time for all astrologers.

This book has been motivated by the authors' desire to increase our understanding of astrology by the inclusion of insights from women of the past and the present, and by looking towards the future role of women in the world.

The Knot of Time

On a personal level each person's birth chart provides her with a way to understand her present reality and her past by interpreting the planets' positions at birth and movements since that time. It also allows her a view of the future, for the planetary movements can be charted for many years to come.

The horoscope provides for each of us a knot in time where all three strands of past, present and future are twisted together; we can trace the interweavings of this knot to make sense of the individual pattern of events within our lives.

References

1   Ruperti, Alexander, *Cycles of Becoming*, CRCS, 1978.
2   *Encyclopaedia Britannica* 'Paracelsus'.
3   Jung, C G, *Synchronicity*, Princeton University Press, 1973.
4   Apart from the important work of many contemporary women astrologers, the following writers in particular have turned their attention to reclaiming astrology for women.

Francia, Luisa, *Berürhe Wega, Kehr' sur Erde Zurück*, Verlag Frauenoffensive, Munich, 1982.

Lionne, Crystal, *Feminist Astrology*, booklet distributed by Matriarchal Publishing Company, PO Box 113, Encinitas, California 92024, USA.

Moonfire, Blue, *The Matriarchal Zodiac*, available from Silver Moon, 68 Charing Cross Road, London WC2H 0BB.

Messmer, Phoenix and Bärbel, *Venus Ist Noch Fern*, Come Out Lesbenverlag, Munich, 1979.

Thorsten, Geraldine, *God Herself – The Feminine Roots of Astrology*, Avon Books, 1981.

2
The Story in the Skies
How Astrology Developed from Its Earliest Beginnings

Astrology did not develop as a separate and clearly defined subject; it was part of religion, science, mathematics, healing, drama, poetry and song. As the study of patterns and meanings in the solar system, its branches today are as interwoven as its roots were in the ancient world. Here we have chosen to tell astrology's story without a rigid definition of the subject, to reconnect astronomy with astrology, science with magic, and the practical and political with the spiritual.

Earth Mother/Sky Mother

There was a time before the counting of years when people watched the stars and the Moon. Some travelled to Australia; some crossed into the Americas. They lived in Africa, in Asia, in Europe, and everywhere the stars lit their nights and led them on their journeys.

Women watched the waxing and waning of the Moon and found from her cycles a way to calculate the timing of menstruation and pregnancy. Only through imagination can we discover the lives of the ancient wisewomen, though we have traces of the Goddess they honoured, the bones they marked and the 30000 BCE caves they painted. Some of the earliest artifacts from Ice Age Europe are incised bones, often marked with red ochre. They seem to be calendars of the Moon and of women's cycles. Some are engraved with animals and plants showing seasonal chan- 6500 BCE ges, some with the female form.[1] An incised bone from the Congo shows similar calendar marks.[2]

The study of the heavens evolved from a spiritual urge to understand the nature of the universe, as well as the need to create a functional calendar. The roots of astrology lie in the neolithic people's relationship with earth, sky and water. In Old Europe they made images of a Great Goddess who moved in the earth as Snake Mother, in the waters as Fish Mother and in the skies as Bird Mother.[3]

c5000 BCE

Abstract ideas about the Moon's cycle, the rotation of the seasons and the life cycle are depicted on cult-dishes and on figurines of the Great Goddess of Life and Death. A decorative four-armed cross seems to represent the four corners of the world (north, south, east and west) and the four seasonal turning-points of the year around which the later zodiac was to be arranged. Earth and sky seem to be contrasted and to have been formed from the two halves of the cosmic egg laid by the Goddess as Bird Mother. As the Snake Goddess she winds around the 'whole universe', over Sun, Moon and stars.[4]

5000 BCE-4000 BCE

Rock art confirms the pre-eminence of a goddess. At Aounret in Algeria there is a huge and mysterious female figure wearing the crescent horns of the Moon.[5]

Long before the zodiac was elaborated, skywatchers in the Northern hemisphere studied the stars that surround the Pole star, which was seen as the axis on which the heavens turned.[6] In particular, people watched the constellation Ursa Major, the Great She-Bear (known to us as the Plough or Dipper). The monthly position of the Bear Goddess' tail at nightfall was used to announce the arrival of the seasons. The same Great Bear was known to the Greeks as Artemis, and in the Far East the constellation was associated with Ma Tsu Po, the Queen of Heaven.[7] Throughout most of the ancient world a supreme goddess was thought to regulate the movements of the heavenly bodies.

c4000 BCE

The temples of the goddesses were the original centres of culture and invention. From the temple of Inanna at Uruk in Mesopotamia comes some of the earliest evidence of writing.[8] Astrology emerged as the study of the Moon's movements through the starry sky and it seems likely that the majority of early astrologers were priestesses. The Greeks were later to call Babylonian astrology 'mathesis' – 'the learning' – and from this word comes mathematics. The root 'ma' ('mother') suggests that

c3000 BCE

'mathesis' was originally the 'mother-wisdom' which came from the learned women of tribe or temple.[9]

The Time of Change

c3000
BCE

The elaboration of astrology and the observation of the planets' movements against the background of the constellations coincided with a great change in the organisation of society. Men began to take over more of women's functions in the temples, often dressing in women's robes. As the economy depended more on individual rather than on group property, so men became stronger in the palaces and homesteads. Gods, previously the consorts or brothers of goddesses, became pre-eminent; princes took to themselves the power they had previously derived from a 'holy marriage' to the Goddess in the shape of the priestess-queen.[10] The worship of the Great Goddess of earth and sky was no longer universal. The changeover took many years, however, and at this time women still retained many rights and privileges.[11] It is not possible to date this change pre-

3102
BCE

cisely, although Tantric Indian tradition places it at 3102 BCE, the beginning of Kali Yuga, the 'Age of Misery', when few men, it was said, would any longer be able to recognise women as manifestations of the Shakti (divine cosmic energy).[12]

c2700
BCE

During the Sumerian culture in Mesopotamia there was both a priesthood under a high priest and a priesthood under a high priestess.[13] A cosmology was evolved that influenced the whole Ancient Near East, the classical world, and eventually mediaeval Europe. The Sumerians envisaged a world surrounded by water, with Sun, Moon and planets in a dome-shaped firmament, and they believed that human life was affected by these celestial bodies.[14] The earlier Snake Goddess coiling in the heavens became the Goddess Tiamat, the Great Dragon who was the Milky Way. She was called 'the body of water in the sky' and her name gives us the word 'diameter'.[15] People learned to identify the rising of certain constellations with the equinoxes, and so evolved a stellar and solar calendar more accurate than the lunar one.[16]

In Egypt the earliest representations of the heavens show the Sky Mother as a great cow whose milk splashed the skies with stars. The skylore of the early Egyptians was to be developed into a complex religious and philosophical system. Egypt's unique geographical site helped to make this possible. The Nile provided a thoroughfare from the African highlands and linked the continent with Asia and Europe. The mingling of many rich cultures led to the expansion and deepening of knowledge.[17]

2600 BCE   The building of the pyramids followed the earlier development of tombs. It has been suggested that the long passages out towards the stars from the burial chambers of the pyramids were built for starwatching, but it seems unlikely that the pyramids were repeatedly entered for observations. The astrological alignments of burial chambers may have been for the benefit of the dead person. The passages were probably made to guide the soul towards the Northern stars (which never set and so represented immortality to the Egyptians).[18]

C2500 BCE   The Goddess Seshat was said to have given the arts of architecture, calculation and astronomy to the people and she is shown in a relief picture making astronomical alignments.[19] It has been suggested that this relief in fact depicts a priestess dressed as Seshat, which could indicate the active role that women still took in astrology, religion and science at this time.[20]

A caste of male astrologer-priests emerged in Egypt who wielded great political power. (The High Priest of Heliopolis wore a spotted panther-skin to represent the starry sky; his title was 'Chief Astrologer'.[21]) Over time the Gods Ptah and Thoth took over Seshat's role.

The rising of the star Soth (Sirius) gave the Egyptians the key point of their calendar. Soth was the star of Au Set, known to us as the Goddess Isis.[22]

c2500-2000 BCE   In India a complex civilisation existed in the Indus valley, focused around the cities of Harappa and Mohenjo-Daro. From Mohenjo-Daro comes evidence of a zodiac of eight signs.[23] The Harappans traded far afield, possibly even with the Sumerians, and seals on the bales they exported showed six animals which may have represented the seasons.[24] It is possible that an early Indian astrological system, based on six or eight signs, had some influence on the Babylonians.

The Indus civilisation honoured a goddess and people bathed ritually in the rivers. Then came the influx of Aryan peoples from the North who established the caste system and worshipped male gods with fire sacrifices. The two cultures intermingled and both influences are to be found in the Hindu religion to this day.[25]

Around the world the change from a matriarchal to a patriarchal religion often coincided with the introduction of the solar calendar, and the Sun became newly identified with the increasing power in the hands of men, though in many cultures it had previously been seen as a goddess.

c2000
BCE

The earlier Northern Europeans seemed to have seen the Sun as female. People built circles of stone and wood that enabled them to mark seasonal cycles, and these may have been used to predict eclipses of Sun or Moon. Stonehenge is the most famous of these but stone circles are also found all over Europe, in the middle East, in Kenya and Northern Africa.[26] All over the same area there are temples and holy sites oriented to the rising of certain constellations or stars. At Avebury in Britain the earth mounds that were constructed appear to represent the Earth Mother's body. Festivals at Avebury seem to have been celebrated seasonally when certain stars rose at dusk.[27] The annual cycle of vegetation on earth was paralleled by the annual cycle of the rising of constellations in the heavens. The Chinese had a comparable philosophy behind their divination systems that were based on patterns discernible in both the sky above their heads and the earth below their feet.[28]

The Elaboration of Astrology

c1600
BCE

In Babylon the religions of the goddesses continued strong, though surrounded by the newer worship of Marduk and other gods. In the religious centres observation of the planets was mixed with weather lore and more general omens from animals and birds.[29] The planets were originally called 'wild goats' because of the way they seemed to wander amongst the stars, but later each planet became associated with a particular god or goddess.[30] Legends told of the killing of the Dragon-Goddess

Tiamat by the god Marduk (Jupiter) and of the rape of Ereshki-
gal (the Underworld Goddess) by Nergal (Mars). We may take
these myths as political commentary on the change from
matriarchal to patriarchal religion.

The astrology of Babylon focused particularly on the planet
c1500   Venus which represented the Goddess Ishtar. The planet has a
BCE   cycle of visibility and invisibility that has fascinated many cultures, and this became the basis for a major ritual in the worship
of Ishtar. As the planet became invisible the Babylonians said
that the Goddess had gone to the Underworld and all desire was
stilled until her return as Morning Star.[31]

Ur and then Babylon were the centres of skywatching, and
Babylon was famous for its 'hanging gardens', which were probably terraces built on the step-sided ziggurats. The latter were
pyramids with platforms dedicated to each of the five known planets and the Sun and Moon, painted in their traditional colours.
The most famous ziggurat was called Ba-bel, meaning 'god's
gate'. From the roofs and windows of the ziggurats the planets
could be observed. People from all over the Ancient Near East
came to Babylon to wonder and to learn 'Babylonian numbers',
as astrology was called, and it was from astrology that mathematics developed. To the unsophisticated observer the mixture of
native languages was incomprehensible and the ziggurat was
recorded in the Hebrew writings as the 'Tower of Babel'.[32]

There is a tradition linking the ziggurats and the whole building of Babylon with a legendary queen Semiramis or Sammura-
mat. Thought to be one of a series of incarnations of the Goddess
Ishtar, 'Semiramis' has been identified with at least two vigorous
historical queens of Assyria in later times.[33]

c1450   In Egypt constellations were painted on the ceilings of tombs;
BCE   it was believed that the soul needed star maps as guides. If the
soul moved towards the zodiac constellations the person would
reincarnate, if towards the Northern stars the soul would achieve
final liberation. The Goddess Nut, Mistress of the Celestial
Ocean, was shown holding the sky, or with the thirty-six Egyptian constellations marked on her naked body.[34] At the birth of
an infant it was said that seven Hathors, midwife Goddesses
with prophetic power and associated with the seven planets,
would appear to announce the child's destiny.[35]

Astrology permeates the cultures in the Ancient Near East, and it is hard to say precisely who taught whom. The Hebrew peoples had arrived in Canaan around 1700 BC from Ur of the Chaldees. Some say their forefather Abraham was a wise astrologer and a priest of the Moon, and that Sarah his wife was the matriarch of the tribe.[36] We know there was astrological
c1300
BCE
knowledge amongst the Jews in the fourteenth century BCE. Women were rulers as well as prophets in Israel, and the oldest writings of the Bible tell of the matriarch Deborah. She had prophetic powers and skill in battle strategy, and she foretold how the Israelites' enemy Sisera would fall.[37] In the Song of Deborah she says that 'the stars themselves fought against Sisera', and the implication here is that the right astrological moment was chosen by her for the battle.[38]

c1250
BCE
In thirteenth century Canaan, the Sun was portrayed as the hero Samson who travelled through the zodiac performing miracles of strength. He was at his height in Leo (when he slayed a lion) and weakest in Aquarius, the sign called 'Delilah' in Hebrew. She cut his hair, symbolising the shortened rays of the weakened winter sun in Aquarius.[39]

It is unclear exactly when the familiar twelve-sign zodiac was formalised from the variety of systems (some with eight, eleven, eighteen, twenty-eight or thirty-six parts) used by different peoples. Gradually, from the tenth to the seventh centuries BCE, the twelve-part zodiac came to be adopted widely in the Ancient Near East.

Samson's Greek counterpart, Heracles, was said to be bound to the wheel of the Goddess Omphale. She sat at the hub of a great wheel of stars, and he had to follow its course – as the Sun has to pass through each sign of the zodiac. Heracles performed one of his twelve labours each month.[40] These myths may originate in India, where it was said that Aditi, the Goddess who is Infinity, gave birth to the twelve Adityas, the heavenly lights which will shine forth at Doomsday. The spirit of the zodiac was Kalanemi, the 'Rim of the Wheel of Time', the serpent who ate her own tail.[41]

C1100
BCE
While zodiac stories were elaborated in the Ancient Near East, astronomical observations were being carried out farther afield. Priests of the Shang Dynasty in China engraved

bones and tortoise shells with questions for divination. Those that have survived show that eclipses, stars and novae were studied.[42]

c500
BCE
The great Babylonian Empire had been war-torn for centuries by the time astrology became highly developed there in the fifth century BCE; nevertheless, Babylonian astrologers, known as Chaldeans, carried their expertise to neighbouring nations.[43] An individual horoscope could be drawn up from planetary observation and tables.

The Egyptians, too, were revered for their philosophy, and Greeks came to Egypt to study and for religions initiation. The cultures of Egypt, Babylon and Greece had many links. The Babylonians had abandoned their original eighteen-sign zodiac for the more familiar twelve signs we know today.[44] Six constellations were said to be carried on the back of the dragon Tiamat and six on her belly. Her head and tail marked the Moon's Nodes that might predict eclipses. Later the zodiac was seen as the girdle of Ishtar, Queen of Heaven, the other constellations in the sky covering her dress.[45] The twelve zodiac signs we use appear to be a combination of Egyptian and Babylonian constellations and it is probable that the Indian zodiac made a contribution to this.

The original Greek approach to the heavens was descriptive; individual planets were named 'the fiery star' or 'the luminous star' but later the names of goddesses and gods were adopted after the fashion of the Babylonians.[46]

500
BCE
The Greeks were interested in the movements and cycles of the planets, which were considered to have the rhythm and harmonies of music.[47] Women astrologers, such as Aglaonice, were sometimes regarded as sorcerers, as they could predict eclipses.[48] Because of the supposed association of women with sorcery they were especially vulnerable as astrologers, ever since the loss of women's status as 'learned mothers'.

Harassed by foreign invaders, Egyptian rulers often retreated to Meroe and Nepata, the cities of the Upper Nile. The Sicilian historian Diodorus records that the Egyptian people originally came from this area, which was called Ethiopia by the Greeks, and the Egyptian civilisation seems to have been truly African in origin.[49] 'Ethiopia' (the present-day Sudan) was the

birthplace of Nefertiti, the black princess of Egypt, and a domain of the Goddess Isis. The stars could be watched from the highlands and pyramids and sphinxes were built at Meroe.[50] Later Greek historians were to be impressed and awed by Meroe's strong dynasty of warrior-queens.[51]

It seems likely that a complex astronomical calendar was evolved in Eastern Africa. At one ancient site, now known as Namoratunga II, nineteen standing stones were raised in rows that seem to have been aligned to stars and constellations.[52]

Many parts of the ancient world suffered from increasing warfare and political instability, which put astrological knowledge in jeopardy. In China scholars criticised the despotic Ch'in regime, and in retaliation all books were burned except some classical texts of medicine and agriculture.[53] Astrological divination just survived, but we do not know how much was lost. In the ashes lay most of the traces of the goddesses and holy women of ancient China. The books that remained were edited by Confucian scholars to support their own patriarchal worldview.

Only stories remain of Xi Wang Mu, the Mother Goddess. As the Celestial Year Tree she was mistress of the beasts of the months that gathered under her branches.[54] A few references survive to the Goddess Hsi Ho who created the heavenly bodies and the ten days of the Chinese week.[55]

c200 BCE
Under the Han dynasty, all phenomena visible to the naked eye were catalogued and named.[56] The names of the star groups were often political in tone – for example 'Crown Prince' and 'Minister of Works'. Astrology was interwoven with the life of the court and civil service. A Ministry of State Sacrifices was set up to respond to celestial portents, and astrologers were powerful figures in the hierarchy.

c200 BCE-0CE
In Athens and Rome during the first centuries BCE many women worked in the sibylline tradition. Originally the sibyl lived at a site where divine inspiration was believed to emanate from the earth. She might convey this in ecstatic utterance or by a symbolic message.[57]

There were ten famous sibylline shrines, and the evidence seems to indicate that the tradition originated in Africa and Asia.[58] One of the sibyls, Sabbe or Sambethe, was believed to be

Jewish, the 'daughter of Noah', though other authorities claimed her as the daughter of the famous Chaldean astrologer, Berossus.

Sibylline oracles in verse form, siding with oppressed peoples, were circulated in Athens from the fifth century BCE onwards. They drew upon both Babylonian astrology and Persian philosophy to predict doom for wicked rulers.[59]

The popular faith in sibylline wisdom allowed many women in the first century BCE to support themselves by their intelligence and intuition, giving divinatory counsel to clients in Athens and Rome. It was at this time that horoscopes became available for all who could afford them, and both astrologers and clairvoyants were sought after. The historian Pliny maintained that the study of the heavens was the business of women, and he notes the widespread belief in women's supposed skill to cause eclipses by enchantment.[60] Juvenal said in his sixth satire that two of women's gravest faults were their susceptibility to astrology and to oriental cults.[61]

The proliferation of astrologers coincided with the growth of the Isis religion in the Graeco-Roman world. Greek and Roman women were attracted to this living Egyptian religion at a time when the Goddess-worship in their own countries had been largely suppressed.[62] Men, too, were devotees of Isis, and Apuleius, the author of the *Golden Ass*, saw the Goddess clothed in stars in his ecstatic trance. She told him that: 'It is my will that controls the planets of the sky'.[63] It seems likely that a symbolic progress through the signs of the zodiac was part of the initiation into the Mysteries of Isis. Some Egyptian temples appear to have been divided into twelve parts, and may have been used for astrological religious rites.[64]

In the first centuries BCE and CE, astrological and religious ideas were interwoven concerning the fate of the soul after death. Many believed that the soul would pass through the 'heaven' of each of the planets, divesting itself of the qualities inherited from each planet at birth. The naked soul would eventually reach the eighth heaven, to live with the gods and become a star in the sky.[65]

c50 BCE   The Romans were impressed by the learning of the Druids, the priestesses and priests of the Celtic peoples, and particularly

by their knowledge of astrology, natural sciences, fate and rein-carnation.[66] From the evidence we have it is likely that Druidic astrology might equal the Babylonian in complexity, but no written records exist. Yet discoveries of carved granite shapes in Scotland confirm the geometric skills of a society that did not use writing.[67] The Druids believed that sacred knowledge should not be contained in writing, and their oral tradition was later to be fed into, and suppressed by, Christianity.

Some say Britain was the legendary land of the Sun Temple 'at the back of the North Wind'. The stars could be observed from the hilltops of Britain and Ireland, where the ancient earthworks, and sometimes chalk figures, were constructed. The 'Long Man' (or Woman?) of Wilmington in Sussex may be a starwatcher making astronomical alignments with two rods.

Irish myths describe the division of royal halls into twenty-eight or seven sections which reflect the days and phases of the Moon, and thirteen trees were held sacred to the lunar months.[68] The Earth marked the time with trees, just as the heavens marked the calendar with the rising of the constellations. The Celtic Goddess Arianrhod turned the starry wheel of the zodiac, the 'Silver Wheel that Descends into the Sea', and each month another constellation disappeared into the Western Sea with the Full Moon.[69] The Lady who turned the Wheel was Ariadne and Arachne in Greece, the spinner who weaves the web of the horo-scope. The Romans called her Fortuna and told how the one who was riding high on her wheel would be thrown down and how the one who fell would rise as the wheel turned. The Scandi-navians shared these ideas, for they saw the heavens turning around the distaff of the spinning Goddess Frija[70] and their feast of Yule ('jul' means wheel) celebrated the wheel of the year.[71] The wheel is shown in the Tarot pack, and the concept of the Goddess who rules fortune has survived as Lady Luck.

Astrology under Threat

c20
BCE

In spite of the popularity of astrology it did not always find favour with the rulers in Rome. Augustus had 2,000 Chaldean

books burned as a warning to those who thought to pay too much attention to foreign wisdom. Astrology might lead to subversion as contemplation of the eternal and mighty planets could diminish the reputation of the more temporal emperors (many of whom set themselves up as gods). Tiberius banished astrologers from Italy, but many Roman rulers did have their own astrologers. They lived a precarious existence, either in high favour, or, if the predictions were either wrong or unfortunate, in danger of summary execution.[72]

Astrologers were safer in Egyptian Alexandria, the cosmopolitan city where esoteric sects flourished and many women lived independent lives.

Alexandria was the home of Claudius Ptolemy, the astrologer who formalised the Chaldean system into a pattern of signs, elements, houses and aspects which has influenced all Western astrology.

Following the fall of Jerusalem in CE 70, Alexandria became as much a Jewish city as it was Egyptian, Greek, Roman or Babylonian. Many of the Alexandrian Jews were great astrologers and debate raged within their community about astrology for hundreds of years. Some believed it was against God's law, and that the Jews were exempt from planetary destiny because God had taken Abraham above the heavens.[73] They referred to the Sibylline Oracles, where, in spite of the popular association of sibylline prophecy with astrology, the Sibyl maintained that the art must be rejected by believers in the One God.[74] She ridicules the over-dependence on omens of the Babylonians and contrasts this with the Jewish concern for care of the oppressed, of widows and of orphans.[75]

Jewish astrologers nevertheless defended the art. They could quote the Torah to show that the signs in the heavens were God's handiwork; they could claim the twelve sons of Jacob (and hence the tribes of Israel) to be the origin of the zodiac signs.[76] They noted that there were also twelve prophets, and interpreted Ezekiel's vision of 'wheels within wheels, with eyes on their rims' as a vision of the zodiac. The debate encouraged Jewish astrologers to incorporate more ethics into their practice.

The Jewish diaspora spread astrology widely. Jews from

c30 CE

c 150 CE

c 230 CE

Babylon were valued astrologers at King Ardashir's court in Persia. They exchanged knowledge with the Zoroastrian priests, the Magi, who observed and interpreted conjunctions of planets.

During a major part of the first two centuries CE Christianity was illegal, and even more suspect than astrology and magical knowledge. The unorthodox gnostic Christians brought astrology into their understanding of spiritual destiny. They considered god to be female as well as male, and both women and men preached and taught.[77] In the gnostic work 'Pistis Sophia', Jesus is shown teaching his disciples the meaning of the influences of the planets and the zodiac on the human soul.[78]

However, when Christianity had become more established, Christian fanatics attacked pagan sanctuaries. In CE 379 the temple of Hathor at Denderah in Egypt was despoiled and the huge statues of the Goddess mutilated. The ceiling remained, c 385 CE its star-covered vault and zodiac circle beyond reach.[79]

Alexandria's Museum (the dwelling place of the Muse) was a repository of astrological, historical, philosophical and religious documents, reputed to number 500,000 volumes. The main Museum and library were destroyed in a civil war in the third century CE. The Serapeum (a healing shrine of the Isis religion) was converted to a Christian church in 389 CE, and a subsidiary library was burned by Christians in 391 CE.[80]

At the turn of the fifth century Hypatia, the great pagan philosopher, mathematician and astronomer, was associated with the Museum. It is recorded that she was consulted about the c 400 CE construction of an astrolabe, the astrological calculating tool of the ancients. In 415 she was savagely murdered by monks and a mob of Christians.[81]

Christian emperors martyred many whom they declared 'magicians'. In some areas people burned their own books to escape accusations of witchcraft.[82]

c 550 CE In sixth-century Galilee, however, a synagogue was built at Bet Alpha which shows how astrology had come to be fully accepted by the Jews of this area. The mosaic floor depicted two scenes from Judaic tradition on either side of a representation of the twelve signs of the zodiac and the chariot of the Sun.[83]

c 780
CE

Much of the ancient knowledge that survived the book-burning was contained in the city of Byzantium. It was threatened by the fanatical icon-smashers, who also destroyed centres of learning where holy images were kept. A temporary respite occurred during the reign of the woman Emperor, Irene, who instituted a period of religious toleration.[84]

From Byzantium emerged the 'Hermetic' manuscripts that were to fascinate and inspire mediaeval alchemists and kabbalists. They were said to have been written by the legendary 'Hermes Trismegistus', an ancient magician from Egypt. A manuscript entitled *The Virgin of the World* recounts the instructions of Isis (sometimes thought to have been a priestess-initiate) to her son Horus in all the arts of magic, the mysteries and astrology. Hermetic teaching emphasised the complete equality between women and men.[85]

Astrology in the East

Under threat in the Christian world, astrology was able to develop in India. Indian astrologers claimed great antiquity for their tradition.[86] Interpretations were developed for the lunar zodiac, the twenty-eight mansions of the Moon that could pre-date the solar cycle of twelve. The lunar zodiac was said to be presided over by twenty-eight beautiful star goddesses. Each one spent one night of the month making love with the Moon-god Chandra, thereby releasing a different psychic energy into the world every night.[87]

642
CE

In the seventh century CE Buddhism and astrology were brought to Tibet from India. The Chinese Princess Kong-Jo married the first Buddhist King of Tibet and brought with her, it is said, the Chinese calendar of twelve animals that had originated in Central Asia.[88] The two systems were to be combined and used in parallel in Tibet.

In Korea an observatory was erected during the reign of Queen Sindok, its design emphasising the twenty-eight sections of the lunar zodiac. From 675 CE celestial events could be studied and interpreted at the new observatory at Asuka in Japan.[89]

The stars were used as metaphors in Buddhist thought; the North Star was shown as a Buddha sitting on a lotus, the still centre of the whirling heavens.[90]

Stars over the Americas

In the Americas a system of planetary observation was being developed from the first centuries BCE and CE. It achieved a high level of accuracy in the calculation of planetary cycles, unparalleled until the twentieth century.

In Teotihuacan, Mexico, there were elaborate observatories. Living so near to the Equator provided a special opportunity to regulate the calendar. On summer solstice a watcher by the Pyramid of the Moon would experience bright sunlight with no shadow, an unearthly noon.[91]

c200 CE

In the Peruvian Nazca Valley we can still see enormous representations in the desert of animals, birds and insects,[92] now thought to be pictures of constellations.

C550 CE

The shrine of the Moon Goddess Ix Chel on Cozumel Island in Mexico is believed to have been a holy place for women.[93] Ix Chel was said to be married to the Sun god but to have many infidelities, marked by the Moon's conjunctions with other planets and stars.[94]

In Mexico Venus was seen as Kulkulkan, the son of the Mother Goddess. The planet was watched from the Caracol, the spiral observatory at Chichen Itza, where Mayan priestesses and priests lived in a ceremonial city never inhabited by ordinary people. Like the peoples of the Ancient Near East, the Meso-Americans thought astrology important enough to dedicate the resources and worker-power of their community to build massive edifices.[95]

c 850 CE

While Europeans considered the world to be only a few thousand years old, the Mayans counted in units as large as three million years.[96] Each day and each moment was ruled by a different deity. Parents consulted the astrologer at a birth to find out to whom their child would owe devotion.[97]

Astrology was also extensively developed amongst the Aztecs.

Details of their system survive to the present day, from which a horoscope can still be interpreted.[98]

In North America many different tribes created 'medicine wheels' with stones and wood, allowing measurement of the sun's passage and the stars' rising. They built earthworks on the c1000 hilltops, and it is thought it may have been women who built the CE massive artificial mounds at Cahokia in North America.[99]

Evidence has been found that indicates that American tribal people observed the Crab Nebula Supernova in 1055 CE, and recorded this extraordinary celestial event on rocks.[100]

Legends of the Sun, Moon, planets and constellations were part of the sacred mysteries of medicine women and men. A more recent Pawnee star-chart, painted on buckskin, was designed to be drawn up into a medicine-bag, the star-pattern protecting the sacred objects carried.[101]

The Anasazi people of the south western part of North America left many ruins suggesting astronomical knowledge. Their descendants, the Hopi, maintained this interest in the sky and it is likely the astronomical methods were very ancient. The Hopi appointed watchers to time the Sun's standstill at solstices and the appearance of the Moon's first crescent each month. These watchers did not have the power and immunity from criticism of a priestly caste, for anyone who could offer a more accurate observation was encouraged to do so.[102]

Starlore in the Pacific

c1200 From 1160 CE the Great Migrations began and continued for
CE hundreds of years: people from the Pacific homeland of Hawai-iki travelled by canoe against ocean currents to Aotearoa (which was to be called New Zealand by Europeans). Maori legends suggest that their advanced navigational skills came from knowledge of the stars.[103]

Pacific peoples named the constellations envisaging the heavens as a dome and practised both astronomy and astrology.[104] In some areas navigators were trained in formal schools; in the Gilbert Islands the rafters of the training house were so arranged

that they represented parts of the sky and constellations. In central Polynesia legends tell of the navigator Hiro who learned all his skills in the school of the wisewoman Brave Hearted.[105]

Pagan Survivals in Europe

1000-
1300
CE

Like the North Americans, the Northern peoples of Europe had once known a comparable tradition of both shamanism and astrology; the shaman could walk between the worlds with the spirit people and knew the lore of the heavens.[106] The pagan peoples of Northern Europe – Celtic, Norse and Anglo-Saxon – continued their own customs long after their countries had been officially converted to Christianity.[107] For prayer Norse peoples turned towards the Pole Star which they saw as the axis of the sky.

The old religion of the Goddess and the Horned God (her consort) survived underground in Europe. Covens met at Full Moon and celebrated their annual festivals.[108] Beneath the facade of Christianity the older religious urge stirred and found its expression in the Arthurian legends. King Arthur was a Sun King, Guinevere the Moon Goddess, the knights could be seen to represent the stars. The Round Table was a new version of the Zodiac Wheel of Arianrhod. The story of Parsifal and the Holy Grail is another Sun-hero myth, like those of Samson and Hercules; Parsifal having had to pass through tests and initiations in each sign of the zodiac.[109] The ancient work known as the 'Prophecies of Merlin' contains many references to signs and planets which seem to come as much from ancient British star-lore as from astrology imported from Roman sources.[110]

Astrology in the Arab World

The threatened astrological system of the Ancient Near East was to find its home amongst the Arab peoples and the Jews who lived amongst them.

A strong awareness of the sky had continued in the Arabian deserts. The planet Venus was named al-Uzza, the same powerful Goddess once called Ishtar. Mecca was the sanctuary of the Kaaba, a black meteoric stone sacred to the shrine of the Triple Goddess.[111] It is not clear whether the nomadic society was ever a matriarchate or exactly what place there was for women sky-watchers at the time of Muhammed. He taught submission to the will of Allah, but seems to have improved the diminished condition of women at this time, prohibiting female infanti-cide.[112] The prophet came from the 'people of Q're', otherwise Kore the Virgin Moon, and the Goddess' crescent Moon and Star became the symbol of the new religious movement.[113] The Koran recognised the importance of the stars to a nomadic people:

570 CE

'He it is Who hath set for you the stars that ye may guide your course by them amid the darkness of the land and the sea.'[114]

In newly converted Iraq, Baghdad grew from a village into a cosmopolitan city where the Indian, Persian, Greek and Jewish cultural legacies mingled with the achievements of Arab scholars. At the 'House of Wisdom' mathematics was developed and planetary calculation made far more accurate.[115]

c850 CE

By the twelfth century CE astrology was widespread in Islamic countries. The astrologer Atrush predicted correctly that the Afghani princess and poet Rabiah Balkhi would shine as the light of a star to the world, and would meet with a tragic death.[116]

Astrologers feature in *The Arabian Nights*, and in Nights 254 to 247 the slave woman Tawaddud gives a dissertation on the astrological elements within medicine.[117]

Some Arab women had access to formal education, and there were many women poets, scribes, religious teachers and mystics.[118] Women became unusually prominent as mathematicians and philosophers in Moorish Spain at a time when these subjects were part of the astrological world-view, and we can assume that these scholars were familiar with astrological calculation.[119] There were universities and academies all over the Arab world and West Africa. The stars were named and catalogued, and medicine used astronomical diagnosis and timed doses according to planetary indications.

C1250 CE

As with many originally nomadic peoples, the Arabs' loyalty to the Moon was strong. The zodiac used increasingly was the lunar one of the Moon's passage through her 'mansions'. As each mansion (or twenty-eight part division of the sky) was called after a letter of the alphabet the Moon's movement was said to spell out the 'Divine Word of the Creator'. Philosophy, number, astrology and mysticism were intertwined.[120]

Astrology Faces Christian Orthodoxy

c1250 CE

A few Christian scholars had kept astrology alive and learned from continuing pagan sources, but much of the art had to be recovered from the Arabs and from Latin texts in the era of intellectual expansion in the thirteenth-century CE. The convents and monasteries were centres of learning, and astrology could not for ever be excluded.[121]

The Virgin Mary had taken on most of the attributes of the Goddesses of the Moon and Venus, and she was shown in a robe as deep blue as the night sky, with Moon and stars around her, like Isis before her.[122]

The mediaeval world – Christian, Jewish and Islamic – was fascinated with cosmology: the order of the heavens, the planets and the stars. In the twelfth century women mystics Hildegarde of Bingen and Alpis de Cudot saw visions of the universe more accurate than the accepted notions of the time, which remind us that scientific experiment is not the only way for discoveries to be made.[123] The Abbess Hildegarde was interested in astrology and suggested that Jesus might have chosen astrologically favourable moments for miracles.[124]

As astrology became more acceptable to the Church, theologians discussed the problems of free will and destiny. One churchman associated the twelve apostles with the twelve months of the year.[125]

Astrology was deeply embedded in the world-view of the alchemists of the Middle Ages. Alchemy was a mystical philosophy and included an attempt to reintroduce the power of the female into a male-dominated cosmology. Alchemists saw

wisdom as Sophia, the Great Mother who ruled the elements, and drew ideas from the gnostic and hermetic writings. As a system of experimentation with minerals and elements, it is said to have been invented by Mary the Jewess whose writings influenced all those who came after her.[126] The correspondences between planets and metals were of prime importance. Alchemy was said to be 'convenient for women', and male alchemists studied the writings of the scholar Cleopatra. Many other women alchemists were to follow.[127]

c 1375
CE

Perenelle Flamel flourished in Paris in the last part of the fourteenth century. She and her husband claimed to have transmuted gold from base ore after many years of trial.[128] Contrary to the ideas of the uninformed public, serious alchemists were not trying to make gold in order to become rich; the tiny amount they might accrue after years spent on the work was negligible. By undertaking transmutation of elements they sought spiritual transmutation. Astrology was crucial for timing and guiding the experiments, and was now more accessible through the works of astrologers such as Guido Bonatti, who was accused of writing 'as if he wanted to teach women astrology'.[129]

Perenelle's husband spent years searching for a Jewish sage to help him decipher an old document, at a time when the Kabbalah was being developed amongst the Jews of Spain. The Kabbalah was the Jewish mystical system influenced by gnosticism and Greek ideas and based on the Judaic spiritual experience. The universe was seen as the clothing of the Deity, which was bejewelled with the 'sephiroth'.[130] These were ten spheres which collectively symbolised the full spectrum of existence, beginning with the origins of the universe itself and descending successively through the spiritual worlds of the zodiac and the planets, and finally to the material world. The Kabbalah brought the Goddess back to Judaism in the guise of the Shekinah or Malkhut, the Mother of the World or Divine Presence.[131]

Astrology was an abiding interest in Jewish intellectual life. The blessing bestowed upon Abraham in Genesis (24.1) was interpreted as the gift of astrology. The Talmud stated that each human being had a celestial body, the 'mazzal', a patron star which perceived things unknown to the person concerned. The mystical kabbalistic work the 'Zohar' takes astrology for granted

and tells how: 'there is not a single blade of grass in the entire world over which a star or planet does not preside, and over the star one [angel] is appointed . . . '[132]

Many rabbis were accomplished astrologers; one such is said to have studied astrology in the bath so as to steal no time from study of the law. The six-pointed Shield of David was said to be King David's six-pointed horoscope.[133] Professional Jewish astrologers were held in high esteem in Spain under both Moorish and Christian rule.[134]

The grudging toleration of Jews in Christian Europe alternated with massacres and expulsions. Astrologers and alchemists who were nominally Christian may have offered some protection to the Jews, whom they respected.[135] Yet sometimes alchemical documents came into their hands from the property of persecuted Jews and their obsession with penetrating Jewish secrets seems opportunist and invasive.

At the same time there were alliances of the oppressed. Alchemists and astrologers were themselves in danger of being accused of heresy, and their own relationship with the Church was precarious.

1310 CE   The Council of Trèves in Lorraine condemned as witchcraft: 'observation of the stars in order to judge of the destiny of persons born under certain constellations, the illusions of women who boast that they ride at night with Diana or Herodias and a multitude of other women.'[136]

The tradition of the female oracle or sibyl could no longer be an open one. However, the poorer people could not be prevented from creeping out at night to the houses of wisewomen, for divination, healing and counsel. The many women herbalists, though they seldom had access to formal education, were probably influenced by the widespread belief in the association of the planets and the Moon with certain plants. It is also quite possible that remnants of older traditions of astrological medicine (such as the Druidic) were preserved within folk-medicine. Unfortunately these women healers were vulnerable to accusations of sorcery.

It is difficult to estimate accurately the number of 'witches' executed, but the figure of 300,000 has been widely repeated in scholarly works.[137] The figure may far exceed this. We can

assume that women who knew starlore or were clairvoyant must have died amongst them, for they would have been likely targets. There were villages in Continental Europe where few women at all survived the persecutions.[138] Those who died probably included some adherents to the old religion of the Earth and Moon Goddess, as well as midwives and healers who threatened jealous doctors, and an enormous number of women who never practised anything associated with witchcraft.

Where women had not been so systematically persecuted it is likely that they were intimidated by example into abandoning medicine and divining. 'When a woman thinks alone,' said the *Malleus Maleficarum* (the Church's approved guide to the identification of witches) 'she is evil.'[139] It was dangerous for women to watch the sky or interpret its patterns.

A much smaller number of men were executed for witchcraft, although the legend of Dr Faustus kept the image of the satanic practitioner of magic before the public gaze. Two men who have been identified with Faust and who survived were the Swiss Paracelsus and the French Jew Nostradamus.

Paracelsus developed his revolutionary theories of medicine from contact with gipsies, healers, sorcerers, and wisewomen in the countryside.[140] He travelled widely, educating himself in the wisdom that the academic circles had forgotten. He introduced into astrology the idea of the *inter*relationship of the planets and human life (rather than control by the planets). This concept was further developed by Jung in the twentieth century.

c1540 CE

Nostradamus was an innovative doctor but achieved his greatest fame from his clairvoyant prophecies, some of which have seemed to be relevant to events in the twentieth century.[141]

The methods of the inquisition and witch trials were exported to the Americas. In 1562 the last stronghold of the Maya fell to the Spanish and the conquistadors seized the annals of the

c1560 CE

Mayan culture. An eye-witness relates: 'We found among them a great number of books written with their characters, and because they contained nothing but superstitions and falsehoods about the devil, we burned them all, which they felt most deeply, and over which they showed much sorrow.'[142] A few of the Mayan 'codices' survive, one showing a priestess in front of

an observatory, which gives us a hint of the role women had played in this culture.[143]

After an era of pogroms, of witch trials, inquisition and conquest, little remained in Europe of traditional esoteric wisdom.

The astrology we inherit today is truncated and incomplete; it is a record of the scholarly, the upper class and the masculine tradition. To fill out the one-sided tradition we have inherited, we have to search deeply into folklore, into memory and into ourselves, to follow clues that can never be adequately substantiated to satisfy the academic world.

Astrology in an Age of Science

European thought was reaching away from intuitive and traditional sources of knowledge towards scientific rationalism. The scientific aspects of astrology, however, (chart calculation and the computation of planetary cycles) continued. Great astronomers, such as Tycho Brahe, and, by popular repute, Newton, were also astrologers, but astrology and astronomy had begun to part company.[144] The wisewoman re-emerges as astronomer c 1650 in the shape of Maria Cunitz who simplified the astronomical tables, and in the many women astronomers who followed in her footsteps.[145] However much men have claimed the rational-scientific approach as their own, it has not been alien to women. Nevertheless, many women (and some men) have felt uncomfortable with the division of thought from feeling and intuition, and have continued their own way of learning; this has been largely unacknowledged.

The woman herbalist, aware of the Moon and sometimes of the planets, continued to practise wherever she survived the witch-hunting.[146] The medical profession harassed and outlawed her, and she had still to fear accusations of sorcery. Eminent male astrologers practised in British cities, but their slightly safer position did little to protect women in the countryside.[147]

Astrology never died out. It continued to be practised in Asia without any break, and in Europe it was still in evidence throughout the 'Age of Reason'. Though no longer part of the

official world-view, the curious discovered it none the less.[148]

The roots of astrology survived in folk-legend, though often
the celestial origins of the myths and fairy-tales were not realised. The notions of guardian angels and of fairy godmothers
echo the seven Hathors of the planetary spheres who visited the
Egyptian newborn, and the planetary angels of the Kabbalah.

c 1650   From the seventeenth century comes documentation of the
Anakara astrologers: Islamised Jews living in Madagascar who
used a lunar system of great antiquity. Malagasy astrologers
observed the heavens directly and their astrology has survived
into the twentieth century.[149] People's movements to preserve
indigenous cultures have often helped to save astrology, along
with the native magical and religious systems. (Madagascar, in
fact, had a strong queen in Ranavalona I – 1828-1861 – who rejected European culture and brought back Malagasy ways.[150])

Chinese scientific developments and astrological divination
co-existed without tension. In India, too, the distinction
between astrology and astronomy never became so rigid as it did
c 1724   in Europe. While the West was developing the telescope,
Muhammed Sha built a massive 'naked eye' observatory outside Delhi. Gigantic and convoluted structures enable accurate
observations to be made. While built for function rather than
form, the observing platforms reproduce the harmony of planetary movement. Their shapes are mandalas, and are impressively beautiful.[151] The scope, depth and antiquity of Indian
astrology has never been fully explored in the West, and astrological histories tend to minimise the Indian contribution to
astrology's development.

This limited vision, however, was not for Helena Blavatsky,
the Russian aristocrat and medium who founded the Theosophical Society. Theosophy had roots in hermetic philosophy (the
teachings of Hermes Trismegistus), in the Kabbalah and in Eastern religion. A strong connection was forged between London
1877   Theosophists and the Arya Samaj, a Hindu organisation in
Madras.

Annie Besant, together with many other feminist and socialist
women, became involved in Theosophy in the US and in Britain,
and the movement allowed scope for women as thinkers, teachers and leaders.[152] While supporting alternative medicines, such

as homeopathy, Theosophy also provided a forum for the development of astrology.

Astrology in Europe managed to accommodate the initially shocking discovery of a 'new' planet, Uranus, in 1781 and subsequently Neptune in 1846. The science recovered from these unforeseen events and underwent a revival in the nineteenth century. By the time Pluto was discovered in 1930 astrology was being developed as an interpretive art relevant to twentieth century concerns and needs.

c 1925 In the 1920s the American astrologer, Dane Rudhyar, put astrology on to a new and deeper psychological basis by pioneering the modern humanistic approach to the horoscope.[153] By the middle years of the twentieth century, astrology was becoming more respectable because of the interest of psychologists. Jung investigated many horoscopes and Jungian astrologers have made chart interpretation a path to self-reflection and self-development that recalls the approach of the alchemists.

c 1950 In the 1940s and 1950s Michel and Francoise Gauquelin published statistical research in France that shows a relationship between the position of certain planets at birth and eminence in certain professions. Their statistical methods have not been faulted, and their rigorous work brings new respect to astrology.[154]

Many Astrologies

There are more astrologers working in India today than in the rest of the world put together; nearly every village has its astrologer. The rites and passages of life are assisted by astrological advice, and the Indian astrologer calculates a variety of other charts from the natal horoscope in order to examine different themes. The mathematical system used is only now being paralleled in the West by computer-assisted charts.[155] Many Indian astrologers also use the ancient lunar zodiac, as well as the more familiar solar one. Tradition says that both systems are necessary, for the foetus in the womb has both a solar and a lunar *chakra* centre.[156]

The Chinese divinatory system as a rigid state institution was not abandoned until after the death of the Manchu Empress Tzu Hsi in 1908.[157] The system is immensely complex – and does not rely heavily on the movements of planets through the signs.[158] Rather, the Chinese have studied the patterns of Jupiter's and Saturn's cycles and have compiled from these a system of recurrent eras based on a sixty-year span. They use a lunar zodiac and a table of beasts that rule the hours of day and night. The twelve animals that rule the years have been popularised as 'Chinese Astrology' in a fashion similar to the simplicity of 'Sunsign' astrology. In fact, Chinese divination like the horoscope requires an understanding of the many subtle and various factors that go to make up one instant in time.[159]

Tibetan astrology draws on both the Indian and Chinese systems. It is integrated with traditional Tibetan medicine into a healing system in which women as well as men become proficient after long study.[160]

The Kalachakra, Tibetan esoteric astrology, teaches through yoga and meditation how to attune the human body with the cosmic patterns of the planets and so further spiritual evolution by transcending time.[161]

Astrology is still a major part of life in South East Asia and is practised in Buddhist Thailand by midwives whose detailed astrological knowledge is brought into play to illuminate and assist delivery.[162] The science has often been associated with midwifery, for she who officiates at the birth knows the time of the child's arrival and sees the starry skies when she steps outside during the long nights of labour.

Anthropologists have collected many Moon, Sun and star myths from people around the world. A story from the Nullarbor Plain in Australia tells how Star Girl threw glowing embers into the air which became stars, and a very similar tale is told by African Bushmen. The Passamaquoddy Indians tell that the stars are birds made of fire who sing with their light, and cut a road for the soul in its journey through death.[163]

It is clear there are many systems for naming the constellations, and many astrologies. Often wisewomen and wisemen from tribal cultures have been reluctant to name the constellations and

make everything clear for the researcher. Star knowledge is usually sacred, and often secret.

A recent controversy concerns the Dogon people of Mali and the importance of the star Sirius in their culture. They appear to have known for generations that Sirius has a dark companion-star which is extraordinarily dense, that Jupiter has moons and that Saturn has rings. (They also tell that Sirius has a 'planet of women'.) Jupiter and Saturn could not be observed in this detail without a telescope and Sirius' dark companion needs advanced skywatching equipment. Some say that a missionary told these facts to the Dogon who quickly incorporated them into the ancient wisdom of the tribe.[164] However, when we know of Hildegarde of Bingen and her strangely accurate vision of the universe, and of Jonathan Swift who named the moons of Mars before they were discovered, we can imagine more intuitive ways of acquiring knowledge than the possession of a telescope.

The Ituri pygmy people call Saturn the 'star of the nine moons', and a Southern African tribe appears to have known for a long time that the earth goes round the Sun. A very old tribal song says: 'I shall worship you and go round you, as the earth worships the sun.'[165]

Some parts of the African continent have long astrological traditions.[166] Ethiopia, for example, preserved the art in its monasteries. There are many Arab and Jewish influenced astrologers on the East Coast, and ancient stone circles exist which seem to have been astronomically aligned.

Western Africa has a history of complex and intellectually advanced civilisations. Not very far from the Dogon were the mediaeval universities of Gao, Timbuktu, Jenne and Sankore, and the Mellestine Empire where women had much power and were highly respected.[167] The Queen Mother of the Ashanti was regarded as the daughter of the Moon, and wore silver to indicate her connection with the 'female aspect of God'.[168] Symbols of the Triple Moon-Goddess Ngame are found, together with a ring of animals which are the clan totems of the Akan peoples.[169]

While conclusive evidence of an astrological tradition originating in Sub-Saharan Africa is hard to find, we cannot be certain that such a tradition did not exist. We know much of ancient Egypt because Nile dust preserves, while in many other

parts of the African continent damp heat and insects rot and eat away artifacts.[170]

Truly to appreciate the breadth of astrology's past we have to abandon not only an ethnocentric vision, but also the linear concept of 'progress'. The skywatchers in the past saw returning cycles in the heavens, but noted the way no combination of cycles ever recurred. The overall pattern was always new. Spiral forms, which are found all over the world in rock art and ancient artifacts, hint at an understanding of the spiral as synthesis of both linear development and circular return. More accurately than either the wheel or the straight line, the spiral gives us an image for a process of rediscovery on an ever deepening and wider level.

Modern astronomy reveals the spiral path of all Earth dwellers.[171] Though the Earth moves in a nearly circular orbit around the Sun, the Sun is itself travelling at great speed to keep its place within the galaxy. Our planet describes a spiral in space as it accompanies the Sun.

References

1   Marshack, Alexander, *National Geographic Magazine,* January 1975.

2   Cornell, James, *The First Stargazers,* Scribner, 1981.

3   Gimbutas, Marija, The *Gods and Goddesses of Old Europe, 7000-3500 BC,* University of California Press, 1982.

4   Ibid. pp 89-111.

5   Branigan, Professor K (ed), *The Atlas of Archaeology,* St. Martin's Press, 1983, pp 138-141.

6   Ferm, V (ed), *Ancient Religions,* The Philosphical Library, NY, 1950 (Section by P Ackermann).

7   Walker, Barbara, *The Woman's Encyclopedia of Myths and Secrets,* Harper & Row, 1983, p 59.

8   Mallowan, M E L, *Early Mesopotamia and Iran,* Thames & Hudson, London, 1965, pp 59-65.

9   Walker, Barbara, 1983, op. cit. p 71.

10   Ibid. p 620.
11   Roberts, J M, *The Pelican History of the World*, Penguin, 1976, p 72.
12   Walker, Barbara, 1983, op. cit. p 248. The role of women as skywatchers cannot be adequately assessed from the surviving early evidence.
13   Ferm, V, 1950, op. cit. (Section by S Kramer).
14   Kenton, Warren, *Astrology – the Celestial Mirror*, Avon, 1974.
15   Walker, Barbara, 1983, op. cit. p 199.
16   Ferm, V, 1950, op. cit. (Section by P Ackermann).
17   Oliver, R and Fage, J D, *A Short History of Africa*, Pelican, 1962, p 20.
18   Cornell, James, 1981, op. cit. p 109.
19   Krupp, E C (ed), *In Search of Ancient Astronomies*, McGraw Hill, 1979.
20   Fagan, Cyril, *Zodiacs Old and New*, Anscombe, London, 1951.
21   Hastings, James (ed), *Encyclopedia of Religion and Ethics* (Vol 12), 'Sun, Moon and Stars', Fortress, 1926.
22   Lamy, L, *Egyptian Mysteries – New Light on Ancient Knowledge*, Crossroads Press, 1981.
23   Cirlot, Juan, *A Dictionary of Symbols*, Routledge & Kegan Paul, 1972. (Refers to Jorge Quintana's 'El Gobierno Teocrático de Mohenjo-Daro'.)
24   Roberts, J M, 1976, op. cit. p 134.
25   Sen, K M, *Hinduism*, Penguin, 1961.
26   Cornell, James, 1981, op. cit.
27   Dames, Michael, *Avebury*, Thames & Hudson, 1977.
28   Carus, Paul, *Chinese Astrology*, Open Court, 1974, p 55.
29   Holden, R W, *The Elements of House Division*, L N Fowler, 1977.
30   Russell, Eric, *Astrology and Prediction*, Citadel Press, 1975.
31   Perera, Sylvia Brinton, *Descent to the Goddess – A Way of Initiation for Women*, Inner City Books, 1983, p 13.
32   Walker, Barbara, 1983, op. cit. p 87; Gleadow, Rupert, *The Origin of the Zodiac*, Jonathan Cape, 1968.
33   *Encyclopaedia Britannica*. 'Semiramis'; *Chambers's*

Encyclopaedia; *Everyman's Encyclopaedia*; Frazer, James, *The Golden Bough*, Macmillan, 1955.

34   Lamy, L, 1981, op. cit.

35   Durdin-Robertson, Lawrence, *Goddesses of Chaldea, Syria and Egypt*, Cesara Publications, Eire, 1975.

36   Walker, Barbara, 1983, op. cit. p 890. *Encyclopedia Judaica*, Keter Publishing House, Jerusalem, 1971; 'Sibylline Oracles', 'Astrology'.

37   Dobbin, Rabbi Joel, *Astrological Secrets of the Hebrew Sages*, Inner Traditions International, 1977, p 119.

38   *Judges*, Chapters 4 and 5.

39   Walker, Barbara, 1983, op. cit. p 217. Dobbin, Rabbi Joel, 1977, op. cit. p 115.

40   Walker, Barbara, 1983, op. cit. p 739.

41   Ibid. p 10 and p 488. O'Flaherty, Wendy Doniger, *Hindu Myths*, Penguin, 1975, p 339.

42   Cornell, James, 1981, op. cit. p 211.

43   Roberts, J M, 1976, op. cit. p 80.

44   Holden, R W, 1977, op. cit.

45   Durdin-Robertson, Lawrence, 1975, op. cit.

46   Cumont, Franz, *Astrology and Religion Among The Greeks and Romans*, Dover Publications Inc., New York, 1960.

47   Ibid.

48   Chicago, Judy, *The Dinner Party*, Anchor Press/Doubleday, NY, 1979, p 123.

49   Diop, Cheikh Anta, *The African Origin of Civilisation – Myth or Reality*, Translated from the French by Mercer Cook, Lawrence Hill and Company, 1974.

50   DuBois, W E B, *The World and Africa*, International Publishers Co, Inc., NY, 1965.

51   Sweetman, James, *Women Leaders in African History*, Heinemann Educational Books, 1984.

52   Cornell, James, 1981, op. cit.

53   Roberts, J M, 1976, op. cit. p 430.

54   Colegrave, Sukie, *The Spirit of the Valley – Androgyny and Chinese Thought,* Virago, 1979.

55   Stone, Merlin, *Ancient Mirrors of Womanhood (2 vols)*, Beacon Press, 1987.

56   Cornell, James, 1981, op. cit. p 214.

57   Walker, Barbara, 1983, op. cit.

58   *Encyclopedia Judaica*, 1971, op. cit. 'Sibylline Oracles';
     Diop, C A, 1974, op. cit.

59   *Encyclopedia Judaica*, 1971, op. cit. 'Sibylline Oracles';
     and *The Jewish Encyclopedia*.

60   Walker, Barbara, 1983, op. cit. p 71.

61   Papon, D, *The Lure of the Heavens – A History of Astrology*, Samuel Weiser, 1980.

62   Witt, R E, *Isis in the Graeco-Roman World*, Thames &
     Hudson, 1971.

63   Apuleius, *The Golden Ass*, translated by Robert Graves,
     Indiana University Press, 1962.

64   Durdin-Robertson, Lawrence, 1975, op. cit.

65   Cumont, Franz, 1960, op. cit.

66   Gleadow, R, 1968, op. cit.

67   Critchlow, Keith, *Time Stands Still*, Gordon Fraser, 1979.

68   Rees, Alwyn and Rees, Brinley, *Celtic Heritage*, Thames &
     Hudson, 1961.

69   Graves, Robert, *The White Goddess*, Farrar, Straus &
     Giroux, 1966.

70   Ellis-Davidson and Hilda R, *Gods and Myths of Northern
     Europe*, Penguin, 1969.

71   Sjoo, Monica in *Wemoon Almanac 1986* c/o Musawa, La
     Serre Darre, Pouzac 65200, France.

72   Seligmann, Kurt, *Magic, Supernaturalism and Religion*,
     Paladin, 1971.

73   Dobbin, Rabbi Joel, 1977, op. cit.

74   *Encyclopedia Judaica*, 1971, op. cit., and *The Jewish
     Encyclopedia*.

75   Henry, Sandra and Taitz, Emily, *Written out of History –
     our Jewish Foremothers*, Biblio Press, 1983.

76   Dobbin, Rabbi Joel, 1977, op. cit.

77   Pagels, Elaine, *The Gnostic Gospels*, Random House, 1981.

78   Seligman, Kurt, 1971, op. cit.

79   Brunton, Paul, *A Search in Secret Egypt*, Samuel Weiser,
     1984.

80   *Everyman's Encyclopaedia; Chambers's Encyclopaedia;
     Encyclopaedia Britannica*, 'Museum, Alexandria'.

81   Ibid. 'Hypatia'.
82   Seligman, Kurt, 1971, op. cit.
83   *Encyclopedia Judaica*. 'Bet Alpha'.
84   *Encyclopaedia Britannica*. 'Irene'. *Collier's Encyclopedia*, Macmillan Educational, 1979.
85   Hope, Murry, *Practical Egyptian Magic*, The Aquarian Press, 1984.
86   Parker, Derek, and Parker, Julia, *A History of Astrology*, Crown, 1984.
87   Vajranatha and Klapecki, Lynne, *Tibetan Astrological Calendar and Almanac*, Kalachakra Publications, Kathmandu, 1978.
88   Ibid.
89   Cornell, James, 1981, op. cit.
90   Carus, Paul, 1974, op. cit. p 69.
91   Krupp, E C, 1979, op. cit. Cornell, James, 1981, op. cit.
92   Branigan, Professor K, (ed) 1982, op. cit.
93   Stone, M, 1979, op. cit.
94   *National Geographic Magazine*, December 1975.
95   Cornell, James, 1981, op. cit.
96   Nicolson, Irene, *Mexican and Central American Mythology*, Newnes Books, 1967.
97   *National Geographic Magazine*, December 1975.
98   Tunnicliffe, K *Aztec Astrology*, N Fowler, 1979.
99   Cornell, James, 1981, op. cit.
100 Ibid.
101 Ibid.
102 Ibid.
103 Alpers, A, *Maori Myths and Tribal Legends*, Murray, London, 1964.
104 Hastings, James, 1921, op. cit. 'Sun, Moon and Stars'.
105 Poignant, Roslyn, *Myths and Legends of the South Seas*, Hamlyn, 1970.
106 Matthews, Caitlin and Matthews, John, *The Western Way (Vol I) – A Practical Guide to the Mystery Tradition*, Methuen Inc., 1986.
107 Bates, Brian, *The Way of Wyrd – The Book of a Sorcerer's Apprentice*, Harper & Row, 1987.
108 Murray, Margaret, *The God of the Witches*, OUP, 1971.

109 Ravenscroft, Trevor, *The Cup of Destiny*, Samuel Weiser, 1982.
110 Stewart, R J, *The Prophetic Vision of Merlin*, Methuen Inc., 1986.
111 Lewis, H D, and Slater, Robert Lawson, *The Study of Religions*, Pelican, 1969.
112 Hussain, Freda (ed), *Muslim Women*, St. Martin's Press, 1984.
113 Walker, Barbara, 1983, op. cit.
114 *Koran*, quoted in Parker, Derek and Parker, Julia, *A History of Astrology*, 1983, op. cit.
115 Papon, D, *The Lure of the Heavens – A History of Astrology*, Samuel Weiser, 1972.
116 Fernea, Elizabeth Warnock and Bezirgan, Basima Quattan (eds), *Middle Eastern Muslim Women Speak*, University of Texas Press, Austin and London, 1977.
117 Hastings, James, 1921, op. cit. 'Sun, Moon and Stars'. Papon, D, 1972, op. cit. pp 108-9.
118 Fernea, E W, and Bezirgan, B Q, 1977, op. cit.
119 Chicago, Judy, 1979, op. cit.
120 Critchlow, Keith, *Islamic Patterns*, Thames & Hudson, 1976.
121 Parker, Derek and Parker, Julia, 1983 op. cit.
122 Ashe, Geoffrey, *The Virgin*, Routledge & Kegan Paul, 1976.
123 Chicago, Judy, 1979, op. cit.
124 Gleadow, R, 1968, op. cit.
125 Parker, Derek and Parker, Julia, 1983, op. cit.
126 Seligmann, Kurt, 1971, op. cit. Walker, Barbara, 1983, op. cit.
127 Seligmann, Kurt, 1971, op. cit.
128 Ibid.
129 Papon, D, 1972, op. cit. p 117.
130 Matt, D C, *The Zohar*, Paulist Press, 1982.
131 Patai, Ralph, *The Hebrew Goddess*, Avon/Discus 1967.
132 *Encyclopedia Judaica*, 1971, op. cit.
133 Dobbin, Rabbi Joel, 1977, op. cit.
134 Fagan, Cyril, *Astrological Origins*, Llewellyn, 1971.
135 Papon, D, 1972, op. cit.

136 Murray, Margaret, *The God of the Witches*, OUP, 1970.

137 Parrinder, G, *Witchcraft*, Penguin, 1958. (Parrinder himself thinks the figures are exaggerated; other sources disagree.)

138 Ehrenreich, Barbara, and English, Dierdre, *Witches, Midwives and Nurses — A History of Women Healers*, The Feminist Press, SUNY/College, New York, 1973.

139 Ehrenreich, Barbara, and English, Dierdre, 1973, op. cit.

140 *Encyclopaedia Britannica* 'Paracelsus'.

141 Papon. D, 1972, op. cit.

142 Krupp, E C, 1979, op. cit. p 156.

143 Cornell, James, 1981, p 136.

144 Papon, D, 1972, op. cit. Hone, Margaret, *The Modern Text-Book of Astrology*, L N Fowler, 1978.

145 Chicago, Judy, 1979, op. cit.

146 It was in the seventeenth century in England that the famous herbalist Culpeper published his works on astrological herbalism, which enjoyed very large sales, in spite of incurring the wrath of the medical profession. See Le Strange, Richard, *A History of Herbal Plants*, Arco Publishing Co., New York, 1977.

147 Papon, D, 1972, op. cit.

148 Papon, D, 1972, op. cit.

149 Volguine, Alexandre, *Lunar Astrology*, ASI Publishers Inc, 1974.

150 Sweetman, J, 1984, op. cit.

151 Parker, Derek and Parker, Julia, *A History of Astrology*, 1983, op. cit.

152 Swiney, Frances, *The Ancient Road, or the Development of the Soul*, Bell, 1918. Despard, Charlotte, *Theosophy and the Woman's Movement*, Theosophical Publishing Society, 1913.

153 Rudhyar, Dane, *The Astrology of the Personality*, Doubleday, 1970.

154 Gauquelin, Michel, *L'Influence des Astres — Etude Critique et Experimentale*, Editions de Dauphin, Paris, 1955. Quoted in Dean, Geoffrey (ed), *Recent Advances in Natal Astrology*, Astrological Association of Great Britain,

1977, where Gauquelin's work is assessed and compared with other statistical studies.

155 Addey, John, *Harmonics in Astrology*, Cambridge Circle, 1976.

156 Volguine, A, 1974, op. cit.

157 Cornell, James, 1981, op. cit.

158 Carus, Paul, 1974, op. cit.

159 de Kermadec, J-M H, *The Way to Chinese Astrology – 4 Pillars of Destiny*, George Allen & Unwin, 1983.

160 *The World Who's Who of Women*, Melrose Press, 1982. See entry on Dr. Lobsang Dolma.

161 Vajranatha and Klapecki, 1978, op. cit.

162 Reynolds, Vernon and Tanner, Ralph, *The Biology of Religion*, Longman, 1983.

163 Rothenberg, Jerome (ed), *Technicians of the Sacred*, University of California Press, 1985.

164 Temple, R K G, *The Sirius Mystery*, St. Martin's Press, 1978.

165 Cornell, James, 1981, op. cit.

166 Volguine, A, 1974, op. cit. p 22.

167 Du Bois, W E B, 1965, op. cit.

168 Parrinder, G, *African Traditional Religion*, Greenwood Press, 1976.

169 Graves, Robert, 1961, op. cit.

170 Du Bois, W E B, 1965, op. cit. Also see Mutwa, Credo, *My People*, Penguin, 1971, pp 232-233 for an account of Bantu astrology, and p 171 for a description of the 'Knot of Time' located at Kariba.

171 Blair, Lawrence, *Rhythms of Vision*, Croom Helm, 1975.

Other books used in this chapter are listed in the Mythology, Religion, and History section of the Bibliography.

3
Wheels Within Wheels
The Basics of the Horoscope

The skywatcher of ancient times saw, as we do today, a belt of stars in the heavens which seemed to turn around the Earth. Each group of stars she identified in this belt rose in the East and disappeared beneath the horizon in the West. She compared the starry belt to a great wheel in the sky. She also noticed how the Moon and planets appeared to move slowly around the wheel over a period of weeks or months.

This wheel of encircling stars appears to rise and set because the Earth is turning, showing us different parts of the sky according to the time of day or night. The stars are there in the sky during the day, but we do not see them because of the Sun's light, unless they are revealed by a total eclipse of the Sun.

Dividing the Sky

The constellations in the sky do not all rise and set, and only those that make up the starwheel are known as the *zodiacal constellations*. It was these zodiacal star groups that gave their names to the twelve sections of the sky that astrologers call the *signs of the zodiac*. The zodiacal constellations vary in size but the signs named after them cover an equal expanse of sky. They divide the starwheel in the heavens into twelve equal parts. Each of the twelve signs covers 30° of the 360° circle around the Earth. Only six of the signs are above the horizon at any one place and time; the other six divide up the sky on the other side of the Earth.

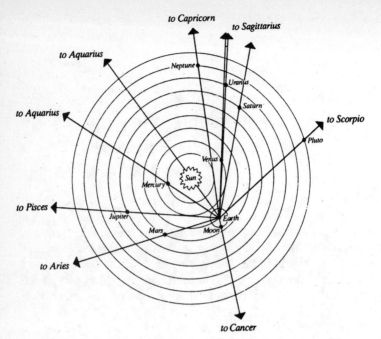

Figure 3.1 *The solar system seen from Earth (not to scale)*

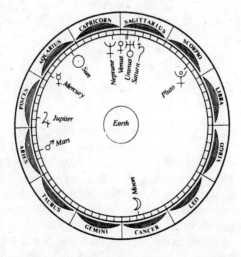

Figure 3.2 *The planets in the horoscope*

The Tropical Zodiac

The beginning of the sign of Aries and, from thence, all the following signs is fixed from the position of the Sun on the first day of spring in the Northern Hemisphere (the Equinox). Because the zodiac signs are fixed from a seasonal point, astrologers refer to this way of dividing the sky as the tropical (meaning seasonal) zodiac.

The twelve signs of the zodiac give us a way to mark the positions and movements of the *planets*.

Planets

The word 'planet' comes from the Greek word meaning 'wanderer'. The planets look like stars in the sky, but seem to wander through the zodiac belt, as they move in orbits around the Sun.

We measure the positions of the planets against the zodiac from the Earth's viewpoint because that is our starting place, not because astrologers any longer think that everything is in movement around the Earth. It is an Earth-centred view that interests us, and although the Sun is not moving around the zodiac it appears to do so because of the Earth's movement. Therefore for astrological convenience we include the Sun with the planets, because this provides a way to chart the Earth's seasonal position. We also include the Moon, although technically it is a satellite of the Earth, because it, too, appears against the zodiac which gives us a way to measure its position and movement.

The *natal horoscope*, the map of one birth-moment, is drawn up from Earth's viewpoint to show the zodiac sign against which the planets, Sun and Moon appear.

Astrologically, the *planets* represent the parts of ourselves which make up the whole of the psyche. Everyone has all ten astrological planets in the horoscope and, very simply, they represent the following parts of the human psyche:

☽ Moon   unconscious self
☉ Sun   conscious, integrating self
☿ Mercury   mental and nervous faculties

♀	Venus	urge to relate
♂	Mars	drive, self-assertion
♃	Jupiter	urge towards expansion
♄	Saturn	urge towards consolidation
♅	Uranus	sense of individuality
♆	Neptune	sense of oneness
♇	Pluto	urge towards transformation

In Chapter 4 the planets are examined in greater depth.

To discover the potential of these planets in combination we learn about them in three basic ways – by their orientation in the cosmos (the *signs*), the positions in which they appear in the heavens according to the time of night or day (the *houses*), and their interaction with each other (*aspects*).

Signs

The twelve signs represent twelve modes in which the planets can express themselves. They are like adjectives describing *how* the planets work.

At a very basic level we can say that the signs offer the following positive and negative possibilities for the planets' expression.

♈	Aries	courageously or rashly
♉	Taurus	productively or obstinately
♊	Gemini	with versatility or diffusely
♋	Cancer	sensitively or touchily
	Leo	powerfully or overpoweringly
♍	Virgo	skilfully or critically
♎	Libra	harmoniously or indecisively
♏	Scorpio	intensely or obsessively
♐	Sagittarius	expansively or extravagantly
♑	Capricorn	constructively or severely
♒	Aquarius	inventively or perversely
♓	Pisces	imaginatively or confusedly

The nature of each sign's approach to life is explored in detail in Chapter 6.

The Planets in the Signs

Each planet expresses its own nature according to its sign potential in an individual horoscope. For instance:

Mars (self-assertion), acting through Capricorn (constructively or severely), gives dynamic energy to build or achieve, or the possibility of a harshly ambitious nature.

Moon (unconscious self), acting through Libra (harmoniously or indecisively), gives an instinctive ability to create pleasant surroundings and co-operate with people, together with the possibility of an habitual vagueness.

The planets remain in the signs for varying lengths of time. The Moon passes through all twelve signs each month, remaining roughly two-and-a-half days in each sign. The Sun moves through one sign in approximately thirty days. The approximate dates that the Sun moves into each sign are given below:

Aries	Mar 21-Apr 19
Taurus	Apr 20-May 20
Gemini	May 21-Jun 21
Cancer	Jun 22-Jul 22
Leo	Jul 23-Aug 22
Virgo	Aug 23-Sept 22
Libra	Sept 23-Oct 22
Scorpio	Oct 23-Nov 21
Sagittarius	Nov 22-Dec 21
Capricorn	Dec 22-Jan 19
Aquarius	Jan 20-Feb 18
Pisces	Feb 19-Mar 20

These dates can only be approximate because they vary slightly from year to year, and the exact position of the Sun can be told only by consulting astrological tables (See notes on cusps p 56).

The position of the Sun gives us the Sunsign, which has been

over-used in popular astrology, but which nevertheless is still very important.

Mercury is always close to the Sun from our vantage point and so appears in the same sign as the Sun or in the one before or after the Sunsign. This planet spends a total of roughly one month in each sign every year, and appears to move backwards and forwards in and out of signs. When we see a planet moving backwards through the zodiac, we call this *retrograde* motion; astrologically it means that the planet is less obvious and more subtle in its action. (Any of the planets except Sun and Moon can appear in a retrograde position.)

Venus is also close to the Sun, and so we see this planet, too, in the same sign as the Sun, or in a sign close (within two signs) to the Sunsign. Venus, too, spends roughly one month a year in each sign.

Mars takes anything from one to eight months to pass through a sign, and may appear anywhere in the horoscope. Jupiter and Saturn can also appear in any of the signs.

Jupiter takes roughly one year, Saturn two-and-a-half years, Uranus seven, Neptune fourteen and Pluto anything from around eleven to twenty-nine years to pass through a sign.

From these figures we can see that the placements of the slower moving planets are shared by everyone born between certain dates. For instance, Pluto was in Leo from 1940 until 1955 and those born during this time will share something of their generation's Leonine nature as a background influence to their personalities. Pluto (urge for transformation) acting through Leo (powerfully or over-poweringly) gave this generation a strong (and sometimes dominating) creative urge to change society.

The slow moving planets can be important in a person's chart if they make strong aspects (see Chapter 8) to the faster moving planets (which have more immediate personal relevance) or to the Ascendant and Midheaven (see below). However, the signs they occupy are more significant to the generation than to the individual.

Cusps of the Signs

The division between two signs is called its *cusp*. There are 30° in each sign of the zodiac so that, for instance, 29° of Aries is followed by 0° of Taurus, the sign cusp.

Rulerships

Certain signs allow a very strong expression of each of the planetary energies, and we say that each sign is *ruled* by a planet. The planetary rulerships are given in Chapters 4 and 6.

Originally astrologers knew of seven heavenly bodies. They saw seven as a magical number and associated the planets with many systems, from the days of the week and musical notes to the colours of the rainbow. Each day, note and colour was said to be ruled by one planet, as were the metals. The three 'modern' planets, Uranus, Neptune and Pluto, discovered more recently, have also been found to rule signs.

The Structure of the Horoscope

It is beyond the scope of this book to explain how a horoscope is calculated or drawn up. At the end of Chapter 9 a reading list is given detailing books from which this can be learned. In the following section of this chapter we explain the *angles of the chart* and show how the *houses* are marked into the chart to give readers an introduction to understanding a horoscope once it has already been drawn up.

The Angles of the Chart

At any one moment on a particular part of the Earth's surface a certain degree of the zodiac is rising over the eastern horizon, and this important point of the chart is called the *Ascendant*. Diametrically opposite is the *Descendant*, the degree of the zodiac setting in the west. The axis of the Ascendant/Descendant represents the horizon.

The highest point of the zodiac is called the *Midheaven* (MC) and the *Imum Coeli* (IC) is the point opposite the Midheaven. It is invisible to us because it represents a point in the heavens on the other side of the Earth. These four points give the four *angles* of the chart. The horoscope is a two-dimensional diagram of the three-dimensional sky, and it cannot be looked at like an ordinary map. For people in

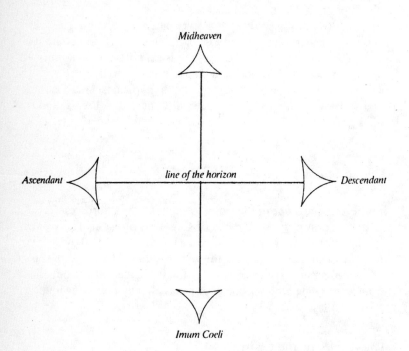

Figure 3.3   *The angles of the chart*

the Northern hemisphere the Midheaven is in the South, and so the easterly and westerly points are drawn in reverse from the positions we would expect them to be on a map of the Earth.

The Ascendant being the rising, or oncoming, point of the zodiac (due to the Earth's rotation) shows the way we reveal ourselves when we first meet people.

The Descendant shows the way we reveal ourselves to people we

know intimately, or it may show the part of ourselves that we only express *through* other people.

The Midheaven represents the way we try to achieve recognition, and the part of ourselves we are reaching towards.

The Imum Coeli represents the part of the self that is most deeply buried in the unconscious.

Houses

While the planets are the 'what' of the horoscope, and the signs tell us 'how' the planets manifest their energies, the houses show us 'where' in our lives the planets express their energies most strongly. For instance, the Seventh House shows one-to-one relationships and the way we approach them.

Each of the houses has a particular theme which summarises a complex of interests and concerns. This is fully explored in Chapter 7, but a brief summary of their themes can be given here.

First House – Self-oriented concerns
Second House – Resources
Third House – Environment
Fourth House – Roots
Fifth House – Play
Sixth House – Work
Seventh House – Partnership
Eighth House – The Mysteries
Ninth House – Exploration
Tenth House – Status
Eleventh House – Ideals
Twelfth House – Seclusion

The twelve-part division of the horoscope by the houses is created by dividing each quarter of the chart shown in Figure 3.3 into three parts. The First, Second and Third Houses lie between the Ascendant and Imum Coeli, the Fourth, Fifth and Sixth between Imum Coeli and Descendant, etc. While the zodiac signs always cover exactly 30° of a circle, the sizes of the houses can vary according to place and time

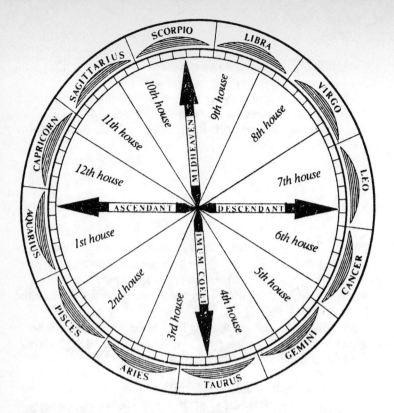

Figure 3.4 *Example of houses in a chart with the Ascendant at 7°*
Aquarius

of birth, and the Midheaven may not be exactly 90° from the Ascendant, as shown in Figure 3.4 above.

The line of the Ascendant is the beginning of the First House, and the sign in which this falls depends upon the time of day, the time of year, and the place on Earth for which the horoscope is constructed. In this example the Ascendant is 7° Aquarius.

The houses create another twelve-part division of the horoscope which is superimposed on the twelve-part division of the zodiac circle into signs. In Figure 3.4 it will be seen that the zodiac circle is marked around the outer circumference, while the houses divide the inner part of the chart. Not all astrologers mark in the houses and signs in exactly the same way, but this method helps us to see the interrelation of the signs and houses fairly clearly. Together, the signs and houses make a wheel within a wheel, reflecting the Earth's

turning on its own axis once every twenty-four hours. The diagram in Figure 3.4 is a picture of one moment in time, but we can see the changes in the way different horoscopes could be drawn up during one day if we imagine the outer wheel of twelve signs as rotating clockwise. One complete rotation of this wheel would take twenty-four hours. If a person were to be born six hours later than the time shown in the diagram (one quarter of a daily rotation) the wheel of signs would have rotated so that Leo would be at the bottom of the chart and Aquarius at the top. Taurus would lie on the right and Scorpio on the left.

Planets in the Houses and Signs on the House Cusps

Any of the areas of life that the houses represent may be emphasised by a planet appearing in the house at birth. The signs that coincide with the beginnings or cusps of the houses show the way in which each person approaches the areas of her life that the houses represent. (This is explained fully in Chapter 7.) In Figure 3.4, for instance, the pattern of the houses is shown as it would be drawn up for someone who has the Ascendant at 7° Aquarius and was born at Latitude 50° 30′ N. Each line marked in the inner circle represents a house cusp or beginning point. In this diagram the beginning of the Second House coincides with the sign of Pisces on the outer wheel. This is described as 'having Pisces on the Second House cusp'.

When a planet falls close to the cusp or dividing line between two houses, it is possible that the concerns of either house (before or after the cusp) will be important to the person.

The Aspects

The *aspects* are the geometrical relationships between the planets, as measured from the Earth. They show us the interrelationship of the different parts of the self within the individual represented by the planets. One planet may make a challenging aspect to another planet, a flowing aspect, or two planets can work together as one combined

energy. When there are many challenging aspects to a planet, we say it has a 'difficult placement', but aspects cannot be seen as simply 'good' or 'bad'. For a more detailed explanation of aspects see Chapter 8.

Dragon's Head ☊ and Dragon's Tail ☋: the Moon's Nodes

The Moon's Nodes are the two points where the Moon's path around the Earth crosses the path of the Earth around the Sun, for the two orbits are not quite in the same plane. These points change slightly every day. The point of the Dragon's Tail (South Node ☋) in the horoscope of an individual shows, by its sign and house position, the instinctual patterns of that person's past. The Dragon's Head (North Node ☊) represents the growing influences of the future towards which the person is moving.[1] Planets making aspects to the Moon's Nodes show parts of the self bound up with this process of self-development.

For instance, Mercury close to the Dragon's Tail in Libra (the sign of balance) could indicate that the person concerned was moving away from her pattern of constantly thinking through all the options and balancing them up before being able to act.

The Natal Horoscope as Blueprint

The different parts of the birth horoscope – the planets and their aspects, the pattern of the signs and houses, the Nodes of the Moon – give us a picture of the complex interactions of energies at an individual's time of birth. The natal horoscope provides us with a blueprint for each person, describing the celestial energies that accompanied her entry into the world.

From that basic pattern we are able to understand the changes experienced in our lives as the planets move on to make new patterns (the planetary transits – see below). The changes they manifest will be experienced differently according to the transiting planets' interaction with the natal horoscope.

Transits

These are the movements of the *present-day* planets through the zodiac. When transiting planets cross or make aspects to the positions of the natal planets in an individual horoscope they represent issues in the person's life that are coming to the fore in the present time.

For instance, Jupiter, the planet of expansion, when *transiting* through Leo in 1979 crossed over the natal planetary positions in the charts of those with planets in Leo. It also made oppositions to natal planets in Aquarius. For people with planets in these signs the urge to travel or to expand their lives in other ways would have become more conscious.

There are almost always some transits occurring for the individual, and this relationship between the present day planets and the planets at birth gives a way to understand the changes and self-development we go through cyclically. More information is given about transits and planetary cycles in Chapter 9, and we refer to the cycles of various planets in Chapter 4.

The Horoscope as a Whole

All the foregoing features of the horoscope need to be seen as an integrated whole.

The subtleties of the interaction of Sun, Moon, Ascendant and planets of the chart can only be brought out by analysis of the whole horoscope. Chapter 9 explains how we may approach the synthesis of these different parts. As we learn to synthesise astrological information we begin to understand the complex meanings of the dance of the planets at each person's birth.

Reference

1   For a full exploration of the Moon's Nodes within the horoscope see Schulman, Martin, *Karmic Astrology (Vol 1): The Moon's Nodes and Reincarnation,* Samuel Weiser, 1978.

4
The Planets

The Planets in Mythology

Many of our ideas about the planets derive from the mythology of ancient peoples. Goddesses, gods, heroines and heroes stir the imagination and overlap with powerful figures we meet in dreams and in art. These are known as *archetypal* figures, which are ancient images shared by all cultures and encountered within the unconscious by the individual. An archetypal figure, an image emanating from the unconscious, is very different from a *stereotype* – a rigid pattern for human behaviour – though the two concepts have sometimes been confused. Astrology does not use stereotyped images to describe actual people, for astrologers are interested in the unique and particular rather than in broad generalisations about individuals.

Many of us have been strongly influenced by the Greek and Roman cultures through our education. Each deity in classical Greece had a distinct personality, upon which much traditional astrological interpretation is based. In this book we question some of the assumptions of these later myths and seek to expand astrology by considering the archetypal figures which preceded the classical stories. These figures lie further back in the past and deeper in the unconscious. We draw directly on Babylonian, Greek and Roman mythologies, and also on African, Asian and European sources, to explore the meaning of the planets. We have also expanded their meaning from other world mythologies.[1]

All the goddesses of classical mythology originate from the Great Goddess of earlier religions. She represents too large a concept to be contained within one or two planetary energies alone, nevertheless only the Moon and Venus were seen to be female in classical mythology.

Yet the many aspects of the Great Goddess readily relate to a number of the planetary profiles. We do not believe that the planetary energies are essentially either feminine or masculine. However, there is a tendency for them to assume a gender within our imaginations and dreams; this process makes them more accessible for us to work with. We refer more to the goddesses than the gods to begin to redress an imbalance which has come from traditional sources.

The planets, because they represent parts of the psyche, show the needs of every human being; the need for an integrated self (Sun), instinctual and emotional needs (Moon), for relationships of all kinds (Venus), for communication (Mercury), for the opportunity to be active (Mars), for a social and/or spiritual connection with the larger world (Jupiter) and the need to learn from experience (Saturn).

The three 'modern' planets show the need to break through old restrictive structures (Uranus), the need for a feeling of interconnection with all life and with the universe (Neptune), and the need for regeneration and renewal (Pluto). Ancient peoples, too, were aware of these last three needs, and included similar ideas in their understanding of the phases of the Moon. The fact that we now know three planets that specifically symbolise these needs shows that we are consciously discovering energies that were always present in the unconscious (which the Moon represents), just as we discover distant parts of the solar system.

In 1977 Chiron was discovered between the orbits of Saturn and Uranus. Astronomers are not sure whether Chiron can be defined as a planet; its orbit is highly eccentric, and it may have come from outside the solar system. The astrological significance of this possible planet is being studied and it seems likely to relate to healing.[2] The names chosen for newly discovered objects in the solar system do not seem to be coincidental; Chiron was the wise healer in mythology.

Between Mars and Jupiter a belt of many thousands of *asteroids* (small planetary bodies) orbits the Sun. Tables are now widely available detailing the movements of four of the larger asteroids (Ceres, Vesta, Juno and Pallas). Some astrologers have considered them to be important astrologically, in spite of their small size, in manifesting the feminine principle because they have been named after goddesses, and to be particularly relevant to personal relationships.[3]

The 'invisible Moon' Lilith has been said to be in orbit around the Earth, though its existence is not countenanced by astronomers. In

the main source of information on Lilith, this hypothetical satellite of the Earth is said to manifest various unhelpful influences.[4] Like the asteroids Lilith has been thought to be particularly relevant to women and to the increasing feminist awareness in the world. (In Hebraic tradition Lilith was Eve's predecessor who refused to submit to Adam.)

In spite of these evocative mythological associations the authors are not convinced that any of the asteroids or the hypothetical Lilith are of particular importance in the horoscope, and have chosen rather to examine the ten traditional astrological planets in the light of feminist awareness.

Astronomers believe that there may be at least one planet to be found beyond Pluto; the implications of this are considered in Chapter 10.

The Planets within the Psyche

Planets are said to be highlighted within a horoscope when they are strongly emphasised by aspect (see Chapter 8), or by sign or house position (see Chapters 6 and 7). One of the most obvious ways a planet is emphasised is by its position near the angles of the chart (see Chapter 3), particularly if it is on the Ascendant or at the Midheaven. Any one of the planets, from Mercury to Pluto, is especially significant if it has a close aspect to the Moon or Sun. A planet works strongly if it is placed in the sign it rules or in its natural house (see the details at the beginning of each planet's description within this chapter).

Planetary transits indicate periods in our lives when we strongly encounter the issues the various planets raise (see Chapter 3). By observing your own feelings and reactions as you read the descriptions of the planets it becomes clearer which of these needs within your self is of special and current relevance to you.

The authors' own work in therapy and personal growth has helped them to understand how one part of the self can feel excluded. A metaphor for this is the anger shown by mythological goddesses or gods when their worship was neglected. An unrecognised part of the self can make a bid for attention, often subconsiously. If ignored,

the hints become less subtle and the neglected part of the psyche may be forced to confront the person in a more direct and possibly shocking way. Recognition of the neglected part of the psyche is the beginning of self-healing, and ways are then found to transform the negative energy of this part of the self into its positive expression.

Astrology helps to put us in touch with every part of the psyche, as well as enabling us to value those parts with which we are familiar. When a conflict is conscious, astrology can name, as planetary energies, the conflicting parts of the self, and provide the knowledge to improve the dialogue between them. It can also help us to see when we have *over*-identified with one particular planetary energy.

The planetary model reminds us of the psyche's complexity and wholeness. By learning about the planets and their archetypes, our inner selves, we can respect their various needs, thereby preparing the way to self-integration.[5]

In ancient times the Moon was the first of the astrological planets to be studied in the sky. While the Moon is the smallest of the celestial bodies commonly used in astrology, it is so close to us that it appears to be exactly the same size as the Sun. The Sun and Moon are known as the two 'lights', the light of day and the light of night. While the Sun's light appears to have a constant and focused qual-

THE MOON

unconscious self
feeling nature; instincts;
imagination; connectedness;
nurturance; belonging
Rules: Cancer and the Fourth
House

ity, the Moon's light appears cyclic and diffuse. There is a mystery in the Moon's soft-focused light which opens up the way to the magical illuminations of the unconscious.

The wisdom attributed to the Moon throughout all cultures and ages is limitless. In their book on menstruation called *The Wise Wound*,[6] Shuttle and Redgrove connect the ancient Sanskrit, Greek, Latin and Polynesian words for spirit and mind (*manas, menos, mens, mana*) with the earliest Indo-European word roots for the Moon and the month (*mas, men, mensis*). The conclusion they draw is that our experience of the Moon has been an integral part of the development of our human consciousness.

To astrologers it is natural that the Moon should play such a crucial role in the development of human consciousness, because it is the only celestial body to move in orbit around our home which is the Earth.

There are many lunar creation myths throughout the world. In Egypt the Moon was the 'Mother of the Universe'; in Polynesia she was Hine, and every woman is a *wahine* made in her image; in Finland the Moon Goddess Luonnatar brought the World Egg from the sea. The sea and/or blood invariably play a crucial part in creation myths, and these two fluids are intimately connected with the cycles of the Moon. Our earliest concepts of time centre on the monthly cycle of the Moon's phases and the corresponding female menstrual cycle and oceanic tidal changes.

Today, research into the Moon's cyclic effect on the rise and fall of fluid levels in the body and sap levels in plants throws new light on ancient folklore. For centuries, gardeners and farmers have followed

the wisdom of planting and harvesting by the Moon, while medical astrologers have always taken serious account of the Moon's position when advising on the timing of an operation. Astrologically, the Moon is said to govern the general conditions of health, and acts as an indicator of how we feel about and care for ourselves. Physiologically the Moon governs the fluids in the body (water, blood, serum, breastmilk, etc) and their levels of balance.

The Moon is a symbol of connectedness. Its phases provide the interconnections between countless polarities; with the Moon's monthly cycle we move through light and dark, strong and weak, fertile and infertile, birth and death, as we go from Full Moon to New Moon and back again. Each night the Moon's size changes, never halting at one point or missing another. The Moon's cycle shows us continual transition, where each step is equally valuable. Lunar energy within us responds to all we encounter daily, allowing us to develop awareness of being: the sense of the importance of each momentary experience.

This lunar ability to live within the moment is the aim of many spiritual practices, because it liberates us from the constrictions of the mind. It is unfortunate that many astrologers have reduced the importance of the Moon to descriptions of its moody, changeable nature, failing to see the wisdom of a more ancient teaching.

With our lunar selves we use our instincts to survive, feel with emotions and create from our imagination. As children we operate from our lunar nature openly and freely, but as adults in 'civilised' societies we often lose contact with this side of our nature. To make the reconnection we need to revalue these lunar gifts. Astrologically, the Moon describes our childhood experience, the emotional foundations and the habitual response patterns which we develop from interaction with our early environment and parents. When we seek to uncover these roots we travel back into the lunar realms of memory and the unconscious, where we find both our personal inheritance and the inheritance of our family and culture. This journey into our past can reveal the early reasons behind our feelings of security and insecurity, and the instinctual ways in which we care for ourselves and others.

This caring and nurturing ability is a strong part of our lunar nature, but a distortion has occurred in astrology by the failure to portray the Moon in its wholeness.

The Moon is most frequently described in astrology texts as representing the protective, nurturing, sensitive and fertile parts of the self. These descriptions draw heavily on the concept of the Moon as the 'Good Mother': the Christian Mary, or Chinese Kwan-Yin. However, world mythologies portray the Moon not only as Mother but also as Maiden and Crone, reflecting the waxing and waning phases of the Moon as well as its full phase. (The Goddess as the full Moon was not only the Mother but the Lady of Power and Sexuality.) The lunar Goddess was portrayed as a trinity by the Greeks: as the maiden Hebe, the queen and mother Hera and the crone Hecate. The Hindu Goddess Kali contained the same trinity as Parvarti-Durga-Uma. Within the Moon as Maiden can be seen the Moon's independent, creative and imaginative qualities, while as the Crone the Moon is wise, a healer who can also bring dissolution and death. In Asia it is said that the true worshippers of the Goddess must love her destructive images as much as her beautiful ones, and as astrologers we can gain much from this advice.

The Moon symbolises the wholeness of life. The growing, life-giving and the diminishing, death-dealing sides of our nature are contained within the lunar images. Through understanding the Moon's cycle we can recognise the part of ourselves that we keep in the dark. This 'shadow' side contains that which is frightening or taboo but also bears the creative seeds of the unconscious.

As we watch the waxing and waning face of the Moon we can contemplate the Moon's phases in our own lives. Our energy is often high or 'lunatic' around the full Moon, low or introspective around the new Moon, and between these two phases we experience gradual transitions as the Moon appears to grow or decrease in size. Everyone reacts differently to this cycle, and each individual's particular sensitivity to the Moon's movement is reflected in the natal chart according to the Moon's position and aspects at birth. As well as responding to the Moon's phases, each of us is often more comfortable on days when the Moon occupies certain signs of the zodiac in its monthly journey. Observing the Moon and understanding her cycles can help women to attune and regulate the menstrual cycle. For all of us, knowing our lunar cycles aids recognition of our peaks and lows of fertility, creativity, imagination and emotional and instinctive responses.

Traditional astrology gave the realm of the Moon to women and

the realm of the Sun to men. However, in many cultures the Moon has been seen as masculine. The Moon represents an integral part of the male psyche, and it is just as important for men to reconnect with the lunar cycle as it is for women to rediscover the solar path. By learning about the Moon in our individual charts we can value the gifts of the unconscious, the wisdom of the instincts and the integrity of the emotions.

Our own star, the Sun, is the centre of our solar system, and the source of the light and life within it. All the planets move in orbits around it, and on Earth our daily experience of light and dark, and yearly journey through the seasons, depends on our relationship to the Sun.

THE SUN

conscious integrating self
self-awareness; self-expression;
confidence; vitality; purpose; will
Rules: Leo and the Fifth House

Contemporary European culture has inherited from the Greeks, and the later Celts, the concept of a male Sungod, but recent research shows that Sun goddesses were just as numerous as Sun gods in earlier cultures. The Hittites reverenced the Sun Goddess as Arinna, the Celts the Fire Goddess Brighde, who gave light to the Sun, while in ancient Argentina the Sun Goddess was called the 'sister of all women'. Similarly, the Australian Wurunjerri people said the Sun was everyone's sister. In Japan the ruling classes once traced their descent from the supreme Sun Goddess, Omikami Amaterasu. The solar deities are often shown as creators. The British Sun Goddess, Sul, gave birth to each new aeon from her belly at Silbury Hill, and in Scandinavia it was said that the Sun Goddess would give birth to a daughter after doomsday and that she would be the Sun of the next creation. The Egyptians believed that each Pharoah was fathered by Ra, the Sun God. The Sun may have been our creator in a literal sense, for one contemporary theory of the creation of the solar system suggests that planetary matter was originally thrown out from the Sun.

In astrology, too, the Sun is seen as a centering and creative force. The Sun in the chart represents the inner flame, a guiding light which illuminates the path of the individual and which acts as an integrating principle for our many selves. The solar path is the journey of the lifetime. In the Tarot pack the Sun card shows a young child, a figure of potential, who is at the beginning of the solar journey. This journey is the one of becoming ourselves and of fulfilling our potential; an individual voyage which, despite the billions of lives on this planet, is unique because it is defined by inner purpose rather than external results. The solar part of us has the courage, strength and will to face the world and meet its challenges. It is the inner self which knows its own nature and direction. By looking at our personal heroines and heroes,

both mythological and historical, we can find in them sparks that ignite the fire of our own sense of purpose. Confident self-expression comes from this knowing of ourselves and our direction; being in touch with solar energy leads to our own creativity. The form of this creativity is unimportant; what is important is our enjoyment of it; that we express ourselves honestly and directly, spontaneously recognising who we are.

One of the biggest set-backs to modern astrology has been the popularised version which takes note only of the sign the Sun occupies. This simplification has both over-emphasised the Sun in the chart, and at the same time devalued the Sun's specific meaning. Knowing the Sun's sign and house position and its aspects in the natal chart helps us to come into contact with our individuality and takes us beyond the generalisations of Sunsign astrology.

The solar process is one of self-integration. We can recognise our many voices and impulses (represented by other factors in the chart) and work towards their synthesis, based on our sense of self and life purpose. Two people who have the Sun in the same sign are unlikely to be very much alike, nor will they express their creativity in the same way; however they will, at a deep level, share similar views of themselves and their life's direction.

In traditional astrology the Sun is said to represent a person's vitality, health and happiness. The twentieth century humanistic astrologer is more likely to say that the Sun's position and aspects relate to our ability to recover from setbacks, heal ourselves and maintain a positive outlook; the underlying theme of the interpretation is the same. When we are depressed, lacking inspiration or feeling devitalised, we are prone to illness; it is the body's expression of our inner state. Today, many forms of healing and therapy work to build up and strengthen our sense of self and purpose, and together these increase the overall life force, leading to cures for many ills. In medical astrology the Sun rules the heart, which is the powerhouse of the body. On a symbolic level the Sun represents the heart also, in its relationship to our generosity, courage, warmth and inner knowledge.

The Sun has been called the masculine principle in astrology, and has been said to describe the man in a woman's life. Some traditional astrologers even assert that a woman should identify herself with her Moonsign, while seeking a husband who represents the qualities of her Sunsign. Through these interpretations astrologers have

encouraged women to project their own strength, vitality, identity and direction on to men. This distortion negates the wholeness which is inherent in astrology, and highlights the necessity for each of us to connect with her own solar energy. As we reach out to the Sun we revitalise ourselves; we become centered, healthy and whole.

MERCURY

mental and nervous faculties
perception; communication;
thought processes; learning ability;
language; acquired skills
Rules: Gemini and Virgo, and the
Third and Sixth Houses

Mercury is the closest planet to the Sun, and it is only ever visible in the twilight of dawn or dusk. This prime position close to the Sun has its disadvantages, for Mercury is hard to perceive next to the Sun's brilliance. Just as the planet can elude amateur astronomers, so its importance in the horoscope can be overlooked by astrologers.

Mercury is the first planetary stepping-stone from the Sun, acting as translator and messenger of the solar consciousness to the realms beyond. The Roman messenger god Mercury has many predecessors and counterparts in mythology. Like Mercury they are often clever tricksters, stealing knowledge from the gods for human beings. The Sumerian Goddess Inanna stole the tablets of destiny for human use, while in Greek mythology Prometheus angered Zeus by stealing fire also for human use; the same trick is carried out by the Maori God Maui on his great ancestress. These gifts mark the opening up of new paths for humankind through greater understanding and skills.

Mercury is the vehicle of all knowledge, representing the thought processes and language which structure our experience of reality. Perception, recognition and the ability to form concepts are Mercurial functions; they enable us to communicate with ourselves as well as with others. Mercury's energy is that of making connections; we use this energy to connect the pieces of information we receive through our five physical senses, and to connect thoughts and ideas.

While the lunar part of ourselves makes gradual transitions between polarities, the Mercurial faculty within us jumps across gaps instantaneously. This process of making connections swiftly enables us to reason, learn and invent. Mercury is visible in both the racing mind and the fast tongue.

A strong Mercury in the chart gives a highly curious nature and thirst for knowledge. Many of the Mercurial gods and goddesses are portrayed as youthful seekers of new information and experiences. When we are in contact with the Mercurial part of ourselves we are youthful students, no matter what our actual age, because we are on the lookout for new horizons and are willing to move towards them.

The problems emerge when it is time to stop; Mercury keeps us going on, restless and speedy.

It is the Mercurial function that brought us language, alphabets, academic learning and manual skills. The Greek forerunner to Roman Mercury, Hermes, is said to have invented music and the lyre. Earlier mythology tells of goddesses who invented all the useful arts and skills: Egyptian Seshat, Babylonian Nisaba, Indian Sarasvati, Greek Athena.

The Mercurial part of the self makes us swift and adept at picking up new knowledge, skills and tricks. However the skills and learning of Mercury are not necessarily accompanied by ethical considerations. This part of the self has a distinctly tricky aspect, and can often be seen in the market place or within the political arena. According to Mercurial reasoning anything can be justified, and we can quite easily be seduced by the brilliance of our own mercurial arguments. Without intelligence, wit and free thinking humankind could not have survived as a species. Yet we have to use the Mercurial function wisely; the development of our intelligence has also given us the means to destroy ourselves and our world. Mercury's gifts can be used for good or ill.

There are many opposites and polarities represented by this planet. The Mercurial god Hermes was seen as bisexual, and as the consort of the Goddess Aphrodite shared her energy as the original 'hermaphrodite'. In the Hermetic mysticism of the Renaissance alchemists the secret of magical power was androgyny, the mingling of the 'masculine' and 'feminine' parts of the psyche. The true intelligence Mercury represents within us is not to be seen as cold rationalism, rather as the coming together of the intuitive faculties of the right hand side of the brain with the logical functions of the left hand side of the brain.

We all have Mercurial energy within us, the ability to make connections, although some are more in tune with this energy than others. When Mercury is highlighted in the chart by position or planetary aspects that person has much to give and to gain from communicating, from acquiring new skills and from exploring ideas and concepts. The same person may find it difficult to choose and commit herself to any one path amongst the range of dazzling possibilities lying ahead. She may spend her time as the eternally youthful inquirer, avoiding the choices and commitments that maturity demands and missing opportunities to fulfil her potential.

In medical astrology Mercury rules the five senses and the nervous system which enable us to take in information and convey messages between the brain and all other parts of the body.

The Sun and Mercury are close in the horoscope (often in the same sign) and it is easy to confuse the mental and nervous faculties of Mercury with the consciousness of self represented by the Sun. Consciousness is something more than just a function of the mind; it can exist even when the mental and nervous faculties of perception and communication are severely impaired. By seeing the solar and Mercurial parts of ourselves as separate we can more readily value Mercury. The Mercurial part of the psyche creates bridges and pathways by which the inner self can travel to meet the external world.

Venus is known as the Earth's sister-planet, because it is our closest neighbour and is similar in size and structure. Venus rotates on its axis in the opposite direction to the Earth, however, so that it could be said that this planet is the Earth's mirror-image. The appearance of Venus in the sky is unmistakable, as either the Morning Star of dawn or the Evening Star of sunset, and the planet has been

VENUS

instinct to relate
love; desire; sensuality; relatedness;
co-operation; ability to create and
appreciate beauty
Rules: Taurus and Libra, and the
Second and Seventh Houses

associated with love in many cultures. The imagery of Venus in traditional astrology has been affected by the European notions of romantic love, but ancient mythology reveals far greater depths.

Often known as 'The Star' (for planets and stars were not always differentiated) Venus formed a trinity with the Sun and Moon in Babylon. Sometimes Venus was personified as the Great Goddess who gave birth to the Sun, sometimes as the Sun's light-bearing attendant. We have found Venus to be of special importance, not only in the cultures from which we learned our astrology but also in Pre-Colombian America and to tribal peoples all over the world.

As the Morning Star, Venus was called Dilbah, Lucifer and Shaher in the Ancient Near East. These deities were active initiators, for they brought in the day, awakening solar vitality. As the gentle and loving Evening Star, Venus was Zib, Hesperus and Shalem. Shalem was said to speak the Word of Peace nightly to the Sun, giving the Hebrew and Arabic words for peace, *shalom* and *salaam*. As Evening Star Venus returns us to the lunar world of the imagination.

The planet was associated with Greek Aphrodite, Babylonian Ishtar, Syrian Astarte and Egyptian Isis. The further back we trace, the greater are the dimensions of these Goddesses, but our astrological understanding of Venus has suffered from more recent reduction of their stature and importance. We need to regain deeper understanding of the principle of love and the nature of desire. (The word 'desire' comes from the Latin *desidere* meaning 'from the Star' – which was the planet Venus.)

The original Venusian goddesses represented love, but not only in the passive, harmonious and sympathetic sense that astrology generally

attributes to Venus. The later Greeks said that Aphrodite was caught in a net in the act of adultery with the God Aries; in earlier times, however, that net was her own and used to draw her lovers to her — formerly she was active, not passive.

Modern astrology has missed much of the vibrant energy of the planet. As Warrior and Huntress in earlier mythology she expressed the fierceness of passion. Many of our most important insights come through intensity of experience in relationships.

Though astrologers have tended to underrate Venus in the last two thousand years, most people are eager to know how Venus is situated in their horoscopes. The desire for love and sexual interaction are often a key to our life-energy. Their denial can bring on depression; the reawakening of love in our lives often initiates healing.

In the ancient world the planet Venus was associated with the myth of the phoenix. Though we may feel burnt by our experience, unable to love again, the Venusian part of the self can be reborn from the ashes like the miraculous bird. Yet we have to learn how to handle this strong force within us. We need to stay in touch with the sensitivity, shyness and need for our own timing that the Moon represents. Otherwise we may feel as though Venus is possessing us, just as the ancients described. (The proper offerings used to have to be made to Venus so that one would be neither possessed nor consumed by her power.) The Venusian part of the self becomes trapped in its own net if we fall in love without having first made a truly equal connection. The experience can be devastating and bewildering, so overwhelming us that we feel we cease to exist without the object of our desire. Paradoxically, we also lose ourselves when we are with her or him. Frustrating and self-denying, this form of obsessional love is rarely returned or respected and often feels as though we have landed on the planet Venus, where it is immensely hot, under great atmospheric pressure, and where sulphuric acid falls like rain.

We need to desire and be desired in a way which is positive for the whole of ourselves; this means perceiving our own desirability and beauty and recognising our own boundaries and our need for a slow unfolding. The Venusian part of ourselves is open to other people. It is by making sure we listen to the other person's experience (instead of being trapped within our own) that we can transform unbalanced passion into much calmer depths of love and shared intensity. At times Venus may lead us to extremes of emotion, but paradoxically

she also enables us to achieve balance and harmony within ourselves.

The Venus part of the self has abundant vitality and a sensual delight in the whole of life. We can see the Venus archetype in the Balinese Goddess Rati ('Erotic Delight'), the Tantric Goddess Shakti (cosmic energy) and the Greek muse of erotic poetry called Erato (The Passionate One). Sexual energy used to be seen as the primary life force. The sexual exchange was honoured for its spiritual as well as emotional qualities, and the intensity of sexual energy was known to contain healing powers.

Sexuality, sensuality and love were once thought of as integral parts of a whole whose expression was far wider in scope than the act of love. This energy is strongly present in humanity's very early artworks. Rounded statues of large women embody the Venusian principles of sensuality, warmth and love, as well as the wider attributes of the Great Goddess. The Venus figures reach out, with arms open.

Love opens the heart. No other emotion has its intensity and endurance. Venus tells of the love we have for lovers, friends, children, animals and plants, and for whatever arouses our affections. The planet represents the part of the self which sees beauty in daily experience, opening up the way to creativity, showing us how to enhance the environment and make fine objects. Passion can be shared in many ways, not only through sexual/emotional relationships, but by working with someone else on an intensely loved project, or by joint creative expression. Artistic or musical collaboration has some of the unique flavour of a love affair.

The vibrant energy of Venus carries us out into the world, motivating us to engage with life. Without the loving connection with others that Venus brings, we are in a vacuum, alienated and disorientated. We miss the sharing of vital energy, and the process of finding ourselves through our involvement with others. Through Venus we are able to experience 'otherness', the importance of someone or something outside ourselves. We expand our boundaries, and the similarities and differences we discover help us to recognise who we are. Even those whom we dislike or whom we identify as enemies help us to know ourselves.

The Venusian part of the self brings our social skills which help us to co-operate and create harmonious and comfortable relationships with others. If we listen to the Venusian desire for peace, harmony and sympathy to the exclusion of all else, however, we can be led

towards a false peace which rests on shifting undercurrents of hostility and lack of respect. Then we need to remind ourselves of the other Venusian values, of fairness and equality in relationships. To realise these values we may well have to call on the warrior aspects of Ishtar.

Venus' action in the body reflects its refining and balancing qualities. Medically, Venus relates to the twin organs of the kidneys, whose main functions are to balance the fluid levels in the body and to filter and purify the bloodstream. The proper functioning of the kidneys plays a large part in the appearance of the complexion which is ruled by Venus.

Venus rules the things we value most, from relationships, ideals and art to money and clothes. When any of these cherished things are lost we can feel extremely insecure, as if a part of ourselves had disappeared. When we are unable to recover from this sense of loss it is usually because we have found values only in what is *outside* ourselves.

It is by valuing and loving ourselves that we can move towards the widest expression of love. We become able to forgive, to love without possessiveness, to want the best for the loved ones, even if we are deprived of their presence. Loving another person can open channels to a universal and compassionate love, for Venus awakens inspiration and deeper spiritual experience.

It is the same passionate Goddess Ishtar, who was to the Babylonians the compassionate one, 'who walked in terrible Chaos and brought life by the Law of Love; and out of Chaos brought us harmony, and from Chaos . . . has led us by the hand. . . . '[7]

Mars is the first planet lying beyond the Earth in the solar system, and astrologically symbolises the energy which we direct towards the external world. It is a raw and rude force, direct and unsophisticated. The early Indian God Rudra was the prototype for the Roman God Mars, and his name is the source of the word 'rude' in Latin, in its meaning of a primitive deity of wild animals and woods. Mars was

MARS
drive and self-assertion
*dynamic energy; vigour; activity;
daring; anger; sexual drive; ability to
recuperate*
Rules: Aries (and formerly Scorpio)
and the First House

originally a God of trees, leaves and vegetation, and Martian energy is the dynamic renewing force which causes the sap to rise in plants in the spring, and the vitality and sexual drive to rise in animals and humankind.

The energy of Mars seeks initiation, change and growth. Mars has been associated with Aries and Scorpio, the signs of spring and autumn. These seasons are times of change; spring brings change through new life, autumn through death. They are the polarities of the life-death-rebirth cycle essential to all growth processes. When we move towards change sacrifices are often called for. The planet Pluto is now seen as ruling Scorpio and the growing energy of Mars needs to be accompanied by a Plutonian process of cutting away from past dead attachments, which can only hold us back.

The Martian life energy has always been associated with the courage to face death, just as the springing corn must later be cut down at harvest. In the oldest myths in Indo-European cultures we find the Martian gods of vegetation and corn portrayed in very different roles from the one we associate with the later Roman war God Mars. Originally the vegetation god personified the courage to die in the annual sacrifice to the Earth, the source of life, and his blood ensured the fertilisation of the land each spring. To die for the land brought initiation and spiritual awakening to the vegetation god through his sharing of the strength and wisdom of the Goddess as her consort.

The image of the war god seems to have emerged in the Ancient Near East at a time when nations were increasingly in conflict with their neighbours. At the beginning of this time it was often the goddesses who displayed the fighting qualities. In Roman mythology it

was originally Mah-Bellona, the serpent-haired Mother of Battles, who oversaw all warrior activity. Even in later classical Greece the Goddess Athena was a warrior of cool intelligence who always over-came the fiery war god in battle. The later Mars represented only heedless fury and carnage, an unhelpful image of our Martian energy.

Though his connection with sacrifice may shock us, the picture of the vegetation god is a more inspiring one as it stems from the wild power of elemental nature. The spirit of the greenwood survived in England as Robin Hood, and gives our children a more positive Mar-tian archetype than the soldier. The greenwood spirit protected the forest, its wild creatures, and the peasant folk who lived around its borders, from the oppression of feudal war lords.

We also find the virgin hunting goddesses, Greek Artemis and Hindu Sarama, to be deities of the forest; though associated primar-ily with the Moon they also provide us with archetypes of Martian courage and independence.

These different mythological figures show us how we may express our own Martian energy either positively or negatively. Although we no longer test our endurance through voluntary sacrifice, at times we push ourselves and our energies beyond what we have known to be our limits. From these ordeals of Mars we emerge strengthened and with a renewed sense of self.

Martian energy inspires us to feats of courage and initiative; the person who has Mars strongly placed in her chart is prepared to sail single-handed around the world, even if she sacrifices her life to the sea in the attempt. The risk she faces gives her a sense of freedom and adventure, a sense of choice. She needs to feel free to do as she wills with her life and vitality, in spite of the urging to caution from those who love her. This Martian urge to risk a glorious death needs to be acknowledged within us, although it can be manipulated to sup-port war.

The Martian drive to express one's vigour and capacity for achieve-ment cannot healthily be repressed. Rather, the Martian part of the psyche needs to be channelled into areas where courage and daring are life-sustaining.

We show Mars by assertiveness, drive, and sexual energy. These instincts are basic to survival. With Martian energy we stand up and make ourselves known in the world, fighting for what we want so we can move towards our goals. Mars governs the means to action,

though not necessarily the values and beliefs that impel us to act. Like Mercury, Mars is a vehicle; through Mars we convey ourselves not in words but in actions.

The archetype of Mars is a dynamic, vigorous and competitive figure. She is found in Atalanta, the Amazonian athlete who delighted in her ability to run faster than any man. She challenged each of her suitors to a race, and they were killed if she won. The survivor was the man who threw down the three golden apples of Venus, which she stopped to pick up. Only the Venusian desire for personal interaction can halt the Martian speed and determination to win. We can listen to the Venusian part of the psyche when our Martian energy drives us recklessly, for it helps to include more of who we are. Mars and Venus need to be in relationship within us, and in balance. We can misuse the Venusian desire for co-operation or our Saturnian caution to repress our Martian vitality. When our energies are blocked, or our drives frustrated, we feel angry because our needs for change and growth are being denied.

When Martian energy is suppressed and anger is allowed to grow below the surface it can overwhelm with its violence and aggression, confronting us with our ability to harm both ourselves and others. Unrecognised, it can also draw angry people and situations towards us. Identifying the source of our anger usually brings us to areas where our personal worth is being ignored. By recognising the roots of our anger we can find the means to resolve and express it positively, and accept responsibility for our own power. Then we can see the positive qualities of anger: honest, clearing and energising. It is Mars which gives us the courage to face the frightening and destructive aspects of anger, and we can learn to contain Martian energy within the loving part of the self (Venus) and guide it through the integrating solar consciousness.

Sexual desire for another is a function of Venus, while unfocused sexual drive is an expression of Mars with its initiating, dynamic qualities. The recognition of the life energy within our sexual drive is an important step towards accepting the whole of our sexual nature. Within a sexual relationship Martian drive unites with Venusian desire and love, while celibacy offers us the opportunity to learn how to redirect (rather than repress) sexual drive into acts of creative vitality.

The denial of our growth processes and suppression of sexual drive and anger lays foundations for bitterness and resentment. Ignoring

the Martian self can be an important contributory factor in chronic illness. Illness or depression may be a last resort method of asserting these needs or expressing anger. Though facing the needs of Mars can be one of the most terrifying steps on our journey towards self-integration, the acceptance of Martian energy allows us to become balanced and healthy.

Like the Sun, Mars shows our recuperative powers from illness or from any setback. The energy that makes the sap rise helps our strength to return. Physiologically, Mars is related to the muscles, red blood cells and flow of adrenalin which initiates the 'flight or fight' response to a threat from the outside world.

Traditional astrology has labelled Mars a 'masculine' planet and has encouraged women to discover its energy in the men in their lives. This reinforces women's conditioning to suppress their needs for growth, sexual expression, anger, assertiveness and power, and men's conditioning to over-identify with these energies. This imbalance eventually produces passive roles for women and violent roles for men, yet as many women as men have Mars strongly highlighted in their charts.

Family and social attitudes affect us considerably in the way we can act out our Martian energy, and it needs Martian courage to stand up against these expectations of feminine weakness and masculine strength.

The Martian self is honest and direct. Our actions speak louder, and with greater sincerity, than our words. The Martian energy needs to be honoured, for through Mars we learn to remain always in touch with our own growing strength.

Jupiter is the largest planet in the solar system, two-and-a-half times more massive than all the other planets put together. The mythology and astrology of Jupiter emphasises related themes of wideness, growth and authority.

JUPITER

urge to expansion
growth; exploration; natural wisdom and authority; social involvement; ethics; belief; optimism; generosity; opportunity
Rules: Sagittarius (and formerly Pisces) and the Ninth House

Roman Jupiter and Greek Zeus were said to be the supreme gods who enforced law and justice. Like Babylonian Marduk, also associated with the planet, the natural law they upheld had originated from the earlier Great Goddess. Zeus' mother Rhea and the Babylonian Tiamat were the creators who handed down sacred law to humankind. In early Greek communities it was the Goddess Themis who personified the natural social order where women were honoured and respected, children cherished and the land protected and revered. Zeus was said to have married Themis before he married Hera, the Queen of the Gods, and it is from these two consorts and his mother Rhea that he derived his authority.

In astrology Jupiter represents the part of ourselves which involves us with society and leads towards philosophy and religion. Many people today feel out of touch with the Jupiterian part of themselves. The patriarchal Jupiter, enforcer of law, has been translated by astrologers into images of the judge, governor, policeman and priest, concepts which may feel outmoded and uncomfortable. It can help to understand Jupiter within ourselves if we look to the very ancient cultures where law and religion were part of the teaching of the elders and wisewomen of the people. In many tribal societies today this situation still exists and the maintenance of order is understood to be a way of remaining in harmony with the land. Such cultures offer us by their example a way to appreciate the Jupiterian instinct within all of us.

The Jupiterian part of the self reaches beyond the individual and her immediate relationships to seek a place in the outside world. It looks for a basis of shared beliefs which will enable us to interact meaningfully with our community.

We are social beings, and if we fail to express the Jupiterian part of

the self we become isolated. Once separated from others there is a danger that we can inflate our own importance so that we see ourselves as the central consciousness of the world, for Jupiter can lead to self-aggrandisement if its energy is not expressed positively.

The Jupiterian part of the self seeks a broader perspective on life and a deeper awareness of its purposes, leading us to contemplate the meaning of existence. In its original Latin form, 'religion' meant relinking or reunion, and was close in meaning to the Sanskrit word *yoga*. Jupiterian energy searches for a comprehensive and coherent world-view which will give a sense of purpose to our actions. For many people the religions and philosophies which answered this need in the past have become devoid of meaning, leaving them with an existential crisis, without the sense of being linked or tied to a greater whole. The crisis centres around the need to create our own ethics if we no longer wish to inherit a social morality from the religions of the past.

Without the positive expression of Jupiter we find it hard to deal with the planet's negative side. Jupiter's action is expansive and can be excessive. In societies where many people lack a sense of meaning and coherence we often find the excesses of over-consumption and materialism filling the gap.

Jupiter traditionally rules travel, exploration and ritual. Many European travellers have migrated to Third World countries in search of enlightenment in response to the Jupiterian demands for a more meaningful existence. There has also been a renewed interest in the teachings of all ancient cultures, and a search for new mythologies, ceremonies and rituals. The quest for new goddesses and gods is apparent in the contemporary proliferation of cults around royalty, movie stars, politicians and spiritual gurus.

Ultimately the answers that Jupiter seeks must come from within ourselves. Jupiter gives us an abundance of faith, even gullibility, but the Jupiterian part of the self will not always be content for us to follow others, rather it demands recognition of our own wisdom. The understanding that the planet gives enables us to create personal myths, symbols and rituals. Our awareness of resonances and connections in our lives allows us to string together the details and events of day-to-day existence to provide personal coherence. Jupiterian energy allows us to make wider connections, both spiritual and political.

It is the Jupiterian vision which makes the connection between the

exploited Third World work force and the cheap imported goods on sale. We create symbols with Jupiterian understanding, so that we can look at a spider's web and see the interconnectedness of life. We weave ourselves into the fabric of existence by making such connections. The Jupiterian self needs not only to understand its place in the workings of the world, but also to contribute to the community by passing on that understanding.

The Jupiterian part of the self leads us to develop a belief system and a sense of purpose. Our newly acquired wisdom inspires us with enthusiasm to teach others. If Jupiter is well-integrated into the horoscope we are able to teach with generosity and humour, but if Jupiter is over-emphasised or involved in difficult aspects we may become fervent preachers and moralists. Jupiterian authority comes from our own insights, and these need to be contained inwardly and shared with others only in appropriate ways and when they want to listen. The social energy of Jupiter also includes a sense of fun which helps us avoid the pitfalls of pomposity and arrogance when we assume the roles of teachers and leaders.

In medical astrology Jupiter is connected to the liver, fat, digestion, blood sugar levels and body weight. These are areas of the body's anatomy and physiology which quickly reveal the results of Jupiterian excess in the diet. Over-indulgence in food and drink can be a sign of lack of purpose and meaning in life. Searching for and discovery of our deep needs is a more helpful approach to related health problems than concern with dieting. The excess of Jupiter can also derive from an over-enthusiasm for 'the good life'. The counteracting Jupiterian quality is a love of exercise, movement and the outdoors, all of which contribute to a healthy body and mind.

Traditionally Jupiter was known as the planet of good fortune, as people who had Jupiter prominent in their charts were seen to be 'lucky'. The Jupiterian 'luck' stems from the ability to approach life optimistically, with faith in the goodness of others and with an open heart. When we are attuned to these Jupiterian qualities, we attract benevolence back to ourselves and are more readily able to recognise the opportunities around us. When we connect with the Jupiterian themes of individual purpose and meaning of our existence we can relate them to the world we live in. It is only then that we can feel the sense of hope and confidence that leads to a true generosity of spirit.

SATURN

urge to consolidation
commitment; self-knowledge;
wisdom from experience; maturity;
self-discipline; reassessment;
structure

Rules: Capricorn (and formerly Aquarius) and the Tenth House

Before the discovery of Uranus in the eighteenth century it was believed that Saturn was the outermost planet of the solar system. Consequently Saturn was portrayed astrologically as the planet of limitation, coldness and darkness, carrying the message of human mortality. Some past societies portrayed Saturn as the Grim Reaper or the Lord of Karma who kept all in their place, usually by dealing out misfortunes such as poverty and illness.

By journeying back into ancient knowledge we gain a different perspective on the attributes of Saturn. One of the characteristics of the Saturnian part of the self is that its true worth is not displayed through outward appearance but is contained on a deeper level. A story which has a strong Saturnian ring is that of the Greek Goddess Medusa whose face was supposed to be so terrifying that it turned men into stone. However, the 'face' of Medusa was actually a serpent-haired mask (also worn by the Goddess Athena) which represented female wisdom. One part of this wisdom is the acceptance of death which will one day turn us stony hard and cold. The mask acknowledges the fateful aspect of human existence, along with a deeper spiritual understanding of life and its source.

The Greek god Chronos, the forerunner of Saturn, was characterised as Father Time. The earlier Crone Goddess, 'Mother Time', is found throughout European mythology under a number of different names, while in India the Goddess Kali's name means 'time'. The sickle of time (which is made from the crescent of the waning Moon) gives us awareness of the finite number of years we have to live. If we are to use the full potential of these years we need to commit ourselves to what we value as important. The Saturnian energy is self-disciplined and serious in its ability to follow through commitments and lay down foundations for the future. It is the Saturnian part of the self which understands the need for limits and structures in order to find fulfilment in life. At the same time Saturn's energy confronts us with the questions of what is important and what our priorities are. When this part of the Saturnian process is ignored, and these

questions go unanswered, we risk becoming 'petrified' into a life devoid of meaning, just as the myth tells of those who did not understand Medusa's wisdom being turned into stone.

Working in harmony with the Saturnian part of the self enables us to use the wisdom of experience and reap rewards from time. An overdose of Saturn's energy can, however, create the workaholic who sees life as a constant struggle, and who feels grudging towards those who are not constantly involved with work and duty. It can be helpful to remember that part of the Saturnian process is also the Saturnalia, a time out for enjoyment and the breaking of everyday rules, when usually stern Saturn becomes the Lord of Misrule. Through the Saturnian concern with limitation we can also find a way to liberate individual consciousness. Saturn was called the Black Sun or the Sun of the Night by ancient Chaldean astrologers, because this planet was seen to be similar and yet opposite to the Sun. Both the Sun and Saturn represent the desire within us to find an integrating consciousness for ourselves. Our solar approach towards this goal is youthful and self-expressive, centering around opportunity. The Saturnian approach, however, is mature and reflective, centering around difficulty.

In her important book *Saturn, A New Look at an Old Devil* [8] Liz Greene writes that 'Saturn is connected with the educational value of pain', even so 'it is not an enjoyment of pain which Saturn fosters, but rather the exhilaration of psychological freedom'. Through Saturn we connect with the teacher and healer within ourselves. The most solid and valuable lessons learned in life are those based on our own difficult experiences which, even while they are painful and frustrating at the time, offer us much wisdom in retrospect. When we are in touch with the Saturnian part of the self we have the ability to perceive the buried treasure within the landslide of the disaster. With pain comes disillusionment, but in that disillusionment we can find an inner knowledge based on our own tested values, rather than easy assumptions derived from the values of others. Through this inner knowledge we discover our individual worth.

When Saturn is emphasised in the chart by its placement or aspects, the individual concerned is likely to be fairly serious and much involved with making sense of the difficulties she has encountered. However Saturn is placed in the chart it shows us where our hardest work is in life, and accordingly where we can gain the most.

The Saturnian side of ourselves is fearful, and along with fear

come feelings of guilt and a lack of confidence. Fear is universal, but what is unique to every individual is the particular stimulus that excites fear most strongly. Whether we fear subways, heights, poverty, intimacy or death, the opportunity which the fear offers is the same for each of us. The area where our fear concentrates is a place of self-discovery and self-understanding. It is one thing to know ourselves when we are strong, but it needs the maturity of Saturnian vision to accept ourselves when we are weak. When we deal with the fearful place of darkness and coldness within us that Saturn represents we move towards wholeness. We face the barriers and limitations that we place on ourselves; the step which lies beyond is the assumption of our own responsibility for lifting these. Saturn can bring us through fear to self-knowledge and self-confidence.

Often we embark on this journey towards self-knowledge during the years of the 'Saturn return', between the ages of twenty-eight and thirty, when Saturn has completed its first cycle of the zodiac since birth. For the ancient world the snakes in the hair of Medusa symbolised the understanding of continual renewal. After a process of Saturnian self-examination, at any time of our lives, we move on with renewed purpose. Saturnian wisdom informs us when it is time to leave behind the past and its dreams, so that we can place our lives firmly in present realities. Often the spur towards this is the experience of a time when nothing seems to work. The lessons of Saturn frequently appear in the form of depression, loss, frustration or illness. Such setbacks can be signs that we need a period of reassessment. One of the original functions of Satan (a close relative of Saturn) was to be an adversary; someone who tested and judged by asking trick questions or posing problems which had to be solved. The Saturnian self asks many questions: 'Who am I? What am I doing with my life? Is this relationship right for me?' While these may tax us, especially when the answers call for major life changes, the questions initiate a process by which we remain in contact with our feelings and directions and stay true to ourselves.

The answers to which Saturn guides us are not always easy, but they are liberating. Saturnian wisdom is based on the knowledge that we are responsible for our own lives and the course in which they are heading. Coming to terms with the leading role that we play in our own lives is not a matter of shouldering the blame but of taking the wheel. It is helpful to carry a sense of our innocence along with an

awareness of responsibility. It is not easy to reach the point where we realise there is no situation or person to blame for our frustration but that in fact our predicament is the result of our own attitudes and actions. The awareness of individual responsibility, however, leads us to realise the power we have in creating our lives. This in itself is the most effective prescription for healing Saturn's ills. The healing power of the Saturnian process is hinted at by the medical symbol for a prescription, which derives from the planetary symbol of Saturn that astrologers use.

Medically, Saturn rules the skeleton, the skin and connective tissue. These anatomical parts structure and form the body, just as the Saturnian process structures the psyche. The aging process is also attributed to Saturn. An archetypal form of Saturn is the old woman or man, whose maturity, wisdom and experience are shown in the wrinkles of time.

When technology gave astronomers and astrologers the opportunity to take a closer look at the solar system they discovered that Saturn was not the last planet of the solar system; at least three more planets lie beyond. A close-up view of Saturn shows not a place of coldness and darkness but a planet of astonishing beauty, surrounded by brilliantly-coloured rings. Saturn always deserves a closer examination, because with this planet nothing is ever as it first seems. Invariably the closer we look and the more we question, the greater are the insights we gain.

URANUS

sense of individuality
originality; invention; eccentricity;
genius; rebellion; revolution;
idealism; tolerance, detachment
Rules: Aquarius and the Eleventh
House

The planet Uranus is a rule-breaker. Its axis of rotation is more horizontal than vertical, so that at times the equator is the coldest part of the planet. Uranus was discovered in 1781, through the work of Caroline and William Herschel, and it is the first of the 'modern' planets sighted beyond the orbit of Saturn.

With the discovery of Uranus a new concept of the cosmos began to emerge. The discovery of a 'new' planet broke what had been perceived as the Saturnian bounds of fate. It led to an astrological reappraisal of Saturn, as well as the development of a revolutionary Uranian consciousness.

The discovery of Uranus heralded the start of a new era, as it coincided in time with the American and French revolutions and the beginning of the Industrial Revolution. Our contemporary astrological understanding of Uranus is as a planet of revolution, humanitarian ideals and technological invention; its unusual rotation suggests the planet's association with eccentricity and originality.

We can also look to mythology to help us understand a newly discovered planet. The myths of the Greek God Uranus have gone through many changes. Originally he was the consort of the Great Goddess as Urania, the Queen of Heaven. The name Urania survived in Greek culture as the muse of astrology, just as the planet Uranus today is the ruler of astrology, astronomy and space technology.

In later myth we find that Uranus (or Ouranos) has taken over the rulership of the heavens from the Goddess, and has become the lover of Gaea, the Earth. He is castrated and overthrown by his son Chronos; subsequently Chronos himself is ousted by his own son Zeus. Historically these myths are reflections of the struggles in Greece between the original matrifocal and various successive patriarchal societies. The instinct to rebel initiates a repeating cycle as the new order becomes the status quo and is itself confronted and overthrown. Uranus represents the process of continuing revolution.

Within the psyche it is the Uranian energy which searches idealistically for a brave new world and opposes authority with a heightened

perception of oppression. The experience of adolescence is often a Uranian process, because it is a time when we are at odds with entrenched conventions, seeking our individuality and independence.

The value of Saturnian structure and form may need to be learnt before Uranian energy and ideals are expressed, giving to these Uranian ideals a realism and practicality. Unceasing rebellion without any regard for Saturnian structure produces only continuous upheaval and chaos. (The aspect formed between Saturn and Uranus in the natal chart indicates how well we are able to balance these energies.)

Those who have Uranus highlighted in their charts are often described as being 'ahead of their times', with a clear and possibly prophetic vision of the future. This vision is often accompanied by feelings of being misunderstood and isolated in the present. Conventional society does not easily tolerate eccentricity in the genius or in the misfit. Disapproval of the outsider comes from unconscious censorship of the Uranian streak in all of us – our eccentricity and originality are held in check. The outsider may be an individual or group who dissents, or maintains a subculture outside the mainstream of society. The established order resents disturbance and controls or destroys outsiders in its attempts to repress 'otherness'.

An indicator of the health of any society is the room it allows for difference, for human contradictions. The eccentric is vitally important, for her 'otherness' gives a fuller identity to her community.

The Uranian urge manifests itself through the use of shock and humour to challenge society. Buffoons and clowns can also be healers; in the Greek myth of sorrowing Demeter she is mocked and startled out of her grief into laughter by the old woman, Baubo, who suddenly exposes her genitals. In a similar way, controversial performers mock, heal and at times outrage society through their art. In American society the role of the shocking outsider has been taken by Bette Midler, Janis Joplin, Lenny Bruce and Richard Pryor. Many Uranian performers are Jewish, Black, homosexual, or non-conformers, outsiders to the mainstream culture. In England the original working-class punk culture manifested Uranian energy with its need to shock and mock rigid convention. Outsiders have special and disturbing insights into the society from which they are wholly or partially excluded. When a society will not listen to such individuals and groups important though unpalatable truths are missed, as well as a richness of diversity.

There is a very narrow dividing line between those society laughs at and those it locks away. There can be genius and flashing insight within the state we label madness, painful but essential truths which often cannot be safely articulated in the 'sane' world. Women especially often find themselves in this position, being outsiders in a society dominated by masculine consciousness. The autobiographical writings of many women authors document this experience as they tell of the forcible exclusion that accompanies the label of madness.

Each of us contains a 'mad' or 'outsider' part of the self which does not conform to social expectations.[9] It is a precious and unique part of the psyche, yet imbalances can arise for the individual who sees herself so much as an outsider that unconsciously she becomes arrogant and leads an existence divorced from reality. The compulsive rebel chooses a path of loneliness and alienation if she cannot at some point recognise her need to 'come in from the cold'.

Through experience we learn to find our kindred spirits with whom we can share our ideals and insights, balancing the Uranian part of the psyche with the lunar need to belong and the Venusian need to love and be loved. Our awareness of our own unique individuality is strengthened and supported by feelings of kinship and connection. This process of finding peer support was a theme of the 1960s during a time of Uranian upheaval and change in society.

Images associated with Uranus include the earthquake and the lightning bolt. The shock tactics of Uranus surprise us into discovering unknown areas of ourselves and our society; its flashing insights irrevocably change our perception of the world, exciting and revitalising us with the vision of new landscapes.

The electrical energy of Uranus is reflected in medical astrology by its association with the brain waves and the impulses of the nervous system. Uranus also relates to the flow of energy in the body, known as *prana* in India and *chi* in China.

The three outer planets, that is, Uranus, Neptune and Pluto, are said to act as the 'higher octaves' of Mercury, Venus and Mars respectively, as they express these three more personal planets' concerns on a broader level. As the higher octave of Mercury, Uranus relates to global telecommunications; it is typical of Uranian energy to leap instantaneously over national borders, as it constantly seeks ways of breaking through boundaries to experience the new and the different.

Since the discovery of Uranus the world has gone through rapid

change and upheaval. The potential in Uranian technology both excites and terrifies us, and the world is still coming to terms with its implications. Increasing diversity in societies allows greater individual expression, as well as alienation. As we enter the Uranus-ruled Age of Aquarius we are inspired by visions of new possibilities in ways of living, healing, relating and communicating.

NEPTUNE

sense of oneness
dreams, fantasy; illusion;
compassion; empathy; psychic
perception; boundlessness; ecstasy;
transcendence; mysticism
Rules: Pisces and the Twelfth
House

Neptune was first sighted in 1795, but the fact that it was a planet was not realised until 1846. This confusion of identity is typical of the Neptunian energy, which has the chameleon qualities of changing appearance, defying easy definition. Historical events in the mid-nineteenth century helped astrologers in their understanding of Neptune's nature. In the European medical world ether was introduced as an anaesthetic, and the technique of hypnosis developed. At the same time that medicine was finding ways to induce sleep and trance, the European art and literary worlds were being swept away by the dreams and imagination of the Romantic Movement. Whole communities, from Europe, China and India, went in search of promised lands, led on by fantasies of a better life. The Gold Rush was on, and hopes were high. There was an understandable urge to escape from desperate poverty and existing social realities. The urge to escape also surfaced with the growth of new pastimes – magic lantern shows and photography. Mind-altering substances became more accessible worldwide, particularly alcohol, tobacco and opium. At the same time there was a proliferation of new religious movements, including Mormonism and Spiritualism. Religious and spiritual beliefs began to spread, or be imposed, from culture to culture. Whereas the discovery of Uranus coincided with the opening up of new ways of thinking, the discovery of Neptune accompanied an opening out to new dreams, visions, fantasies, states of consciousness and mysticism.

Mythologically Neptune has a strong association with the sea. The sea is a universal symbol for the beginnings of life and for the unconscious. In mythology and dreams the sea represents a source of inspiration and a renewer of life. The Babylonian Goddess Tiamat and the Indian Goddess Kali were both referred to as 'The Deep' from which life emerged. The Near Eastern Goddess Mari symbolised the primeval waters and is shown with a deep blue robe and pearl necklace. Some deities were said to be born from the sea complete with magic powers, such as the Greek Aphrodite and the Maori Maui.

The number of fantastical sea creatures in myths and fairy tales,

from mermaids to sea-serpents, reflect the alluring beauty and hidden dangers of the sea, and the Neptunian energy. The Neptunian part of the self seeks a state of oneness which has no boundaries of space or time; like the sea it is a formless, unceasing flux. The awareness of being at one with all of creation is central to mystical experience. This awareness is sought through meditation, prayer, chanting, trance, fasting and dance. Those who surrender themselves to the ecstatic energy of Neptune through these disciplines go beyond the veils of Maya, or the illusion of reality, to join the universal source of life. In many cultures the Shaman or Medicine Woman acts as the bridge between the spirit world and the world of matter. A gruelling training opens the way to psychic and spiritual experience. Shamanistic wisdom emphasises the importance of incorporating the Saturnian qualities of self-discipline, maturity and endurance in the Neptunian quest for enlightenment.

Neptune is the higher octave of Venus and Neptunian sensitivity is attracted to Venusian creative fields, and especially to the non-verbal arts -- music, dance, photography and art. Film and theatre also provide for the Neptunian need for fantasy and empathy with others. Through Neptune's energy we feel we become one with what we create in the heightened attunement of the creative process. This creativity can have a transforming, magical quality for the viewer and listener, as well as for the creator.

The Neptunian energy within us transcends personal boundaries and develops compassion; we are not able to do harm to other living beings if we truly believe they are part of ourselves and we a part of them. While Uranian energy jumps over national boundaries, Neptune does not even perceive them; this part of ourselves experiences one world, one universe. Focus on the spiritual and the imaginative deflects us from the desire to accumulate excessive wealth or to wield power over others.

The Neptunian healing energy of loving kindness and compassion is known as 'Karuna' in the Tantric tradition and as 'caritas' in Latin (significantly, modern English lacks an exact translation). In past cultures it was particularly temple priestesses, such as the 'devadasis' of India and the Holy Mothers of Japan whose work was to express love and compassion to the community. One of the ways this compassion could be expressed was sexual, and the Sacred Harlot is an archetypal representation of Neptune with her combined talents to love, heal,

forgive and prophesy. In the past she was revered and honoured, and this archetype is personified in Christian culture by Mary Magdalene.

The energy of Neptune is not an easy one for human consciousness to contain because it overflows the boundaries of self and time. When the Neptunian part of the self takes over others describe us as being 'in a dream' or 'spaced out', because we are, in a sense, out of ourselves. While few of us consciously apply our Neptunian energy to achieve states of mystical unity, we all contain Neptune's yearning for oneness.

Humankind has used many aids to enhance awareness – mind-changing drugs, alcohol with its history of the ecstatic wine cults of Dionysus, tantric sexual practices, music from tribal drumming to rock and orchestral concerts. To use the Neptunian energy well we need to retain our increased awareness after the experience for it to enhance our whole lives. The imaginative sensitivity of the Neptunian part of the psyche is allowed to develop if we use to the full whatever experiences we have had rather than constantly seeking to recreate them.

Any Neptunian activity, whether meditation, drinking alcohol or the development of a vivid fantasy life, can be used as an escape route from experiencing pain, boredom or disillusionment in our daily lives. When used in this way these activities lose their creative, transformational qualities and act to numb us from reality.

The self-destructiveness which can result is the very real danger within the Neptunian ocean. The parts of ourselves we need to call upon when this danger threatens are the solar consciousness and the Saturnian self which together provide the shoreline of self-awareness, self-knowledge and self-discipline. Tracing the root cause of a self-destructive habit very often reveals the Neptunian self, weakened through lack of recognition and spiritual disillusionment. The Neptunian self needs to be able to express freely feelings of love, connectedness and sensitivity.

Those with Neptune highlighted in the chart have a special need to find a channel for this energy. Often they pick up and experience the feelings of others. Without natural or trained ability to shield themselves this can make for feelings of extreme vulnerability or even craziness.

Medically Neptune rules the lymphatic system which separates out and destroys harmful foreign bodies and poisons within the system. If

the immune system cannot distinguish between what belongs to us and what does not, the defence system breaks down and we are left open to disease. The Neptunian part of ourselves needs this protection, physically, emotionally and psychically, to filter out the harmful things we can pick up from the external world. Our Solar, Saturnian and Uranian energies can come to our rescue when we feel too open and vulnerable by re-establishing a sense of individuality and boundaries.

Many natural psychics have been classified as mentally unstable, an idea which Doris Lessing explores in *The Four-Gated City*.[10] Recognition of these talents and training in the wise use of them can often provide a stable, more Saturnian, framework. Many strongly Neptunian people are natural healers, and all of us use the Neptunian part of ourselves when we care compassionately about our fellow human beings.

A frequent problem with Neptunian caring for others is the absence of acknowledgement; women in particular have been expected to care for others without return or recognition. While the Neptunian part of the self may consciously insist that recognition is unnecessary, unconscious resentment can build up, leading to the martyr syndrome and emotional blackmail. At the same time the person cared for is not truly helped if she becomes passive and dependent on the carer or healer. It can help those with Neptune strongly placed in their charts to make sure that they feed themselves with imaginative material and have alternative outlets for their energy through creative expression.

We need to experience beauty and magic to satisfy the Neptune side of ourselves, to give ourselves time and space to find the moments of transcendence in everyday life. Then our Neptunian sensitivity can offer us a way of relating to the Earth and its inhabitants which is loving, accepting and truly healing.

PLUTO

urge towards transformation
initiation; confrontation;
elimination; death; rebirth and
regeneration; power; crisis
Rules: Scorpio and the Eighth
House

The discovery of another new planet in 1930 meant that both astrologers and astronomers had to undertake some urgent rethinking. Astronomers needed to expand their conception of the size of the solar system by over one third. Astrologers were faced with the task of expanding their consciousness beyond even the spiritual heights of Neptune to perceive the meaning of the new planet. An important astrological signpost was provided by the eleven-year-old English girl who named the planet Pluto, the Roman God known as both the Lord of the Underworld and the Lord of Riches. Before long, astrologers were beginning to characterise Pluto as the planet of death, rebirth and transformation.

The underworld is commonly portrayed in world mythologies as both the chamber of death and the womb of birth, usually ruled over by the Crone Goddess. In Norway, Hel the Queen of the Underworld brings death to all, even the gods; in Hawaii the sacred cave door to death leads to the volcano Goddess Pele; in ancient Greece dead men were said to be admitted to the bridal chamber of the underworld Goddess Persephone. The Native Americans and Hindus share a belief in rebirth from the womb of the Earth, following their reunion with the Earth Mother at death. These mythologies give us a wider perspective on death than contemporary cultures commonly provide. Viewing death as part of an inevitable cyclic process helps us to gain an acceptance of the passing from one stage of life to another, reducing the terror with which we approach death today. In the Tarot deck the card of Death is seen positively, as a card of liberation from the past which clears the way for new beginnings.

Astrologically, Pluto introduces us to the concept that there are many deaths we face within a lifetime, and that the death we commonly recognise as the end of life is just one more transition point. Death is like the chrysalis from which the butterfly emerges; it is a cocoon of transformation.

Pluto's discovery came in an era of hardship and disillusionment in world history. The 1930s were the midpoint between two world wars,

when the world economy crashed. Fascism and organised crime were on the rise and nuclear weaponry was being developed. This was a time when humanity lost much of its innocence about human nature, as these phenomena made our hatred, greed, cruelty, racism and violence more visible. Since then, humanity has lived with the knowledge that we belong to a species which is capable of genocide and global destruction.

Pluto is associated with the process of elimination. Pluto's action is like a boil which brings the trapped poisons up to the surface, usually with great pain and ugliness. This century has seen the human race confronted by its own poisons in the form of world wars, nuclear weapons and global pollution. The eruption of a boil, however, is part of a healing process which both allows the body to eliminate toxins and warns us that we are overloaded with internal rubbish. Pluto tells us that the world's present toxic state could be transformed into a healing process if we face the present situation and deal with it, rather than repress, ignore or surrender to it.

When a person is chronically sick a crisis of acute illness provides the opportunity for the elimination of toxins and improved health in the future, and the world crises of this century have been accompanied by a new awareness of ways to healing. As humanity has lost its innocence, so methods of transformative healing have evolved which work from deep levels within ourselves. Analytical psychology was developed between the wars, and was followed by developments in psychotherapy. We are learning ways of working with the unconscious that parallel ancient healing wisdom, while introducing the new wisdom that comes from recent experience. With these therapeutic methods we can start to face the horrific aspects of human nature, and to work with their results. In dealing with the destructiveness of humanity, neither ignorance, repression nor forgiveness can bring about real change. The change has to come from a conscious awareness of our shared human depths, and a willingness to act on that awareness.

Whereas the energy of Neptune ascends and accepts, the energy of Pluto descends and confronts. We meet the Plutonian part of the self through the experience of deep confrontation. This confrontation breaks down and transforms us by its intensity. The areas of life in which we are most likely to encounter this type of confrontation are indicated in the natal chart by Pluto's position and aspects. The

Plutonian path towards regeneration and transformation leads down to the murky depths of our nightmares. In her book *The Descent to the Goddess*,[11] Sylvia Brinton Perera uses the ancient Sumerian myth of the Goddess Inanna's descent to the underworld of her sister Erishkegal to illustrate this downward journey. It is a journey of importance, both personally and globally. The descent is neither easy nor pleasant; for Inanna it entailed being stripped, killed and hung up to rot. In a graphic way this myth represents the process which strips away our old identities and props, kills off past behaviour patterns and takes us beyond innocence. The process of initiation is neither painless nor quick, but its outcome is a rebirth of self and a renewal of spirit. We emerge unencumbered by the dead weight of the past. Plutonian energy enables us to face what terrorises us through our own neuroses, traumas and repressed fears. The decision to take this step to self-confrontation may be made consciously or unconsciously; once the descent has started it is not important. We need to be aware that the underworld also contains the power and strength required to meet the pain and the fear. After the descent comes the ascent. Once the work of confronting old fears, blockages and taboos has been accomplished, we are able to emerge regenerated with a strong life spirit and a powerful faith in our ability to survive.

The energy of Pluto works along the axis between 'holding on' and 'letting go'. This axis has much to do with the proper use of power. It is essential that we understand both these energies to maintain balance. The wisdom of knowing when it is appropriate to 'hold on' and when it is appropriate to 'let go' comes with experience. We can hurt ourselves by holding on to a relationship, job or ideal which on a deep level we know to be dead. At other times we can destroy what we value through releasing fears, rage and insecurity. The Plutonian journey involves this right use of power and control. We all have personal power, although some have a greater awareness of this than others. Until we have been through some of Pluto's initiating rites we are likely to misuse this power through ignorance or fear.

Those with Pluto highlighted in the chart have a particularly strong drive and need to confront the deepest parts of the self. If the confrontation is resisted they often tend to transfer Plutonian energy into possessive or dominating patterns of behaviour. A strong Pluto gives a great power to influence others; self-knowledge is needed for this power to be handled wisely.

With the experience of the Plutonian journey into the self, however, comes the skill to assist others with the descent, and the self-knowledge to avoid abuse of the power this will confer. It is important for strongly Plutonian people to find a way to use their experience, for they can be transformative healers and teachers. Without some positive channel, their intensity can feel like a time-bomb. Pluto's energy contains a powerful force which, if used wrongly, can be destructive, but keeping the lid on Plutonian energy only increases the chance of this happening. We can turn ourselves into volcanoes by holding on to our more powerful energies. After a lifetime of repression even the most apparently meek and timid person will explode. The explosion may be an internal one in the form of destructively progressive illnesses or emotional breakdown as the repressed part of the psyche breaks through.

Physiologically Pluto rules the vital functions of elimination and regeneration. When the bowels and bladder cease to work, the body becomes overloaded with its own toxins. The genitals, also located in the pelvis, express the sexual energy which welcomes new life.

We can be destroyed by keeping Pluto's energy in check. By daring to enter the underworld, however, we discover the riches that Pluto governs. The Plutonian energy is that of our most powerful drives and emotions. It contains possessiveness, hatred, revenge, obsession and rage. In this same energy we find sexuality, courage, faith, integrity, trust and willingness to go through transformation and rebirth. When personal and social moral codes prevent acknowledgement of the destructive elements in human nature we lose access to the creative and generative force of Pluto. The consciousness of Pluto demands that we acknowledge all that we feel, and accept the responsibility to choose what we act upon.

We can bring our Plutonian awareness into the community and on to a global level as we face the present crises. This allows the transformation of defeat and despair into strength and faith. As we recognise the Plutonian healing crisis that is occurring throughout the world we gain the necessary insight to take action. The Mandarin word for crisis is *weiji*. The *I Ching* gives us a deeper understanding of *weiji* as a time when there is an opportunity for change, for a transition from disorder to order.[12] Beyond breakdown lies rebirth.

References

1   In order to illustrate the planets' meanings from mythology, the
     authors have drawn on the source books to be found in the
     'Mythology, Religion and History' section of the Bibliography
     (p 278-83). A particularly rich source has been Barbara Walker's
     The Woman's Encyclopedia of Myths and Secrets. *The New
     Larousse Encyclopedia of Mythology*, Patricia Monaghan's *The
     Book of Goddesses and Heroines*, Merlin Stone's *Ancient Mir-
     rors of Womanhood* (2 vols) and Lawrence Durdin-Robertson's
     The Goddesses of Chaldea, Syria and Egypt have also been used
     extensively.

2   Lantero, Ermione, *The Continuing Discovery of Chiron*,
     Samuel Wieser, 1984.

3   Dobyns, Zipporah Potenger, *Introduction to the Asteroid Ephe-
     meris*, TIA Publications, Los Angeles, 1977. Donath, Emma
     Belle, *Asteroids in Synastry*, Geminian Institute, Dayton (Ohio),
     1977.

4   Jacobson, Ivy Goldstein, *The Dark Moon Lilith in Astrology*,
     (published privately), California, 1961.

5   For more information on planets readers are referred especially
     to the following books:
     Arroyo, Stephen, *Astrology, Karma and Transformation*,
     CRCS Publications, 1978.
     Cunningham, Donna, *An Astrological Guide to Self-Awareness*,
     CRCS Publications, 1978.
     Mayo, Jeff, *The Planets and Human Behaviour*, L N Fowler,
     1972.

6   Shuttle, Penelope, and Redgrove, Peter, *The Wise Wound*,
     Gollancz, 1978.

7   Stone, Merlin, *Paradise Papers*, Virago, 1977.

8   Greene, Liz, *Saturn: A New Look at an Old Devil*, The Aquar-
     ian Press, 1977, pp 10-11.

9   The authors are grateful to Ewa Wojakowska for her help in
     understanding the Uranian principle as it manifests in society.
     See her article 'New Perspectives in Psychiatry' in The Institute
     of Psychosynthesis Yearbook Vol III, c/o 1 Cambridge Gate,
     London NW1 4JN.

10   Lessing, Doris, *The Four-Gated City*, Panther Books, 1972.

11 Perera, Sylvia Brinton, *Descent to the Goddess – A Way of Initiation for Women*, Inner City Books, 1981.
12 Wilhelm, Richard, *I Ching*, Routledge & Kegan Paul, 1968.

5
Understanding the Signs
The Four Elements and the Three Qualities

Greek astrologers evolved a way to understand better the nature of the twelve signs of the zodiac. They categorised the signs according to the four *elements* of their philosophical system and the three modes of activity called the astrological *qualities*.

Figure 5.1 shows the way the zodiac signs are ascribed to the *elements* and *qualities*.

The Four Elements: Fire, Earth, Air, Water

The four elements help us to understand the nature of the world we experience. Each has a strong imaginative association for us.

The Persian Magi considered all four elements holy and their philosophical system influenced Greek astrologers. In a Hindu myth Great Mother Kali distributes the elements to give life, with water forming blood, earth producing the solid body, air giving breath and fire making vital heat. There are many symbols assigned to each of these elements; the objects carried by the Greek Goddess Nemesis are a cup symbolising water, a wand for fire, a wheel for earth and a sword for air. These symbols later gave rise to the four suits of the Tarot cards as well as our modern playing cards.

These elements are very much part of our everyday thought and speech. We talk of finding ourselves 'all at sea'; 'high and dry'; 'fired up'; 'burnt out'; 'stuck in the mud'; 'well grounded'; 'full of wind'; with our 'heads in the air'; all highly graphic descriptions related to the elements.

Astrology provides an indication through the natal chart of how we

Figure 5.1 *The wheel of the zodiac*

respond to the four elements. The twelve signs of the zodiac are divided into these elements as in Figure 5.2.

Each set of three signs in one element is called a *triplicity*.

In traditional astrology the watersigns and earthsigns are thought of as feminine while the firesigns and airsigns are seen as masculine. In astrology there has been an underlying bias towards 'masculine' air and fire which have been thought to be purer and closer to the spirit, while 'feminine' earth and water have been seen as baser matter. These concepts have been inherited from Aristotle. It is important that we no longer perpetuate these value judgements.

Earth and water energies share an orientation towards the past and present, with an emphasis on sustenance, commitment and values. Fire and air energies are orientated towards the future and stress innovation, independence and philosophies. Each element is a way of approaching, perceiving and expressing ourselves to the world.

Most people tend to identify closely with one or two of the elemental modes of consciousness (for instance, someone feels herself to be a 'fiery' person). The elements with which an individual is less familiar seem to her to be natural to others rather than to herself ('My daughter

is an earthy person; I'm not'). However in fact each of us contains all four of these modes of consciousness in varying proportions. This elemental model can be a useful framework for understanding both ourselves and others, while at the same time it provides fresh insights into our various relationships.

Astrologers have related the elements to Jung's idea of the four functions of intuition (fire), sensation (earth), thinking (air), and feeling (water). Jungian astrology suggests ways we can balance the elements within the personality. For a full exploration of this, Liz Greene's *Relating*[1] is a most helpful book, and Marie-Louise von Franz's *Lectures on Jung's Typology* [2] provides the background theory.

The Elements in the Horoscope

An emphasis on an element occurs with the placing of the Sun, Moon, Ascendant or a number of other planets in any of these elemental signs. For example, a chart would have a predominance in the air element if the Sun and Venus were placed in Libra, Mars were in Aquarius and Uranus were in Gemini. However, working out the strength of an element in the chart is not just a matter of counting up the number of planets placed in the signs of each element; it is important to remember that the Sun, Moon, Mercury, Venus, Mars and Ascendant and Midheaven are stronger in impact within the chart than the five outer planets. An element is said to be of low significance when there are no planets in any of the signs of one element, or where there are just one or two planets in the element. For example, someone who has Pluto placed in Leo but in no other planets is said to be low in fire. It is relatively rare to find natal charts which are perfectly balanced; most of us have an abundance or scarcity of placements in one or two of the elements and this is no great boon or tragedy in life. What the elemental distribution shows is the element(s) we are most naturally in tune with (those emphasised) and the element(s) we need to work with on a more conscious level (those under-emphasised).

As well as helping us to understand the four basic modes of consciousness within the self, the elements provide an introduction to the signs of the zodiac.

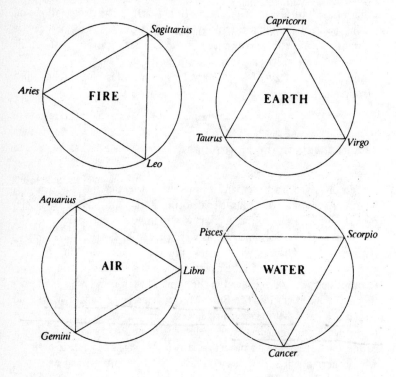

Figure 5.2 *The four elemental triplicities*

Fire

The energy of fire is hot, moving and dramatic. It is an energy we exhibit with fiery passions, flaring tempers, heated debates, blazing beliefs and great warmth. The fire type lives from the heart, approaching life with a natural confidence and optimism, inspired by her quest in life. There is a true romanticism in fire, which is greatly excited by what lies just over the fence or across the world – the greatest adventure, the perfect lover, the enlightened teacher. Aries, Leo and Sagittarius may have different goals; they share a similar style in pursuing them.

The fiery perception is visionary and intuitive. When operating from fire energy we go with the hunch, following our initial response impetuously and enthusiastically, leaving our rationalisations until later. To be in tune with this way of operating we need to be in tune with ourselves; in other words, we need to be self-centred. The latter term is often used as an accusation against fire types, but to be centred within ourselves is not in fact a negative process; it is something we can all benefit from. It is true, however, that being over-fiery can result in a lack of sensitivity in relating to others. When fired up, we revel in our own dynamism and intensity, and can easily forget that not everyone is so strong in their sense of personal identity and mission. We can best use our fieriness to inspire ourselves and others with the belief that anything and everything is possible. This is the talent which lies behind the leadership qualities of the firesigns.

When Aries, Leo and Sagittarius are emphasised in the natal chart, creativity becomes very important as it is a natural form of self-expression. The fire signs enjoy the limelight and are not self-conscious. It is the fire part of ourselves which demands to be recognised and which feels angry and frustrated when taken for granted. When we feel this way it is important to express and act upon it, otherwise our fiery self can become bitter and low in energy. Fire needs fuel, and the fire in us needs new experiences, recognition and joy to prevent burnout and apathy. Without fire life can become meaningless, and identity crises may immobilise us. To feed our fire we must greet each day as an opportunity to create our life anew.

The fire of *Aries* is expressed through action and initiation. Aries is called the pioneer as she seeks out new frontiers, fascinated by what

lies ahead and constantly on the move towards it. She directs her
energy towards self-reliance and self-sufficiency.

Leo's fire is a joyful energy of self expression and creativity. Leo
needs an audience to share her gifts with, as she seeks a relationship
of recognition and awareness between herself and the outside world.

Sagittarius uses her fire to look for adventure in the world of
expanding consciousness as she searches for meaning in life. This last
fire sign is socially orientated, especially in her concern for the teachings of the world.

Earth

Earth's energy is instinctive, formative and grounded. To be earthy is
to be in touch with the senses through which we know and connect
with our world. Our earthiness turns our attention to the external
world, gives us a base from which to operate and forms a sense of our
own effectiveness. The Earthsigns represent the 'doers' of the zodiac
who, with their feet on the ground, show the way to making visions
and ideas become real. The earthy type has the realism and practicality to perceive how the world works, and this enables her to participate effectively in the scheme of things.

Our earthy senses seek to make an order out of the randomness of
matter. Our earthy side delights in acquiring and using skills which
enable us to carve out what we want from life. The earthy person has
great persistence and self-discipline in following her goals, along with
patience and stability which comes from an understanding of the
slow, organic nature of growth. There is a natural humility inherent
in the earthy perception which stems from an awareness of place in
the universe. It is an awareness which never undervalues the cog in the
wheel. Those people who have an emphasis on earth in their charts
are often attracted to manual skills and crafts, because these combine
practicality with creativity, and open the way to self-sufficiency. We
use our earth energy to find ways to stand on our own two feet. The
earth worker has an instinctive respect for and sensual delight in the
material she uses, because she values the gifts of the Earth. The earthy
perception can see that ecological awareness makes sound sense
because the world, which sustains and nurtures us, must be protected.

Earthy people are at home in their bodies, and often enjoy working on and caring for the bodies of others. Our earthy side never under-values the worth of gentle massages, fragrant baths and tasty meals. Over-identification with this physical awareness, however, can lead to a mistrust of what lies beyond the physical plane, which earthy types can show through a fear of death or a scepticism about spiritual matters. With too much earth we can get stuck in the mud or bogged down, losing vision through over-concern for practical details. With-out earth, however, there is no matrix of life, no ground to stand on. When we feel ungrounded it is time to attend to the material resources which sustain us.

Taurean earthiness is displayed in a sensual, concrete way, directed towards establishing a good quality of life for all. Taurus works with great determination and thoroughness towards her goals, without losing her sense of beauty and enjoyment.

The earth of *Virgo* is geared towards establishing a sense of order. Virgo has the ability to analyse whoever or whatever she encounters to increase the understanding she has of herself and the world. She looks for useful ways to share her knowledge and skills with others.

Capricorn's earth is constructive and dedicated, looking for ways to a better society through her work. Capricorn takes her awareness of personal responsibility to the world seriously, while she enjoys gaining the skills she needs to reach her goals.

Air

With air energy we freely connect; ideas, people and cultures come together through the communicating skills of the air element. To let in air we need to open our windows, and the airy type is always open to new ideas and insights to increase her knowledge of the world, ensuring broad-mindedness and constant youthfulness. The airy world is an ideal one; we all build castles in the air, but strong air types can build entire cities in their search for perfection. This airy search calls for a system which, whether philosophical, political, psychological or spiritual, can promise, and often produce, a brighter outlook for our-selves and the world. The air element emphasises humanity, for none

of the symbols associated with the Airsigns, neither Gemini (the Twins), nor Libra (the Scales) nor Aquarius (the Water-Bearer) are animal, and the prime airy concern is the progress of humankind towards greater civilisation. The ideals of our airy selves can lead to pain, however, for if our heads are in the clouds, contact with earthy reality can produce jolting shocks.

When we observe the world from an aerial view, we gain a broader perspective by being able to distance ourselves. We use our detached airy energy to be more objective. Airy people can act as the eye in the tornado, remaining still and calm within life's activity as they serenely view its patterns. Not all airy types are intellectuals but the airy mind makes brilliant connections to find harmony and balance. The aesthetic of air is classical and elegant, producing, for example, music based on systems, or buildings constructed on philosophical ideals.

Despite the emphasis on ideas and ideals, air types are people-orientated, loving company and conversation, and with strong social needs. However, airy people often feel frightened by what they perceive as the irrational and overwhelming nature of the emotions, which threatens their position of detachment. Others may accuse the airy person of being 'cold', but they misunderstand the airy need for maintaining openness, fairness and harmony in their relationships with others.

If we lack air we feel suffocated, for we cannot communicate with others, gain fresh insights or plan for a better world. When we are feeling like this we should circulate more, to open ourselves up to the breezy energy of change.

Gemini's airy energy is directed towards words and ideas, loving to talk, write and learn with speed and breadth of scope. Gemini is like the child who approaches the world asking 'Why?', and is greatly fascinated by each new piece of information she encounters.

The air in *Libra* is expressed through energy for relationships, and the ideals of love and peace. Libra's happiness lies in harmony and beauty, and she is naturally attracted to social and artistic interactions.

Aquarian airiness has a global scope which looks for a better world through far-reaching concepts. Aquarius is an innovator who is often ahead of her times in her vision of the direction in which we could all be going.

Water

Water's energy is flowing and strong. There is an ancient primeval force around water which is reflected in the number of creation myths which begin with a flood. Water contains hidden depths and mystery. The animals associated with the water signs – the crab (Cancer), the scorpion (Scorpio) and the fish (Pisces) – are all very ancient creatures, usually well-hidden from the human world and strongly instinctual. The watery side of ourselves is our emotional nature and our unconscious; it is our sensitivity, our vulnerability and our imagination.

Watery people have a very natural empathy for others, as well as a subtle perception of the complexity of human beings and their motivations. They will naturally seek out close one-to-one relationships of all sorts in which they can explore their emotional selves. A predominance of water in the chart often gives healing and counselling ability, for watery people give support, listen well and accept the full range of human emotions.

The feelings we encounter with water know no bounds; they range from overwhelming fears and obsessions to unconditional love and trust. Water needs to be contained or else it will drain away, and often the watery person needs to feel contained within a circle of security. This can take the form of a committed relationship, a special private space or spiritual practice.

When we establish an external tranquility there is more safety for us to take the plunge into the unconscious, a step vital for realising our full potential. Without our watery perceptions we would feel bewildered by the interactions between ourselves and others. For the watery person who gives a great deal of attention to others, however, it is crucial to remember her own emotional needs and to see that they are met, otherwise she may be left undernourished and resentful.

The watery perception is subjective, seeing the world in personal terms as a collection of people similar to those already known. While this can lead to difficulties in perceiving broader social issues the watery nature understands the emotional realities we all share – which go beyond cultural and sexual divisions.

Through water we feel our way into the world, often non-verbally: crying, embracing, making love, painting and playing music. These are all activities watery types carry out with ease and imagination, and which act as a release for the floodgates. When we feel ourselves left

high and dry it is to these activities we can turn, to reconnect with the waters of life.

Cancer's water embraces and nurtures those around her, seeking a loving environment from which to venture into the world. Cancer explores her own unconscious through closely connecting to whatever she feels to be her roots, and through a highly imaginative creativity.

The wateriness of *Scorpio* is expressed intensely through an exploration of the hidden parts of human nature and the socially taboo areas of life. Scorpio is drawn to the depths of herself and others, which she investigates by facing her fears and setting herself challenges.

Pisces' water is oceanic; she feels at home wherever she is, and is receptive to whatever she encounters. Pisces seeks a oneness with the world, and the means to express her encompassing vision.

Elemental Combinations

It is relatively rare to find charts which are predominant in just one element; far more frequently a chart shows strength in two or even three elements. What follows are images of the way the elements combine, which may help to look at the way each of us relates to someone who is strong in a different element.

Fire and *Earth* create hot lava, metal alloys and brick. This combination has been called the 'steamroller' because of its force. The faculties of intuition and sensation are considered to be opposite in nature within the Jungian schema, and their combination is extremely dynamic. Fire has vision and confidence, while earth is practical and enduring, so when the two meet something very ambitious in scope usually happens. When they work together fire and earth have tremendous stamina, but if they are in disharmony volcanic fire will unsettle the earth with its restlessness, or earth will smother the fire with its realistic outlook.

Fire and *Air* together mean a great deal of hot air or a raging fire, for fire and air with their similarities stimulate each other and create high energy in the process. The fire-air type is a brilliant communicator and an exciting thinker, usually with a good sense of humour. This gives an invigorating liveliness but too many highs can lead to a

need for some earthiness. When out of balance air can blow out fire, just as the rational thinker can extinguish the visionary. In turn, fire can consume air with its exhausting, ever-expanding energy.

Fire and *Water* produce steam and this is a highly volatile combination bringing passionate feelings with a tremendous sensitivity. It is a tricky mixture because these two elements have such very different natures. Yet fire can bring water courage and confidence in its emotional expression, while water can give to fire the sensitivity to bring its visions into the world in a caring way. However, when fire evaporates water, and feelings are denied, it can lead to emotional instability. If water puts out fire, depression and frustration can result.

Earth and *Air* result in a dust storm; there is plenty of movement but it can be very dry. Working together, earth and air are both practical and innovative, producing some highly effective thinking. The air brings change to the earth, speeding up its work, while the earth grounds the air so that thought can be put into action.

Earth and *Water* produce mud, a sticky combination but with a lot of potential. Earth and water together are good at shaping, as with clay, and steady growth, as with stalagmites. This combination brings serious feelings and conscientious actions. An over-emphasis of water turns the earth into quicksand, where it is easy to get bogged down with feelings of duty. Stressing the earth side can produce stagnant mud which denies the need for change for the sake of emotional growth.

Air and *Water* give us mist, an ethereal combination. Together these elements like to live in the mind and the emotions, but have difficulty dealing with the real world. Thinking and feeling are opposites in the Jungian schema and their effective combination is highly creative, producing imaginative thinking and ability for emotional exploration.

The Qualities

Dividing the twelve zodiac signs into four groups of three signs reveals the *elements* of the zodiac, while the division of the same twelve signs into three groups of four shows the *qualities* of the zodiac (see Figure 5.3). These qualities are *cardinal*, *fixed* or *mutable*.

Each set of four signs of the same quality is called a *quadruplicity*.

Whereas the elements deal with modes of perception, the qualities deal with modes of activity, in terms of both action and response. The distribution of the qualities in the natal chart is calculated in the same way as for the elements (see p 111).

Cardinal – The Energy of Beginning

Cardinal comes from the Latin word for hinge, and it is on the four signs Aries, Cancer, Libra and Capricorn that the zodiac hinges. Aries and Libra begin at the equinoxes, while Cancer and Capricorn start at the solstices, so they mark the seasons in the same way as the cardinal points of the compass mark the directions.

Cardinal activity is initiating, being geared towards making a new start, as often happens with the arrival of each season. Astrologically the cardinal signs are intensively active, enthusiastic in their pursuit of life experiences. When a chart has a strong emphasis on the cardinal signs, the person's life is lived at a rapid action-packed pace. Cardinal sign people prefer to channel their energy into external events, and the way they respond is to react immediately. This can lead to a crisis-ridden way of life. However, this is preferable to boredom for a cardinal type.

These four signs express their cardinal energy in the area where they feel most comfortable.

Aries, as a fire and cardinal sign, loves fast physical action. Always ready for new adventures and explorations, Aries is the 'cardinal of cardinals', happiest always to be at the beginning of a fresh project and to take the initiative.

Cancer, with her watery cardinality, initiates in the realms of feelings and imagination, the areas in which she is acutely sensitive. The explorations which are made are very often creative and the risks taken emotional in nature.

Libra's cardinality works through the air element, encountering the worlds of social relationship and communication. The initiatives here are towards maintaining harmony, working for peace and bringing people together for exciting interactions.

Capricorn's earthy nature grounds the cardinal energy. Capricorn provides the pioneering organisers, responsible leaders and initiators

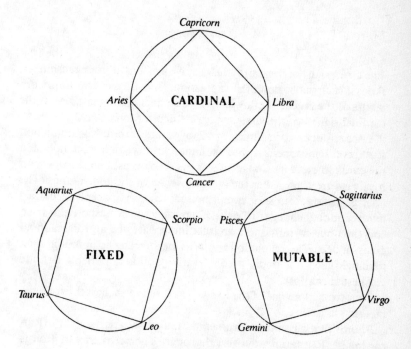

Figure 5.3 *The three quadruplicities of the qualities*

of new communities. This sign's enthusiasm is geared towards the planning and building stages of any project.

All these signs have a love of beginnings, fresh enthusiasm and the courage to take risks as we move onward. The prudent sign Capricorn shows us that risks need not be taken rashly.

Fixed – The Energy of Perseverance

The fixed signs arrive at the height of each of the four seasons – a time of their most powerful expression. These signs are the anchor points of the zodiac. Following on from the initiating impulse of the cardinal signs, the fixed signs provide depth and meaning, through the establishment of a strong sense of values. From this foundation the fixed signs operate with stamina, loyalty, determination and perseverance, and it is for good reason that Taurus, Leo, Scorpio and Aquarius are regarded as the most powerful of the zodiac signs. The fixed signs are not easily compromised; they have deeply ingrained habits and find change difficult. The most common response of fixed energy is one of resistance, and 'letting go' can be a problem in all areas of life. The revolutionary fixed sign Aquarius makes it clear that this need not imply a conservative outlook, rather a definite vision and purpose.

The strong presence of the fixed signs is felt in each of the four elements.

Taurus fixity, combined with earth, makes for great stability. Taurus can be slow at times but very thorough. The persistence of Taurus is put to use in her ability to acquire practical skills which have bountiful yields. Taurean energy is well-grounded, good at taking on great work loads while maintaining a sensual enjoyment of life.

Leo brings together fire with fixity to create strong individuality. There is a natural confidence with Leo which leads to a wealth of self-expression, which is often channelled into creative endeavours. This sign exhibits a dignity, pride and beauty which comes from the knowledge of self-worth.

Scorpio's fixity in the watery realm is expressed by the phrase 'still waters run deep'. Her intense emotional perceptions lead to a passionate engagement with life, so that few areas are left unexplored.

Scorpio's strong connection with the unconscious gives her great depth of understanding, and she has the determination to challenge and confront others with her perceptions.

Aquarius, as an air and a fixed sign, has a far-reaching intellect which she applies to working out her own values. These form the basis of her idealism; Aquarius has a strong commitment to all humanity. Its unswerving quality underlies Aquarian fixity.

Through the fixed signs we can establish ourselves with sureness and stability, which come from the knowledge of our basic precepts.

Mutable – The Energy of Change

The mutable signs coincide with the times of change in the seasons; when what has once been firmly established breaks down to clear the way for the new. It is an unpredictable time which calls for adaptation.

The mutable signs dissolve the fixed quality of the signs preceding them. Mutable energy is open to change, quickly responding to new circumstances and ideas. Strongly mutable types, who have an emphasis on Gemini, Virgo, Sagittarius and Pisces in their charts, are mentally active people whose focus is towards knowledge. They want to change their consciousness, and are always looking for ways to make improvements in themselves and in their lives. Mutable energy gives a versatile and impressionable approach. There is a noticeable duality in all the mutable signs, which gives them a talent for seeing both sides at the same time. However, taken to an extreme, mutable energy can set up a cycle of restless indecision which is hard on the nervous system.

This transitional quality in the zodiac is exhibited in different ways through the four mutable signs.

Gemini's airy mutability gives a mental brilliance, which ranges from lateral thinking to punning. Intellectual curiosity and tolerance are two of Gemini's main traits. Gemini has the ability to change rapidly to accommodate the new concepts she encounters.

Virgo, the mutable earth sign, applies her versatile mind to many practical aspects of life. Virgo keenly pursues useful ways of adapting and improving herself and her life on all levels.

Sagittarius combines mutability with fire in her quest for wisdom. This sign will travel widely to find new truths and meanings in life,

motivated by an intuitive optimism. She approaches the development of her philosophy in a spirit of fiery adventure.

Pisces, being the water mutable, is extremely open emotionally, and has great compassion and empathy. Pisces flows readily into the lives of those she loves, adapting quickly to the newness of each emotional encounter, and experimenting freely with her vivid imagination.

References

1   Greene, Liz, *Relating: An Astrological Guide to Living with Others on a Small Planet*, Samuel Weiser, 1976.
2   von Franz, Marie-Louise, *Lectures on Jung's Typology*, Spring Publications, 1971.

6
Twelve Paths of Possibility
The Signs of the Zodiac

Introduction

In this section of the book the signs of the zodiac are outlined in essence as twelve ways of approaching the world, and as paths of cosmic and human possibility.[1] These delineations are not intended to sum up individuals according to their month of birth. A sign may be highlighted in the horoscope not only by the Sunsign, but by the Moon's placement, by the Ascendant or by any strongly placed planet or combination of planets. When we talk of Aries or Taurus we mean an abstract essence of Aries or Taurus; when we talk of Ariens or Taureans we mean all those who have the signs highlighted, whether this is by Sun, Moon or Ascendant.

To emphasise this broader definition of each sign, we give examples of notable women who have the sign emphasised in their charts in various ways. Usually the women cited have the Sun in the relevant sign, but sometimes it is the Moon or Ascendant which is referred to.

Some people have both Sun and Moon in the same sign, or Sun and Ascendant, and are known as 'double' Aries, 'double' Taurus, etc. They usually display the characteristics of the sign very strongly. However, neither they nor anyone else manifest the energy of one sign alone; some women are cited twice, once under their Sunsign and once under the sign in which Moon or Ascendant appeared at their birth. The description of each sign in its entirety will not apply to the women whom we give as examples any more than it will for others born with a similar zodiacal emphasis. It is not helpful to see Helen Keller, for instance, only 'as a Cancer'. She was a Cancerian woman, but she was also Piscean as she had the Moon in Pisces.

Nearly everyone has several signs emphasised in the chart (see

Chapter 1 p 9). In fact, on the broadest level we can see each horoscope containing all the signs, for all are present, in stronger or
weaker manifestations, and provide various approaches to the parts
of our lives which the *houses* represent (see Chapter 7). Some signs
represent approaches to life which are familiar to us, while other signs
represent ways which are less accessible. Such signs are hidden within
the person, and do not manifest openly in the character or life of the
individual. Even if there is no planet, or angle of the chart emphasising the sign, its possibilities are still there.

We urge you to read *all* the signs of the zodiac, not just those of
your Sunsign, Moonsign and Ascending sign, for in each one there
will be something of yourself. Recognising these hidden parts can
help us to see better the similarities between ourselves and others.
Astrology can best be learned by understanding the signs from the
inside, and by experiencing each approach to life as equally valuable.

Background to the Sign

ARIES
The lamb or ram
The path of action
Approach to life of **cardinal fire:**
initiating, adventurous, courageous,
energetic, impulsive, direct
Planetary ruler: Mars

The first sign of the zodiac, Aries, represents the urge from formlessness into creation. In Hindu astrology the thunderbolt of Aries emerges from the Akasha, the primordial waters of the previous sign, Pisces. Aries symbolises the will to action. The Babylonians did not originally use the ram for this sign but called it 'The Hired Labourer', indicating that the month of Aries was a time of special activity when extra help is needed. This is in tune with Arien energy which is abundant and which can be called on in moments of crisis.

Sheep were of great importance in Sumer and Babylon, the birthplace of the astrology we have inherited – the Goddess Inanna acknowledges this by choosing the shepherd Damuzi as her lover rather than his rival, a farmer.

The ram was revered in Egypt, where various gods were shown with rams' heads, and in Greece. The most famous manifestation was Hermes' golden ram which could fly through the air, talk and reason. Its fleece became the object of the quest of Jason and the Argonauts, and it is not surprising therefore that the ram became the best known symbol for this sign. But it is not the only one in ancient history. There is evidence that the original sign of Aries in Egypt was the ewe, Seret, a symbol of fertility. From the early Hebrew tribes we know that Rachel was reverenced as 'the Divine Ewe', a compassionate Goddess who was the mother of the 'Holy Lamb'. Most suitable of all images for Aries is the lamb, a symbol of spring in temperate climates, for Aries is the sign of beginnings. The astrological year begins on the first day of Aries, the spring Equinox in the northern hemisphere.

The Pioneer

As buds spring into life, hibernating animals waken and sap rises in the trees, the newborn lamb shows a playful enthusiasm that stirs

thoughts of the coming summer. Aries has the lamb's personality: innocent and energetic. The Arien impulse is to leap out into the unknown and, like the lamb, she does not stay lying down for long. The Arien spirit is that of the pioneer, risk-taker and adventurer. Aries initiates new projects and ideas; she crosses continents alone and flies over uncharted seas. She enjoys pushing herself to her limits and discovering new sources of energy beyond the frontiers of exhaustion. Like the young initiate of many tribal peoples she finds herself in situations where her endurance, strength and ability to survive will be tested to their utmost, and she is equipped with the necessary faculties for survival in many dangerous undertakings. She makes decisions fast and her body displays her natural intelligence in action. Later, she looks back at the feats she has accomplished and wonders how she came through alive – yet she will take the same risks again and again.

Not every Arien sets off into the wilderness of earth, sea or sky, for some of the risks she takes are emotional, intellectual, social, political or financial, but she always displays the keen Arien drive. This sign is both fiery and cardinal and so combines the qualities of leaping fire with those of the initiating cardinal sign. Aries' impulsiveness often gets her into trouble because she seldom looks before she leaps, but when she lands in a mess she dusts herself off, laughs and lives to leap again. She does not give herself time to appreciate the dangers she is rushing into. If she did assimilate fully everything that happened to her, she would not be able to grow in the particularly Arien, extroverted way, for caution would inhibit her actions. Aries has the vivid, clear-cut vision of the youthful spirit, and tends to think that others are making mountains out of molehills.

Ideas inspire her; stories of unexplored possibilities capture her imagination, and she rushes off to find them in reality. Aries is the sign that rules the head, and can be strongly intellectual without living in an ivory tower of the mind. The Arien mind has a keen edge; incisive because her understanding is direct, she can go straight to the point. With clarity of purpose she cuts through tangles of muddle, woolly mindedness and sentimentality. She can be impatient with vaguely drifting imagination, whereas she will respond to the epic and the heroic.

The Wisdom of the Fool

Aries' keen intelligence is accompanied by the innocence of the Fool in the Tarot. This 'foolishness' is far from stupidity, rather it is a product of her courage. The Tarot Fool is shown setting out on life's journey with little baggage, inspired by hope and vitality. The zodiac is a circle and after the development of many complex concepts in Scorpio, Sagittarius, Capricorn, Aquarius and Pisces, we return again to the wise simplicity of Aries, clearing away the mental clutter that has accumulated. Zen sages teach of the need to retain or return to the 'beginner's mind', that which includes both doubt and possibility, to apprehend that 'the world has its own magic'. We do not need to load every part of our experience with symbolic interpretations. The Arien simplicity is disarming and she helps others, lost in complexity, towards a clearer vision.

Aries is an exciting companion because she is in tune with the moment. She knows how to be present and to celebrate the amazing fact that she, and everything else, exists. She has never lost her sense of wonder or forgotten how to express joy. The Aries principle is self-assertion, the joyous 'I am, I exist' of the new-born baby who is taken up with her desire to live.

The love of self and of life is the seed from which all other love grows. The zodiac teaches a spiral, not a linear, development, each sign correcting the excesses of the one before. The self-assertion of Aries is the natural corrective of the tendency to martyrdom of the preceding sign, Pisces.

The Warrior

It is because of her simplicity and her natural confidence that Aries manifests as a warrior. She has a driving need to be active; as she thinks, so must she act. She is attuned to her purpose, every muscle obeying her will through an instinctive concentration. With this ability to focus energy into activity she often excels at sport, like Sue Barker with Sun in Aries and Martina Navratilova with the Moon in the sign. Aries is competitive with herself, with her own records, her personal

best. Like American athletic director, Donnis Thompson, she may use her Arien skills as a trainer of champions.

The modern Arien is frequently involved in martial arts, for the meditative concentration on the effective use of the body is an Arien way. Even in the most peaceloving Arien there will be the 'butting' instinct of the lamb, a playful trying out of strength with no destructive intent.

As a warrior, Aries' mission is both to defend her people and herself. The warrior is an image with which many of us are no longer familiar, as we know only the reluctant soldier dying in wars he did not choose, or the brutal mercenary who enjoys making a living from killing. Ideally, the warrior is dedicated to a sacred ideal, respects life, and is highly trained in arts of concentration, meditation, endurance and fighting skills. She is prepared to die in defence of that which is sacred to her, but does not seek war or glory in intimidation. She knows her own power and is treated with respect.

Before the Age of Pisces (which began around 0 CE) warriors were often female as well as male, and in the writings of Greek historians we find reports of Amazon cultures. They were also reported in Asia Minor and Africa. During the end of the preceding Age of Aries the realm of Meroe, upriver from Egypt, was ruled by the Candaces, a dynasty of warrior-queens who were respected and feared by their contemporaries. The long tradition of warrior-women in Africa has in fact lasted to the present time with the famous Amazons of Dahomey. In Chinese opera the swordswoman heroine is beloved by her audience and her legendary roots are deep within popular culture. The Celts, too, were famous for their fighting women. Boadicea is one of many in British, Irish and French history. When Joan of Arc adopted the clothing of the warrior the people acclaimed her readily, perhaps stirred by folk-memories of the women warriors of the tribal Celts.

We see from myth and folk-tale that the true warrior is never brutal or oppressive to the weak: the Chinese swordswomen have a compassionate gentleness; the Celtic heroines protected wild animals.

Aries the Warrior is drawn to all that is vulnerable and defenceless, for hers is a loving impulse inspired by horror of suffering. The modern Arien often finds her inspiration in the Native American vision of the Rainbow Warrior who is prophesied as coming to defend the Earth and her creatures.

Aries often forgets, however, that she herself has the vulnerability

of the creatures she protects; her symbol is the lamb or ram, not the wolf or tiger. Her courage and vitality cover her insecurity, for, though she appears fearless, Aries can feel lost and alone. Action is her solace and gives her a way forward. She is at her best in a crisis; her pioneer qualities make her a natural leader. She hates to face a situation in which she can do nothing, and often rushes in to fix things up where she finds misfortune. Sometimes she can be interfering and too impatient to watch people help themselves at their own pace. Aries can be a fierce mother, battling for her children and their rights, but if she is confined to expressing her Arien energy through protecting them they may be deprived of the opportunity to fight for themselves.

The Arien woman finds the constraints of the traditional female role particularly burdensome. She needs an arena in which to be creative with her skills, to dazzle onlookers, either metaphorically or literally, with fast sword-play. She is happiest with a sparring partner, perhaps in exercising her ready wit in a duel of words. Aries may express her creativity through the use of cutting tools, as carpenter, jeweller or sculptor. More than any other sign Aries needs creative expression or a cause to fight for beyond providing for the needs of her family.

Challenging the World

There are many ways Aries can express her pioneer instinct. The way may be political, like that of Arien Alexandra Kollontai, who was not only a revolutionary but also an accomplished stateswoman. Arien Sirimavo Bandaranaike of Sri Lanka was the first woman in the world to become Prime Minister. Isadora Duncan had both Moon and Ascendant in Aries and her assertive spirit made her innovations in dance memorable and impressive. Bette Davies rejected the glamorous image of the star and fought with all the major studios to play tough and unlikeable parts. Billie Holiday had the Arien drive and courage to refuse the more socially acceptable role of the Black artiste solely as entertainer; she discomforted and challenged her white audiences by singing about racism, regardless of whether or not this was good box office strategy.

Whether a political or cultural fighter, the Arien woman often finds

that society has little room for her. She is frequently forced to assume a male disguise, not because she wants to be like a man, but because this is the only way she can express her vigour and energy in a world which sees these attributes as masculine qualities. Arien Queen Christina of Sweden dressed as a man and was memorable for the active role she took as a ruler.

Adapting to the World

Famous heroic Ariens inspire us and we can learn from these women how the cult of the hero needs to be integrated into a loving and life-preserving culture. The innocence of Aries is lost in the carnage of war, and she soon discovers that the romance of the adventurer wears very thin.

Yet to suppress her desire for competition and need for activity may bring out the aggressive side of Aries rather than subdue it. Arien people are destructive almost accidentally; there is no malice in them, only an impulse to grow that has been thwarted. Their faults are those of an adventurous child – lack of awareness of others' reactions, impatience, impulsiveness and foolhardy bravery. Those who reject the child in themselves and are self-importantly serious will find Aries most tiresome. Aries pooh poohs the kill-joys around her, but she has to learn to modify her behaviour and take part in society if she is not to become an outlaw. For this reason she often seeks places where she can express her exuberance without stepping on someone's toes. Sports may provide her with an untrammelled space, and the older Arien often works with young people who are more in tune with her own energy than are her contemporaries. At work she is often best suited as self-employed, or working alone within an organisation. Ariens have to work at their own pace; few can match their energy or their speed.

Emotional Enthusiasm

Often Aries falls in love with someone quieter, slower and more peaceable, who has all the faults and qualities she lacks. In a relationship she

can be self-assertive and confident, and sometimes her feelings pre-occupy her so much that she can miss what the other person is saying. But, in spite of her tendency to self-involvement, her love is clear and strong and she is a vivid and passionate partner. She brings a fiery energy into a relationship, which is warm and direct, and her honesty cuts through the emotional muddle that can come from defensive-ness. She often provides her lover with a new chance emotionally, for the directness of her passion provides security for a partner who has become inhibited by trying to protect old wounds. Aries excels at wel-coming the new while dispensing speedily with the past, and often her emotional enthusiasm can rub off on to her partner, who borrows some of the Arien courage for a fresh start.

Aries' fervour and initiative in a sexual relationship are usually stressed rather than her sensuality. Astrologers who have not ques-tioned traditional sex roles consider Aries a more comfortable sign for a man than for a woman. Yet, as with most of the signs, we dis-cover in Aries strong images of female sexuality.

As a friend Aries is respected because she is clear about what she wants. She can be trusted to display rather than hide any selfish motives, to put her cards on the table and declare her interests. People are won over by her honesty and are both bemused by and admiring of her colossal cheek. She is always prepared to act on behalf of those she loves, and they know they can call on her in any crisis.

Maturity

Constant activity is not always possible, even for Aries. Illness or res-ponsibilities may tie Aries down and enmesh her in other people's complex lives. She is disconcerted when faced with a reality that does not fit into her clear-cut categories. She finds it hard to hold on to two contradictory ideas simultaneously and she is often at a loss to describe her own ambivalences.

The discomfort she feels is the beginning of a process of self-discovery. With maturity Aries is able to keep the wisdom of the 'beginner's mind', while acknowledging there may not always be an immediate solution to every problem she encounters. This maturity of outlook is often hard for her to attain. Youth is her natural

stamping-ground and the ageing process may be particularly difficult for her. She may need help to smooth the passing into middle age, for she becomes bitter if she feels she has missed out on opportunities for action and adventure. Once the transition has been made, however, her vigour and enthusiasm in later years challenge the ideas society has of what is appropriate to old age. Aries has the dignity of the vigorous and rebellious older woman who breaks the conventional mould. Continued activity (even if no longer physical) is vital to her well-being and happiness; excitement keeps Aries vibrant. The dignity of the active Arien woman is a keynote for the twentieth century.

Nevertheless, despite increasing active possibilities for women, many have forgotten the sense of innocent self-worth natural to Aries. For those women with Aries strong in their charts it is imperative that they rediscover it. All women need to find the Arien part of their personalities (for we all have each sign within us, even if only in embryo) just as all men need to discover the Libran way. The development of the potentials of these two signs is necessary to rebalance a society suffering from the abuse of the Arien urge to action. Arien women may well find themselves as initiators in the necessary changes.

Aries has a strong belief in her own capability, and others can learn from her to say 'I can' rather than 'I can't'. In this, the most clear and direct of the signs, Aries provides a vivid example for those whose lives have become too complex and are weighed down with anxieties and responsibilities. Aries shows us how to assert ourselves, to share some of the inspirational courage of the Arien pioneer who cuts herself off from the tangles around her. Typically we see her alone on the mountain-top, in the desert, or sailing the ocean. She discovers her sense of self and her spiritual communion with the universe through the exhilaration of action. Alone with the elements she is aware of her deep joy in being alive.

Background to the Sign

TAURUS

The cow or bull
The path of nature
Approach to life of **fixed earth:**
steady, determined, calm, sensuous,
productive, fertile
Planetary ruler: Venus

This sign has been known as a bull or cow since the Age of Taurus (from about 4000 BCE to 2000 BCE) when, in various parts of the ancient world, there were religious ceremonies involving sacred cattle. The special significance of cattle appears to date back at least to the last Ice Age. Cave paintings show that horned animals were of special significance, probably because they reminded people of the crescent moon. Many centuries later in Crete bull-leapers were trained to perform feats of daring and the horns of the bull were a central motif in the art of the palace of Knossos. Behind the stories of the Cretan Queen Pasiphae, who mated with a bull to produce the Minotaur, are memories of the divine bull who was the consort of the Goddess. In Canaan the Goddess Asherah took the form of the Divine Cow, and it is her golden calf whose worship is mentioned in the Bible. In Egypt the cow was the most ancient form of the Goddesses Isis, Hathor and Neith. The cow-mother's milk splashed the sky with stars (called the Milky Way to this day), and she was the creator of all things, giving birth to the Sun. Mesopotamian kings claimed their right to rule because they had been 'fed with the holy milk of Ninhursag', the Sumerian Goddess who was sometimes seen as a divine cow.

Older than the myths of Zeus' exploits as a bull, and the rivalry of his wife with his other lovers, are stories of the white moon-cow as forms of the Goddesses Hera, Europa and Io. Classical poets wrote of the constellation under the name of Io, as well as Taurus. The Holy Cow of the early star-gazers was revered in a way few people outside India can understand today. Far from being treated as stupid, the cow was the symbol of the Goddess' love for her creatures, nurturing them with her milk.

The constellation was one of the earliest to have been named, and attracted special attention because it included the Pleiades or Seven Sisters, a tiny but noticeable cluster of stars which has been used all over the world to mark the dates of festivals by its rising.

The major festival of spring, celebrated in temperate climates of

the Northern hemisphere, was the arrival of the Goddess as May Queen, lady of the flowers, and the burgeoning earth. May Eve was celebrated, when the Sun was in Taurus, as the night when the fairies were abroad, when country folk stayed out in the fields and woods. The sign is ruled by Venus, Roman version of the Celtic May Goddess Blodeuwedd who was made by magic from flowers. During May her worshippers sometimes wore green, the fairy colour, to encourage the earth to flower and ripen, and green has always been one of Taurus' colours. Similar festivals have been celebrated all over the world to welcome spring, often with fertility rites. It was to prevent the May night of licence that the Puritans in Britain banned the maypole and the enthusiastic celebration of the May Goddess. The Taurean spirit of sensuality and merriment offered a pagan threat to sober faith, and reminded people of an older religion which saw human love and sexuality as sacred rather than profane.

Affectionate Sensuality

The Taurean personality is touched by the warm sensuality of the flower Goddess, and those born in this astrological month have some of her easy grace and luxurious delight in the physical. They like to demonstrate affection, to touch and be touched.

Both bull and cow were seen as the Goddess' creatures, but it is the calm stability of the cow that Taurus shows rather than the excitability of the bull. Taureans are not usually complex in their emotional lives. They love deeply, simply and long. They tend to be threatened by change in their relationships and develop strong attachments to those they care for.

Taurus is a sensual and exciting lover, reconnecting her partners to their own earth energy if they have lost touch with it. Rather than being driven by passion, there is a slow, easy sense of enjoyment in Taurus that animates all her relationships. To her, affection is a deep, not superficial, emotion and it is the strongest motivating force with her friends, family and lover. Although her very sensual nature could lead her to many sexual experiences, Taurus tends to monogamy because this gives her time and space to develop a deep love. Yet she seems to keep a memory of May Eve's freedoms by sharing her pleasures with

her friends, with a physical rather than sexual openness to many. She does not have the secrecy of her opposite sign Scorpio, but her need for quality of interaction means that she stays in touch with a few very close friends who know her on a deeper level and appreciate her constancy. She will extend her circle generously if other people make the effort to maintain the same level of contact; she likes people round her for warmth and companionship.

Taurus is usually even-tempered, slow to see red but if provoked too far she explodes with anger, rather like the cow who can suddenly become enraged when there is thunder in the air. But this is rare and Taurus' friends usually depend on her affectionate nature. The Taurean impulse corresponds to the phase in an infant's life after birth when she learns what she likes and dislikes. She discovers the pleasures of comfort, warmth and food and dislikes extremes of temperature, discomfort, hunger and pain. The infant enjoys the stimulation of new experience so long as she is safely in touch with her mother's body, and Taureans have the same need to remain in contact with earth-energy at all times. If Taurus feels safe, centred by her experience of the physical and of demonstrative affection, she is prepared to encounter something new. Grounded in her instinctive responses, she is very clear in defining what she likes and dislikes. She does not need half an hour to work out whether she has enjoyed a film; she can usually tell you straight away.

Creative Enjoyment

Taurus has a great appreciation for art and music, a taste in clothes and decor that most people find pleasing, and an ear for harmony. One of the most positive paths for Taurus is through some form of creative work, where she can use her sense of beauty. Making something gives her a deeper sense of her own worth, and she will take a great deal of pleasure in the look and feel of something she has made that satisfies her. She may be an artist and, most especially, a craftsperson, a maker. She likes to make things that are not only beautiful but also useful, for Taurus is always practical at heart. She has her feet on the ground and her aesthetics are influenced by the function of the artifact. This means that Taurus often works in design. She

would not be drawn to a sparse functionalism, however, for her sensuality inspires her to find a synthesis of practicality and pleasure. Whatever material she works with she has great respect for it as a medium, and her designs bring out its essential beauty, whether of clay, stone, fabric or wood.

The Taurean visual sense is unrivalled, and depends on her receptivity to sensual stimuli. When Taurus goes into a room she notices everything within it, aware of subtle gradations of colour and texture. The perception of Taurus is so vital to her that much of her daily consciousness is taken up with absorbing what she sees.

Taurus may be a scientist, interested in the observation and description of the physical world and respectful of the natural laws of the universe. But she will not be very interested in scientific speculation; she wants her information to have been proved and re-proved before she will trust it. For this reason she is less likely to be an innovator, for she has less of the intuitive faculty that allows a leap in the dark. But Taurus does not have to be constantly making new discoveries to be satisfied with her surroundings or her work. She may be an engineer or a mechanic, for she respects matter and is interested to see how it behaves and how it can be organised to be useful.

Whether scientist, mechanic, engineer, farmer or builder, Taurus is neither cold nor detached from her work. Her sensual involvement with her materials brings out the artist and craftswoman, whatever task she is undertaking. She excels because she is not driven by desire to complete her project; she luxuriates in the process rather than jumping ahead of herself and is able to exist within the moment and enjoy it.

As a musician she has the persistence to learn an instrument or train her voice. Taurus rules the throat and the larynx and Taureans are often fine singers, in touch with the potential of the whole body to make music and to express rhythm through drumming and dance. Famous Taurean women include many singers: Ella Fitzgerald, Ma Rainey, Judy Collins, Barbra Streisand and Dame Nelly Melba. The Taurus instinct to create beauty was part of the mystique and manner of Greta Garbo who had both Moon and Ascendant in Taurus.

Many Taureans have a charismatic quality, because they are so aware of their own bodies and so certain of their own reality. They exude not only sensuality but confidence; they understand their own experience because it is firmly grounded in sensation. To others,

whose sense of reality is less definite, Taurus can seem to have an enviable calm, because she does not constantly question and torment herself. Her approach to life is rooted deep in her instincts and she knows how to feed herself with the pleasant impressions she needs.

Her love of quality can be expressed by a gourmet interest in food and drink and a voluptuous appreciation of fine surroundings. When over-indulgence threatens her health she needs to find other ways to pleasure herself – saunas and soft fabrics rather than cream cakes and rare wines. She may have to watch her spending while taking care of her aesthetic needs, although money seems to come to her as easily as she can spend it. Something rich in her personality seems to attract riches to her. Usually she handles money well because she knows what she wants and so has a firm basis for spending and saving.

Luxurious Taurus can be lazy, but there is another side of her personality: committed, persevering and determined. She is prepared to work hard in order to surround herself with comforts, and values the benefits that money can provide. She is also generous to her friends. Taurus is often interested in finance and able to save and invest. Others who are less practical often dismiss her as materialistic, but fail to understand that decisions about money are a way for her to make important choices about what she does value and provide her with a path to self-knowledge.

Earth-Centred

Sometimes Taurus will choose a less comfortable lifestyle, so long as she has strong connections with the earth, and might prefer a simple house with a very large garden, or live in a caravan in the country. She is happy in a rural setting and seldom gets bored because the rhythm of the seasons provides her with the measured change that she needs. Nature reflects her own processes of gradual and centred growth. She has an awareness of the needs of the earth around her and takes responsibility as a caretaker of the land very seriously. She may become involved in ecological campaigns or devote herself to a particular area: her valley or garden. She grows plants for food, healing or for beauty, or she may return her garden to nature, letting it become wildwood or meadow to provide a home for the creatures she loves.

She feels an affinity with trees, especially large trees like the oak, the elm and the cedar, for they have her endurance and their roots reach deep into the earth. Taurus loves and often studies the earth's textures, collecting stones and mineral specimens. She respects people who live closely with the land and shares some of their awe for the processes of germination and growth. Though often a sceptic about 'psychic' matters, the idea of currents of energy running within the earth is not alien to her. She feels her own body as if it were an extension of the earth, and needs to be still and allowed to grow quietly like a tree, adding rings each year to the heartwood. Like a tree she can only grow if she is well-rooted, and so it is imperative for her to have a stable environment. She likes her work to have a sense of continuity, a past and a future as well as a present.

The stability in Taurus makes her specially valuable to any movement or organisation. She often prefers routine and the security of a clearly defined task and chooses a job that provides these things. Whatever work she is doing Taurus constantly reaffirms the value of the practical, the sanctity of the earth and the wisdom of the body. Naturopathic medicine appeals to her because of its respect for the body's mechanisms of self-regulation and self-healing. She is likely to have a gift for massage and may work as a healer. She is open to biodynamics and other kinds of therapy which pay much attention to the body and the messages the body expresses. If Taurus can touch something and experience it with her senses, she will respect and believe.

Taurus likes to be in touch with her body through sports and physical exercise. She is particularly attracted to marathons which bring out her endurance, rather than short sprints when there is hardly time to get going. She is just as likely to be a fine dancer, and Taureans have excelled, like British Margot Fonteyn and Indian Sonal Mansingh. Taurus may take up yoga, T'ai Chi, or one of the oriental martial arts. Self-defence attracts her, not for the excitement of combat, but because if one is truly grounded in one's own body one can best deal with attack.

Fundamentally motivated by affection, Taurus is not insensitive to the needs of others who are in distress; she will usually respond with very practical help. The situation of the hungry, the homeless and the exiled will move her, while she will not waste time sympathising with emotional suffering when she feels it could be avoided.

Taurean Sylvia Pankhurst chose a more practical and less glamorous

reality in the East End of London than her mother Emmeline or her sister Christabel, showing how Taurean commitment can overcome the need for a luxurious environment.

Grounded Realism

As a rule Taurus tends to be conservative in outlook; her ideas, however, may be conservative with a small 'c' only, as many left wing thinkers have had the caution of Taurus, or even tended to a similar ossification in their belief systems as their political opponents. Taurus tends to see her own values as the only ones possible, and readily accepts her reality as the only one. She can also interpret events in a very literal, material way, ignoring more subtle or spiritual perceptions which often unsettle or frighten her in their mystery.

A basically materialistic world view underlies the Taurean faults of over-attachment to possessions and a tendency to see people in terms of her own desires. Taurus is down to earth about her emotional and sexual needs, and her practicality can be insensitive to those who function on more subtle planes. She becomes exasperated by those who elaborate endlessly and may become involved in a spiral of misunderstanding because of her literal interpretation of another person's words. She becomes obstinate and defensive and hangs on to the facts of what has happened in their interaction, rather than looking to the spirit beneath it.

Growing

Through her stubbornness, Taurus risks shutting off from the possibility of change in herself; this can really damage her, although it will take a long time for her to realise what she has missed. But, in spite of the fixed nature of Taurus, it is not a static sign; rather, it is a sign of growth. The growth of Taurus is slow and scarcely perceptible; we do not expect the Taurean spring flowers of the Northern hemisphere to open in front of our eyes, nor for the autumn leaves in the Southern hemisphere to become red overnight. Because Taurus is so hard to

convince or convert her changes are the more impressive and the more lasting when they do take place. She cannot be hurried, but she is worth waiting for. By going at her own pace Taurus teaches others that speed is not necessarily better than slowness, like the tortoise she will arrive at the end of the journey before the hare.

Taurus is guided by her instincts, but does not have to be dominated by her instinct away from meaning and towards literal interpretations. She is engaged in the formative process of learning her own values, discovering what she likes and dislikes on a deeper level than her immediate instinctive responses can guide her to. This process of learning value is explained by the Zulu in their story of the Rain Goddess Mbaba Mwana Waresa, which tells how she made herself ugly to test whether her mortal husband would still recognise her inner beauty.

At an early phase in her development Taurus tends to run away from ugliness and anything which she cannot readily explain but, as she expands her understanding, she becomes more deeply aware of the inner beauty beneath the surface, just as she loves the roots and the minerals within the earth. Always practical and realistic, her intuition works through her bodily instincts and gut responses, and becomes more finely attuned as she accumulates experience through her senses.

Whenever Taurus is unsure of direction or tempted to discount her own wisdom she can turn to the earth, her source, for reassurance and inspiration. She sees there, in the soil and in the growing plants, a confirmation of her own nature, her stability and her ability to create beauty.

'Returning to the source is stillness, which is the way of nature.
The way of nature is unchanging.
Knowing constancy is insight.' *Tao Te Ching*[2]

Background to the Sign

GEMINI

The twins
The path of versatility
Approach to life of **mutable air:**
inventive, communicative, adept,
curious, multi-faceted, quick
Planetary ruler: Mercury

Gemini was one of the earlier constellations to be identified, and in many cultures the two very bright stars were seen as twins. The symbol was a potent one, for the phenomenon of twin births has always fascinated and has become a symbol in the development of ideas. Some cultures have seen twins as specially blessed, or even of divine origin. In West Africa twins have inspired a system of religious observances and a tradition of sculpture. In many cultures twins are made to stand for duality in all its manifest forms: identical doubles, complementary opposites, antagonistic opposites. Antagonistic pairs of twins are typified by Cain and Abel, or by the Celtic idea of the king's 'wyrd'. This was a shadow twin whom, it was believed, would one day overthrow him.

Twins may be polar, but not necessarily antagonistic, opposites; the Chinese, for example, called Gemini Yin/Yang which they show as a male/female pair of twins. Isis, representing life, was often shown with her twin sister Nephythys, representing death, protecting the dead with their winged arms outspread on Egyptian tombs.

The twins most usually shown in astrological illustrations are Castor and Pollux, sons of Leda (a form of the Great Goddess), one fathered by Zeus and one by her mortal husband. When mortal Castor was fatally wounded in battle, his divine brother mourned him so passionately that Zeus placed them both in the heavens as the twins. Gemini is sometimes shown as two women, or as a boy and girl. In many mythologies twins of light and darkness can be found, and behind every set of twins is the more or less shadowy figure of the Great Goddess who bore them. The Goddess is present in the story of the twins Romulus and Remus, the founders of Rome, in the form of a she-wolf who suckled these orphans. She stands for the maternal whole, the completeness that existed before the split into duality.

Making Connections

Gemini is always seeking wholeness, and so whatever path she takes she always wants to explore the other left behind. Many Gemini people have two jobs, two homes, two nationalities and two major relationships. The dilemma of Gemini is how to reach that wholeness and unity, to form bridges between the contrasting realities that she can readily identify. It is her inventive spirit that makes the bridges, creating connections and enabling communication to take place.

Gemini never loses the child's enthusiasm to know. In adult life she is not content with the knowledge she has acquired in her growing, and she continues to accumulate information, learning new languages, with the desire to understand them. She has a keen eye for facts, a quick ear and an ability to mimic. With her love of words and ideas she plays with their meanings and derivations, sometimes making puns that others would groan about. Words and ideas are pieces of a puzzle to her, to be shifted about until she sees a new pattern that appeals.

Gemini has the ability to be interested in practically anything presented to her. Variety is vital for her; her butterfly mind is sudden — she is so speedy and unexpected that few can follow her. Ideas intoxicate her, each one enchanting until another comes along.

At work she needs constant stimulation and flourishes only in fields which provide it. She has an intuitive ability to 'read' her audiences and instinctively adapts what she is saying to suit them. So she often excels at teaching, sales work or advertising. When she gives a talk it is as if she has an automatic pilot which takes care of the details for her. She may make an able politician because of her ability to deal with hecklers with wit and skill, and she usually outsparkles her opponents. Communication delights her, and she enjoys letters, telephone conversations and appreciates the technology that makes greater links possible. Journalism and broadcasting are particularly Geminian fields and, an Airsign, she loves to be on the air as an announcer, DJ, interviewer or personality in chat shows.

Easily bored with routine or repetition, Geminis love the immediate. They may be extremely fashionable because they are in contact with the spirit of the age, the *zeitgeist*, and have an instinct for what is new. Gemini is light and breezy one moment, in the abyss the next, and tends not to be able to remember happiness when she is depressed

or sadness when she is radiant. She is a creature of the moment with a wonderful memory for fact, but her emotional memory is a short one. She needs the ring given to the king in a Sufi story. He had asked for a gift that would steady his ever-changing emotional states, and this ring had the property of stabilising the fluctuating emotions of the beholder, whether in a state of despair or of ecstasy. Inscribed upon it were the words 'This too will pass'.

The Bridge to Feeling

The most changeable of signs on the surface, Gemini finds deep changes very difficult. If someone can offer her an idea which is new and exciting she may be tempted to examine herself in the light of that idea. The danger is that she will engage with it on an intellectual level only, and ignore the challenge to cross the bridge from ideas to feelings. In the realm of feeling she can become lost, having to work out (intellectually) whether she feels something or just thinks she feels it. This distance can make her a puzzle to other people who often see her as unfeeling or superficial. They are upset by her inability to be serious, for when Gemini cannot cope with an emotional situation she jokes her way out of it, and can be insensitive. It is not that she has no feelings, only that she is often afraid of them. She fears loss of control of the mind (her security) over the emotions and unconscious, and part of why she talks so much is her attempt to keep the silence at bay, for fear of what it might contain.

Many Gemini people fear the lesser known parts of themselves, and the popular misconception that Geminians are split personalities can be very distressing. In fact, the lesser known 'twin' self is part of the psyche of all of us, and the duality of Gemini is very far from either true schizophrenia or multiple personality. But Gemini *is* strongly aware of the polarities within herself, between the twin self she knows and the twin she fears. With apparent innocence she pushes away and disowns the twin self that makes her feel uncomfortable. She cannot completely get rid of it, however, and her fear remains as long as she tries to escape from herself, or makes sure there is always a 'back door' open in every situation she enters into.

The maturing process, vital to her development, is to learn to take

responsibility for her actions and feelings, so freeing herself from fear of her inner double. Once she can own her ambivalent or negative feelings towards others she will not feel so split.

Using the Mind

Just as Gemini needs to find out how to still the mind, she also needs to exercise it, to find out what it can do. In the ancient world the workings of the mind were seen as magical and blessed by the gods, as were the inventions that may now seem to be coldly rational, such as the alphabet and the use of numbers. For Gemini to travel beyond the mind she must use her mind to the full.

Unlike her polar opposite, Sagittarius, she tends not to schematise her knowledge into one great belief system, but rather gathers a treasure trove of unsorted facts, like a jackdaw's hoard which may contain discarded scraps of silver paper or solid silver teaspoons. Often dismissed by others as lacking judgement, the Geminian approach has its own advantages. Like the jackdaw's hoard her mind contains unlikely juxtapositions. For her, all that glitters *is* gold, because it is her perception and her experience that matter to her rather than the hallmark of an external assayer. She may be more interested in the wrapping paper than the birthday present.

Her dependence on thought does not mean that Gemini is a rigid or unimaginative thinker. She leaps sideways into the unknown, spanning two worlds. When she encounters two realities that will not integrate with each other, however hard she tries to synthesise them, she finds a philosophical comfort in paradox. She enjoys riddles, apparent impossibilities and trick questions.

Many literary traditions contain the riddles that Gemini loves. The Celts used riddles and paradox extensively; they found a path into the realms of magic through the door paradoxes opened in the mind. Particularly magical times were paradoxical, because they were neither one thing nor the other – between seasons at the Solstice and Equinox, between directions at the crossroads, between day and night at twilight. These are the duskily grey areas that Gemini opens up by her concentration on the black and white world of duality and polarity, the world of twin vision.

In a tradition far removed from the Celts, Zen masters often used paradox as the 'trick' to break the mind of its habits. The Geminian focuses on mind but by her attraction towards riddles and 'tricks' she can find her own way out of the trap that a purely mental approach can set up. For, in her constant search for the 'missing piece' of the jigsaw puzzle, Gemini is not always aware that the part that she cannot get hold of may not be definable in words, or that its very essence may be in its indefinability. If she does not leave room enough for what she cannot know, paradox will escape her. But at some time in her life the urge to document and find out will lead her to face the unattainable, the incomprehensible. This is often a long process for Gemini. She hates boredom because with the lack of stimuli she may have to face herself. In the most still pool her face will be reflected best, and in the most profound silence she will hear her own heart and breathing. So Gemini spends much of her life filling stillness with activity and silence with noise. Eventually she can reach a point where she has exhausted this tactic. By facing the apparently terrifying emptiness Gemini can find in it a peace that has eluded her in all her Mercurial travels.

Grounding

For Gemini it is unfamiliar but helpful to consider the way she holds her body, or the feelings she has in various parts of it. She seldom pays her body much attention, skips meals, and tends to forget her other body functions for extraordinary lengths of time. She needs to sleep and eat well more than any other sign; it is when she is over-tired that she can be silly and irritating, superficial and restless. Then she can lose her friendly sensitivity to others and become inquisitive and unfeeling.

She may be surprised by her own anger or grief that she honestly would not have known were there below the surface. Her fears affect her body very directly. Because she fears being trapped she may be prone to feelings of physical suffocation. She may breathe shallowly or have other problems with her lungs (which are ruled by Gemini), and her emotions may express themselves directly through asthma. (Contrary to appearances, asthma involves difficulty in breathing *out*

more than in, and Gemini takes everything in but often does not give herself time to let out some of the useless information and experiences she has absorbed.) Breathing exercises help her lungs, which are sensitive to stress. Training in self-hypnosis can give her a sense of control and power to determine what she experiences physically, so that her body ceases to be a source of panic for her. Any technique appeals to her which demonstrates the power of mind over matter, for Gemini deeply respects the power of ideas. She benefits from meditation or yoga, for many of her problems come from the scattering of her energies. Crafts are another way she can centre herself, for Gemini rules the hands. Many crafts allow the eye and hand to work together without constant intervention from the conscious mind, and this is restful to Gemini.

The Jester/Trickster

All Airsigns suffer from pain and disillusionment because the world does not conform to the ideal that they have perceived. Gemini carries the pain of the disappointed child around with her, unsure of how to nurture and comfort the screaming infant within. So she often demands social approval and attention from an audience, making herself the jester, the clown whose make-up hides tears. She has the wit and a fund of accumulated information to entertain, and she may make her living by it. At the end of the show she tells herself 'No one would love me if I didn't keep performing', so undercutting the security she has just striven to gain. Marilyn Monroe had the Sun in Gemini and Judy Garland the Moon, their premature deaths underlining the insecurity behind the facade of the successful performer. When insecure, Gemini is sometimes pushed by her own drives, needs and fears to become the trickster living by her wits, the juggler whose hand deceives the eye while the tongue keeps up a fast patter. She is often accused of being emotionally manipulative, but Gemini is not consciously scheming for power or trying to hurt anyone. Sometimes her natural cunning operates almost in spite of herself: Gemini knows that it is a dangerous world out there, and she is sure to be streetwise. She has the naive belief that she can get something for nothing, and as she often does it makes her very pleased, for it reinforces her confidence

about her ability to survive. She believes she can talk her way out of any situation, and usually she can.

When Gemini tells stories she often embroiders them spontaneously – she cannot resist this – and may later come to believe in her additions and improvements. To her it is the idea which is paramount, not the fact. She is in tune with Blake's proverb: 'Everything possible to believe is an image of truth'.

Invention

Gemini does best when she puts her ability to improvise to creative use and tells or writes stories. In the world of fantasy she can become whomsoever she pleases and play all the parts, here her versatility becomes virtuosity. She may need the discipline to hold her stories within herself for a while, not to talk or write them out but to nurse them and allow them to grow.

One of the earliest English women novelists, Fanny Burney, had her Sun in Gemini, and she has been followed by many Geminian writers. Gemini can use words with satirical precision as novelist Ivy Compton-Burnett shows very clearly. Many Geminians write a daily journal (Anne Frank, the most famous of diarists, was a Geminian), and to them it is often their greatest emotional resource. The most flexible of the signs, Gemini can adapt and change to suit practically any situation she is faced with, and this is her enormous strength. A true Airsign, she flows around obstacles. Gemini can be so adaptive that she doubts her own identity. She likes the story of the philosopher who dreamed he was a butterfly, and woke to wonder if he was a butterfly dreaming he was a man. She is much given to wondering. It makes her insecure, but also flexible and spontaneous.

Famous creative and inventive Geminians often show the child-like quality of the sign, the 'Peter Pan' personality. Edith Piaf with her Moon in Gemini impressed her audience with a paradoxical maturity behind a street urchin image. Both Isadora Duncan and Amelia Bloomer who both had Sun in Gemini rejected the narrowly confining definitions of suitable clothes and behaviour for women. From their rebellious examples some of the freedom of the child has been recaptured for women. Neither of them cared how much they were mocked, and were as impervious to convention as the jester.

Finding her Twin

Peter Pan Gemini often prefers to fly away to the Never-Never land of the idealistic Airsign rather than take up adult commitments. She may use a multiplicity of emotional involvements to escape from reality. Typically Gemini is a compulsive charmer who is never sure what she wants from other people. Often she depends on a partner for the security she claims not to need.

However, she has an inner yearning for her soul-mate, a companion, a sister or brother 'twin' who understands her interests. Gemini needs a relationship that will change with her, a partner who will understand her preoccupations and tolerate her inconstancy. She needs contact between them to be very strong on the mental level, and this connection will help them to weather Gemini's emotional confusions.

Whether with lover, partner or friend Gemini always has much to give from her inexhaustible hoard of ideas and experiences. Her interest in her friend is genuine, and she loves her 'twin' (of whatever sign) with unquestioning affection.

The sisterly nature of her love does not mean that it is passionless; it is a bond of great depth that she has with her psychic twin. Yet the relationship is not always an emotional/sexual one; it may be a deep friendship or a bond with a relative. Gemini particularly enjoys the rapport between sisters, brothers or cousins in large families. She relates to her own children with the same sense of ease and freedom, like the dancer and singer Josephine Baker who adopted orphans from all over the world and called them her 'rainbow tribe'.

The Alchemist

Gemini can be very happy and complete in herself, satisfied with her own duality. For she is the alchemist who uses knowledge to transmute the elements, the magician who knows that words are the source of power. She can steal the apple from the tree of knowledge or train her mind to span the twin realms of idea and form and connect inner consciousness with outer reality. She darts from one to the other like swift-footed Mercury who rules her, and lives to tell the tale.

Background to the Sign

CANCER

The crab
The path of imagination
Approach to life of **cardinal water:**
sensitive, emotionally attuned,
nurturing, creative, protective,
tenacious
Planetary ruler: the Moon

Cancer is the least visible of the constellations and has been called by the ancients 'The Power of Darkness'; it is the sign of the gentle darkness of the sea, the womb and the night. Its symbol has most often been a hard-shelled creature: the tortoise, scarab, crab and crayfish. In Egypt the scarab's life-cycle was the symbol of the regeneration and rebirth of the soul, just as the butterfly has symbolised a cycle of transformation. The Sun was pictured as travelling in the boat of the scarab during the hours of darkness, ferried through the night so that it could rise again in the morning. This night-time journey of the Sun had another symbolic level in Egyptian religion; it represented the soul's journey between the daylight of two incarnations.

Both Chaldean and Platonist philosophers saw Cancer as the gate through which souls came from heaven into earthly life. The boat or ark is an alternative symbol for Cancer. In many different cultures the boat represented the womb that carried the child passenger, or the vulva through which she passed into life, for the vulval opening has the shape of a boat.

Because of the long connections of the sign with birth and fertility Cancer has been associated with the Great Goddess as Mother. Robert Graves describes how one of the myths of Hercules emerged from an age of struggle between patriarchal and Goddess-worshipping cultures.[3] In Hercules' fight with the Hydra (which Graves sees as representing the Goddess religion) the crab fought on the side of the Goddess, pinching Hercules in the foot. For this service Hera placed the crab in the Heavens.

Creature of the Oceans

Vulnerable Cancer may be a fighter, concealing her soft inner parts within a hard shell. She is competent, adventurous and can seem very

tough, but the shell has been acquired because the person within is so sensitive. The world she lives in is that of the shifting and tidal ocean. In dreams and fantasies the sea represents feelings, the unconscious, and sexual desire. Cancer is, like the ocean, subject to many moods. Sometimes she is swamped by her own feelings and then, as her 'tide' recedes, she finds herself dry, empty and drained, at her emotional low. Those around her are astonished at her mood swings. But Cancer is consistent and can be relied upon to stay with any project she has started. Her movement is all in the realm of emotion, of tidal moods. Just as the sea is low at one time of the day, so it can be relied upon to be high at a later time. Cancer's ruling planet, the Moon, often described as inconstant and changing, is ultimately reliable. The tiny crescent of the new Moon always reappears after the nights of darkness when the Moon has been invisible. Cancer's mood swings have a firmness beneath them, like the beach whose rocks are only slowly eroded by the shifting tide. She has an awareness of minute changes and cyclic growth, like the sea creatures who are so delicately sensitive to the Moon's pull on the Earth.

Cancer is able to perceive emotional depths in those around her, for wearing a shell herself she is not deceived by other people's disguises. Mary Shelley, who had Cancer as her Ascendant, conjured up in her book, *Frankenstein*, a monster of iron who is a creature of vulnerable emotions inside the shell. The flowing moods of Cancer give her an extraordinary emotional range as a writer, or as an artist with the sensitivity of Käthe Kollwitz who was vividly aware of the experience of the people around her in Germany in the 1920s and 1930s. Cancer may find her expression as an actress like Barbadian Elizabeth Clarke who is also a poet and dramatist.

Practical Sensitivity

Cancer uses her imagination to enter the experience of others. Her sensitivity and compassion are usually expressed in practical ways, and this practicality is an essential balance which prevents her from becoming overwhelmed by her emotional nature. Cancer turns her gaze inward to her own inner life of emotion, imagination and intuition. She looks to the inner life of any group she is involved with, and

may develop her skills of understanding as a psychic. Often she has to battle for emotional and imaginative needs to be recognised. She has a ready understanding of the emotional implications of any change in legislation or the practices of local government and is able to translate figures or the turgid language of official statements into emotionally meaningful images. For this reason she can be one of the best people to have writing for any cause or campaign.

She is particularly interested in the homes we create for ourselves. Her own home expresses her personality strongly and she spends much time on it, making it a place that will allow her emotional retreat. Because of her skill in identifying human needs for comfort and security and her combination of imagination and practicality, she is well equipped to work in architecture and design. She has a sense of 'home' that stretches from the tiniest room all the way to the planet as a home for humankind and other creatures. She is often concerned about ecology and the protection of the earth, worrying that its protective shell is being stripped away. Cancer is keenly sensitive to any danger from exposure, either physical or emotional. She likes to feel that she is 'on the inside', that she *belongs*.

Cancer often limits her concern to those who are 'her own', who share her life or her roots. Cancerian love can be boundless and deep as the sea, and she fears to give herself up to it without restraint. So she fixes boundaries and says 'To these people I will give all I have, but beyond them I cannot share'.

Use of the Imagination

Fear of exclusion makes her unduly sensitive to criticism. She easily feels guilty, and if anyone voices general dissatisfaction she may fear she is the cause. She needs to become a home-maker in the deepest sense, to promise herself a place 'inside' – a spiritual home.

Yet sometimes it is easier for Cancer to find other people to take care of her than for her to nurture herself. If she becomes too dependent she never feels the real security that she wants, and remains easily hurt and touchy, given to worrying. Her enhanced sensitivity that monitors nuances of criticism finds a more positive expression in her extraordinary imagination. She is best employed using it to the

full and not wasting it on her fears. She can develop many psychic skills by following her natural intuition. Her sensitivity and insight allow her to express herself musically as well as in writing and art. Her imagination is her greatest resource; she can use it to transform her fears because she is open to the wisdom of her unconscious. Many of her worries can be channelled into creative interests.

Nourishment, Nurturing and Creative Risks

Because she is concerned with nourishment, both emotional and physical, Cancer can see that food is far more than just the fuel a body needs to keep functioning; she is aware that its quality is important and that the people who grow and cook the food must be satisfied and happy in their working conditions. Cancer rules those parts of the body that are concerned with nourishment: the stomach, the breasts which nourish the infant, the placenta which feeds it before birth, and the womb which contains and protects it.

Cancer has long been associated with motherhood because of the nurturing qualities of the sign. This may not be an easy association, because of society's expectations of women and because so many people have unresolved feelings in their relationships with their mothers. Those who are searching for the 'good mother' may idealise Cancer because she seems to express the nurturing qualities of which they have felt deprived. Cancer may become strongly attached to this 'Good Mother' pedestal; she needs to be needed. It is a dangerous and ungainly perch, for if the admirers spot Cancer's feet of clay they will rapidly demote her. Even when they do not, Cancer will feel frustrated for she cannot have true companionship with those who do not feel themselves to be her equals; pedestals get lonely.

Cancerians are particularly liable to become trapped in situations where they are looking after everyone else. Cancer sees the child within the adult and responds to cries for help, but holds her own tears inside. She knows that inside her, too, there is a hurt and frightened child, but she can use her shell to block off from looking at that child's needs, busying herself with the care of others. Often this is because she is uneasy with her own neediness and vulnerability.

But just as often she can find extraordinary courage to take risks

emotionally, for this sign is the initiator in the world of feeling. Often she makes her feelings known and gets hurt. Cancer feels a driving need for emotional scope and development, for it is primarily through feeling that she learns and grows. The paradox at the heart of Cancer is the tension between her extreme vulnerability, which makes her shut herself off, and creative risk-taking, which puts her out on a limb. She often veers between these two extremes or tries to combine them by taking risks, pretending that she does not care one way or another about their outcome. This 'win some, lose some' nonchalance is belied by the intensity she feels about past hurts. It takes Cancer a very long time to forget a wound, and while she does not actively seek for revenge she does not let the person who has hurt her easily off the hook of her quiet reproach.

She needs a variety of emotional outlets. If she fixes all her attention on one or a very few people she may try to live through those in whom she has invested everything. If she is disappointed she risks becoming bitter and resentful. Often Cancer will not be able to escape from this pattern until she has worked on, and cleared, some of the feelings she has about her own mother. Usually she has a strongly emotional relationship with her mother. Whether idealising or denigrating her, however, she may be hiding other feelings.

The World Outside

It is particularly difficult for Cancer to live in a world that idealises nurturing and caring and expects women to provide these functions, often unsupported emotionally or financially. Because of these confusions, Cancer finds the traditional astrological description of her sign unhelpful. She may have strongly rejected traditional motherhood roles and yet find all her caring qualities defined in terms of their expression in the family. Often her work is unpaid, but Cancer has many other options as a nurturer. She knows how to give other people the protection they need when they enter new and deep emotional waters. This ability makes her effective as a therapist or counsellor. Equally, she may work with the very young, the old and the sick, or may use this energy to nurture a project or nourish a cause. Emmeline Pankhurst chose to be mother to the Women's Social and

Political Union rather than confine her energies to her family. In America black suffragist Ida B. Wells was a family woman but was not traditionally domestic, 'devoted to her children, but hated housework'. She poured her energy into political work and journalism.

Cancer is a born organiser and gets a tremendous amount done in a short time with her intense bursts of energy. As Cancer is a cardinal initiating sign, she has a strong need to be powerful and effective in the world, and if this is frustrated it is important that her work in relationships is appreciated and validated by those around her.

When a Cancerian is aware of her need for a larger sphere of action she feels her restriction intensely. Charlotte Perkins Gilman wrote of her confinement within family and marriage in *The Yellow Wallpaper* [4] where the sense of suffocation becomes almost overwhelming to the reader.

The Cancerian ambivalence about security shows how the forms we create to take care of our needs can become a prison, blocking out all other needs for change, exploration and freedom.

While Cancer rules the home, many overlook the fact that it is also the sign of seafaring. Many Cancerians have been great navigators and explorers, travelling to new shores in their womb-like boats. Once they have a harbour to return to Cancerians will travel far and wide. Cancer has a tremendous urge for discovery, as shown by the aviator Amy Johnson, for example, who had Sun in Cancer. Though she moved through the air rather than water her journeys covered vast expanses of lonely sea.

Cancer's discoveries are not only geographical; she also charts new territories of the mind and emotions. Cancerian Helen Keller pioneered new possibilities for communication and inspired the teaching of deaf and blind children. Her writing is full of images of shackles being broken.

Cancer the voyager can anticipate the buffetings of the high seas and steer her boat with the focused precision of a helmswoman whose body responds instinctively and who becomes one with her craft. As she sets out on an adventure, memories of her home and her past often provide her with the security she needs for her voyage.

Ebb and Flow

Through connections with birth and with the child within, Cancer has many links with the past, not only of her own, but that of whole civilisations and cultures. She is deeply interested in history, and can often feel the emotional past of an object or a place. She has a sense of continuity, of an unbroken cycle of human consciousness stretching back through thousands of years. Possessions are experienced as a sacred heritage and she accumulates many of her own. She likes antiques, enjoying the way an object's past history mingles with her present. Cancer is the sign of far memory, of the possibilities of previous lives and of early memories of this life. Her recollections and acknowledgement of the child's need for love give her a deep and compassionate wisdom. She knows that the emotional voyager needs a climate of loving kindness to nurture her strengths. Her own love is sensitive and aware, and suggests both to herself and others the potential for forgiveness, for being accepted, protected and allowed to become whole again. Cancerian tenderness gives us flashes of memory of a time before separation, of love that seemed unconditional, stronger than any danger. This inspiration gives Cancer her strong spiritual roots. She is happiest when she is amongst others who share her understanding and her mystical nature, and yet allow her voyaging spirit to take risks, to let her be her moody, cyclical self. She needs commitment and stability, a harbour, because her inner world is all ebb and flow. She wants to know others who share her belief in the overriding importance of love; in exchange for that security she will give deep and committed devotion and share her intuitive perceptions. Within a sexual relationship Cancer can be a deeply loving and passionate partner, inspiring her lover to understand the tidal nature of an oceanic sensuality.

Cancer lives like a sea creature who inhabits both shore and ocean, depending on the state of the tide. Sometimes she is on the shore of reality, sometimes in the sea of the imagination. She is acutely aware of her own cycles, of her needs for inner life or life in the world, to be private or to be in relationships. She is in harmony with a fluid existence.

Whether she is light and shining or withdrawn and secret Cancer is the dancer in tune with the pattern, the daughter of the Moon.

LEO

The lioness or lion   The path of
self-expression
Approach to life of **fixed fire:**
*confident, dramatic, commanding,
generous, loyal, playful*
Planetary ruler: the Sun

Background to the Sign

The stars of the constellation Leo were named as a lion from very ancient times. The lion was known as a symbol of power and authority in the ancient civilisations of Africa. The Egyptian and Ethiopian cultures used the lion extensively in their sacred art, and the mystery of the lion-bodied sphinx has captured the imagination of people down to the present day. In the Babylonian myth of the Goddess Tiamat's creation of the world, the 'Great Lion' was one of the eleven creatures she made do battle for her. In the form of Canaanite Anath and Arabic Allat the Goddess herself was shown as a lion. Egyptian Goddesses Tefnut and Sekmet were lion-headed, while the gentle cat-Goddess Bastet changed into a lion when she was angry.

These associations bring out the awe and respect in which the lioness was held and suggest some of the underlying dignity of the sign. The lioness was revered in those days, while she is rather ignored in more recent mythology, lions usually being shown with a mane and honoured as 'The King of Beasts'. But people who live close to real lions know that it is the lioness who does the bulk of the hunting. The lioness-goddess is also playful, and represents the free-flow of female sexuality. Lioness Tefnut represented 'moisture' and Sekmet was associated with sweetness and pleasure; she was addressed as 'the lioness in heat'. We find these themes in pleasure-loving Leo who luxuriates in the sweetness of love-making. Sometimes the lion was shown as the companion of the Goddess; lions accompanied the Sun-Goddesses Wurusemu and Arinna in their pictures and statues. In India the Goddess Parvati/Durga is shown with a lion.

The lion is strongly associated with the Sun – his mane reminded people of the Sun's rays – and in the Northern hemisphere the Sun is strongest at the time when it passes through the sign of Leo. Ancient rulers sat on thrones carved into shapes of lions to emphasise their Goddess-given authority. Remnants of this custom survive in the clawed legs found on thrones and antique chairs in our day. The Goddess, or her representative, was thought to tame the lion by her inner

power, which the creature instinctively worshipped. Stories tell how the nymph Cyrene overcame a lion which was terrorising Libya and was given part of the kingdom as a reward. This image of a woman taming a lion survives in the Tarot pack as the card for Strength: the power and stature of integrity that tames through gentleness where coercion fails.

The Courage for Self-Expression

The woman with the lion is a symbol of the inner power of the spiritually developed Leo, who has the ability to impress others with her integrity without blasting them with ego or dominating her surroundings. But many Leos need to be seen as important in the circles in which they move; they find it hard to be just one of a crowd, and want to feel like a queen and shine like the sun. Though Leo may be introverted (like Emily Bronte) she usually draws attention to herself by some kind of charisma and Leo can be a glorious and unashamed extrovert. She feels that she needs appreciation and acclaim, and this may be more important to her than finding her own peers. Equipped with a flamboyant manner and a flair for the spontaneous, creative gesture, she is a joy to watch and often has a humorous awareness of her regal behaviour. As Leo Mae West says, 'You can't have too much of a good thing' – and here she means herself.

Naturally Leo attracts criticism at the same time as applause. Many accuse her of ostentatiousness and of needing to be the centre of attention. Leo is very hurt by this criticism and usually shuts off from it, hardening her heart against her detractors and concentrating on the recognition she does get. It is easy to knock Leo because she makes herself so visible; when she shows off it is her vulnerability that shows. There is no guile in Leo; she knows what she wants and asks for it with confidence. Often those who criticise her are afraid to ask for the same recognition, though they would dearly like it, and envy lurks behind their reserve. To those who are afraid to express their own creativity and vitality for fear of criticism, the vivid presence of Leo is an active rebuke. Without the Leonine impulse we lack a sense of glory; we feel inhibited by the opinions of those around us; we are unable to speak a word, sing a note or dance a step. As with all the

signs we each have Leo *somewhere* in the chart, and it is this impulse which brings out the creativity of the story-teller, the dancer and the actor who are prepared to accept the gaze of all eyes upon them. Leo is not controlled by self-consciousness, she is animated by consciousness of self. She can no more inhibit herself than the Sun can stop shining, and if others cannot take her confident self-expression, her joy and her vitality, they must protect themselves. If Mae West's diamanté gives you a headache, wear sunglasses. Leo usually understands if some of her friends withdraw when she is 'full on'; providing they are not unpleasant and do not ruffle her dignity.

The power that Leo claims and expresses is the right and proper power of the individual who is in touch with herself; the power of health and vitality, the shining inner light that enables us to heal ourselves when we are sick. Knowing her own power and standing bathed in the light of it allows each person to become the Sun of her own solar system, the integrating centre.

Before we rush to criticise Leo for her exuberance and confidence it is helpful to imagine what the world would be like if everyone were able to shine in the same way. Sadly, most people are inhibited in their self-expression, scarcely believing in their own beauty or goodness. We can see Leo as the one who has not forgotten her solar power. She has the courage to be seen, to take risks with her creativity and face the flak. This is the bravery of all performers which habitual or professional critics cannot understand until they too have exhibited or have performed something of their own.

Underneath her shining exterior Leo is indeed as vulnerable as everyone else. Her need for recognition proceeds as often from her lack of self-worth as it does from her illuminating sense of her own self. When she is truly confident Leo wants only to share; she does not crave an audience but enjoys one. Driven by the craving she makes herself vulnerable indeed, for few will give her recognition when she grasps after it. Her insecure need for recognition and acceptance often alternates, or even combines, with truly creative self-expression. Her admirers are often lovingly tolerant of her weaknesses, of her ego which craves to be encircled by courtiers like the sun surrounded by planets.

Generosity of Heart

Leo is popular. She disarms her friends with her charm and her naturally affectionate nature. The light that illuminates Leo comes from the heart, which is ruled by this sign. She is generous and magnanimous, and makes new friends easily, simply and innocently. She is deeply loyal and steadfast to those she loves, often surprising them, for they wrongly imagine that success will make her fickle. But love is central to her life and to all her experience. Her faith and joy in life give her the ability to warm others. Many rely on her sunny nature to cheer them, and what she contributes to a group cannot be easily quantified. Her great gift is to inspire people to find that confident sense of self within, which she can often do by the example of her creativity. Her creativity may be artistic, but most typically it is in the form of some kind of entertainment. Her creative expression may not be in the conventionally accepted form, however; many women artists and performers have had no means of self-expression except through their houses, their gardens and their clothes.[5]

In her self-expression Leo can be quite open about her vulnerability and her needs, in spite of her tremendous pride. In her act of emotional self-exposure she can be so honest that she does not lose any 'face' or power from it; she has defined her own terms. She acts out her tragedies, but they are none the less deeply felt because she knows how to exaggerate her experience for effect. Leo is always able to perceive the dramatic possibilities in any situation, and likes life to be attended by ritual and celebration. She enjoys parties and marks anniversaries, passages and transitions. She would prefer an elaborate funeral for someone that she loved than to try to deal with grief totally in private. The reserved Anglo-Saxon consciousness finds Leo uncomfortably embarrassing at times, and she is often happier living in cultures which are more expansive.

The Leader

Leo has the ability to hold the central focus in a project or organisation. Her skill as a leader is her ability to inspire, to give faith and heart to the more timid and cautious souls around her. Because she is

not afraid of the limelight she may be a spokeswoman for her cause like Vijaya Pandit, Indian feminist and independence worker, who later became a government minister. By holding the centre together as director or organiser Leo allows less confident people to grow under her guidance. The Theosophical Movement had the very leonine Helena Blavatsky as figurehead and inspiration.

Whether performer, organiser, sportswoman who carries the responsibility in a team, or a large-hearted friend, Leo has sometimes to be careful that her ego does not get out of bounds. The lion carries the Goddess in ancient statues; she is a vehicle and channel for universal love and creativity to come into the world – she did not invent these energies, however, nor can she own them.

While Leo can be very efficient by delegating practical tasks which she would not carry out well herself, she must beware of despising them and passing them on to people whom she secretly thinks to be boring. For Leo can be a snob, interested only in those who have style and charisma. This is her most difficult side, but there is no malice in her. She suffers from ignorance in these matters rather than any deliberate negativity towards others.

Vulnerability

Leo's growth and development come about by facing and hearing the criticisms from which she has always shut herself off. She may be accused of being autocratic, or too dogmatic, for Leo is a fixed sign. The criticism cuts deep. Leo is the fairy-tale queen who thrives so long as her people love her and sickens when her popularity fades. She experiences criticism as lack of love, and feels betrayed by a friend who is not unswervingly loyal. She finds it hard to understand a slight when she is putting out loving energy, or to learn that no one is under an obligation to love her just because she cares about a particular person. Her usual practice is to withdraw if she is not appreciated.

Yet at some time in her life Leo may no longer be able to escape to a new audience. Either she cannot find one, or her sun-shiny power goes behind a cloud and she panics and is depressed by its loss. Continued disappointment can break even the Leo spirit and she is particularly vulnerable to grief, because her heart is so open. Leo may

reach the point where she sees through her own roles, removes the masks and asks herself who she really is beneath the show. Whatever the reason for the lion's wound she will be thrown into a movingly vulnerable state. The mighty lion will be brought down, like the one caught in a net who was freed by a mouse. In another story the lion could not walk for the thorn in his paw which was removed for him by Androcles. In both these stories the lion is helped by the weaker being, and this is often how Leo learns to value those who seem insignificant, how to listen to the quiet and notice the unremarkable. Leo can learn from her opposite sign Aquarius to appreciate the value of every individual.

When Leo realises mistakes she has made she has the healing ability to forgive herself and start again. There is nothing petty about her, and the great heart of the lion enables her to recuperate from the hardest setbacks; she bounces back. She needs help from her friends; simple affection means a great deal to her and the difference it can make should never be underestimated. Gifts, letters, invitations are all balm to her soul.

Room for Joy

Most of her life Leo puts out her own creative and emotional energy so powerfully that she must feed herself with the creative productions of others. She loves dramatic music (whether rock or classical) large-scale theatre productions and epics. She especially enjoys special effects in the cinema because she has a child's imagination and has never forgotten how to play. She needs plenty of fun in her life. She loves games of all sorts – sports, games of chance and games of skill. Although she may be an expert player she never becomes over-serious about her efforts. Most of all she likes to break routine by sudden spontaneous outings. Children are drawn to her by her personal magnetism, and by the fact that she is a natural story-teller. She plays with them unselfconsciously because she herself lives in a fantasy world of heroines, dragons and villains much of the time.

Leo often sees life as a fantasy extension of her own role, an arena for her prowess. She values honour and integrity and her ethics are from the age of chivalry when queens, kings and knights entertained lavishly and lived vibrantly.

From her fantasy world Leo meets children as equals. Because she *is* bigger than they are she does not have to roar so loud, and if she does they love it. Many Leo women have written for children, notably Beatrix Potter and Edith Nesbit. Many famous educators, too, have had Leo prominent in their charts. Maria Montessori had Leo Rising and pioneered the emphasis on play in education. Work with children attracts Leo, but she needs scope to express her personality widely and cannot be hidebound by regulations. Many Leos are teachers, but others prefer to define their own audiences and would rather be buskers in the rain than subject themselves to another authority.

Many Leos are great orators, using their dramatic flair to make political, educational and philosophical points. Anna Julia Cooper was such a Leo – she was one of the first black women to hold a university degree in the USA and she promoted women's education, she said, 'to unlock the feminine side of truth'. The saddest Leos are those who are unable fully to express their brilliance like Zelda Fitzgerald who was born on the cusp of Cancer and Leo and had her Mercury in Leo. Most Leos will never become famous, but they can live happy lives because they are able to shine with creative expression in their own circles.

In relationships it becomes clear how vulnerable Leo is. She throws herself into love affairs and, however impractical the relationship may be, becomes totally involved. Holiday romances are her forte, but she is not casual or exploitative of her partner; she pours into each contact passionate love and longing. She is a great romantic and can easily become sentimental.

She needs plenty of space and time for demonstrations of affection, often assisted by her dramatic imagination. She enjoys arranging an outstanding surprise birthday treat for someone she loves, or meeting someone from a journey with musical instruments and elaborate costume. But flamboyance does not mean superficiality, and she loves her partner, her friend, her sister and her child with a strong and deep love. She is the epitome of every epigram about love that has ever moved us, and Leo is not snobbish about a cliché if it rings true for her. She would always rather have loved and lost than never to have loved at all and she considers the world well lost for love. She makes anything hackneyed or dreary come to life again when she touches it with her Midas touch (for Leo rules gold).

Like gold her love survives all tests; like the Sun's rays it constantly radiates from the fiery Leo heart.

Background to the Sign

VIRGO

The Cornmaiden
The path of clarity
Approach to life of **mutable earth:**
skilful, discerning, analytical,
thoughtful, sincere, observant
Planetary ruler: Mercury

This constellation has long been seen as a goddess, the arrangement of stars suggesting a woman holding a cornsheaf. The notion of the Goddess is so large that it cannot be contained by one sign of the zodiac only, yet we find in Virgo, more than in any other sign, reflections of the beliefs about the Great Goddess held most dear by her worshippers. The Goddess was seen as both the fertile Earth mother and the sanctified virgin, the Queen of Heaven and the woman who lives in obscurity; she was in every woman. Virgo's oldest associations were with fruitfulness and fertility. The earliest name for the sign meant both 'furrow' and 'vulva', for any cleft in the earth was seen as the genitals of the Mother.

Virgo represents the harvest (the mother Demeter) as well as the planted seed (the daughter Persephone). In the Americas we hear of the Mother of Maize and the Blue Cornmaiden, while in Europe people made corn dollies at harvest time to contain the blessing of the Cornmaiden/mother throughout the year.

The apparently paradoxical combination of both sexuality and virginity in the Cornmaiden and mother had no contradictions for Goddess-worshipping peoples. Sexuality was sacred and the word 'virgin' did not imply celibacy or inexperience as it does now. A virgin was a woman who did not belong to any man, who was her own mistress, aware of her powers and her value. She formed relationships and made love when she chose to, but never gave up her right to self-determination.

Many peoples have believed in the power of woman to procreate without the help of a human partner, and children whose fathers were unknown were often called 'virgin-born' in the ancient world. In Babylon it appears that temple priestesses of Ishtar, the qadishtu, were holy virgins (in the ancient sense) who served the Goddess through sacred sexual expression.

It seems that even the famous vestal virgins of Rome, set apart to tend the sacred fires of Vesta, were not originally celibate. It was in

the last years of the age of Aries, however, (up to the first century BCE) that an apparently new concept of virgin sanctity was developing. Sacred celibacy rather than sacred sexuality became the official religious view in most cultures. In the Christian world the Virgin Mary became the pattern for all women, whether nuns or mothers. But within this ideal of sexual abstinence the ancient idea of the Virgin Goddess lived on. The Virgin Mary became the Queen of Heaven, inheritor of the symbols and titles of the goddesses she supplanted. Sometimes the Goddess religion continued underground. In France, churches and cathedrals were built in formation with each other so that their placement on a map marked out the constellation of Virgo – a tribute to the Virgin Mother. The 'Virgo' chapels, churches and cathedrals were centres for many cults and longstanding religious traditions. The Romany people visited them to worship Sara-Kali, the Black Virgin and 'source of the spring of life that flows over the gypsy race'.

Virgo Today

Today, Virgoans find themselves in a time when the word 'virgin' prompts childish sexual jokes about their sign of the zodiac. Many young women grow up believing not in their own autonomous right to enjoy or refrain from sex in their own time (as did the ancient virgins), but in a sanctified virginity that they have to preserve at all costs. Yet they also fear to remain virgins for too long, in case they are ridiculed as old maids and accused of frigidity. The Virgoan has to shake free from all these distortions of the meaning behind her sign. The ancient tradition she can reclaim is that of the autonomous and creative woman, fully involved with the life of her people but very much her own mistress.

As Demeter brought the harvest's fullness to her people, so the modern Virgo is often a gardener or a farmer. She has a deep relationship with the earth and with all growing things, and responds both instinctively and deliberately to repair any damage done to the natural world. She readily understands the complex interrelationships of plants and animals in apparently 'wild' nature, and is excited by the possibility of so ordering an environment that plants too tender for the wild can survive. Virgo would prefer to co-operate with nature

rather than impose her will upon it. She is often described as having green fingers, and Virgoans may be aware of the spirits or devas of natural places and plants. They do not often talk of this to others and they are usually sceptical of flowery descriptions of psychic phenomena; their relationship with plants and places is at once reverential and matter-of-fact.

Mind and Body

At once intellectual and practical, Virgo is the Earthsign that makes the connection between the material world and the world of ideas. To Latin-speaking peoples the Greek word 'idea' seemed to echo the words 'in-dea' or the 'goddess within' and occultists believed ideas emanated from the virgin female soul of the world – a Virgoan archetype. Virgo does not despise the body or consider spirit and mind to be more sacred than matter, for subconsciously she knows that 'matter' or 'material' comes from 'mater', the mother, the body of the Earth she loves and respects.

Virgo is a sign with a highly developed mentality, but a grounded one, for she does not oppose mind and body in the dualistic manner of Gemini. Like that sign she is ruled by Mercury and has a great interest in words as the vehicle of ideas. Two famous poets show us this Virgoan fascination: Edith Sitwell who has the Sun in Virgo and Gertrude Stein whose Moon was in the sign. Virgo brings her very considerable mental powers to whatever project she wishes to serve. She has more astute powers of discrimination and discernment than any other sign; she dislikes anything that is shoddy or second-rate in the world of ideas, wanting to reach beyond easy solutions.

She uses her acute critical and analytical abilities to order her perception of the world, and concentrates on detail both lovingly and precisely. She can study and research any subject that interests her with unparalleled thoroughness, though she may not delve as deeply into her subject matter as Scorpio or range as broadly as Sagittarius. Her concern is for truth, but she does not believe that truth is only found buried deep in inaccessible places or hidden at the ends of the earth; she finds it manifest in everything around her.

Virgo very often has considerable manual dexterity and can produce

fine craftwork. The bountiful Goddess was believed to manifest not only as a Corn-mother but also as patron of the arts of spinning, weaving and basketmaking. Virgo is proud of her work and values it highly in her life. She gains the greatest satisfaction from the conviction that it has been carried out in accordance with her own standards. Her stitching is as neat on the back as it is on the front. Her enjoyment of perfect detailed work with fine materials is an expression of her sensuality and respect for the Earth. For Virgo has a strong awareness of the beauty of physical form as an expression of an idea. As an artist Virgo likes to work with detail, like Chinese–American Yee Wah Jung who has created large facades in mosaic. The Virgoan precision and clarity can be expressed through music as, for example, by Clara Schumann and the modern composer of Hindustani classical music, Prabha Atre.

It is her awareness of the interconnection between mind and body that impels Virgo towards healing. She may work within orthodox medicine as doctor, nurse or health visitor, as a physiotherapist, or in alternative forms of healing. Virgoans have been at the forefront of work on body–mind connections, instinctively drawn to the theory that the physical body reflects beliefs and attitudes of the mind that animates it. She is attracted to schools of thought that maintain that the food we eat can affect experience and behaviour, and she is interested in the purest and most organic foods in nutrition and diet. Virgo works best as an educator, preferring not to sort people's problems out for them but to teach how they may best look after themselves and to pass on her confidence in the body's innate healing ability. While the Scorpio healer is interested in the process of disease, Virgo concentrates on the healthy working of the body, which corrects its own imbalances.

The virgin Hygeaia was believed to have taught the arts of healing to the ancient Greeks, and her modern successor is often a Virgoan dedicated to the task of helping others to achieve the most perfect and efficient working of the body possible within the framework that has been inherited. Just as the virgin priestesses showed the people how to use plants, the modern Virgoan studies herbs or homeopathic medicines, believing in the Earth's abundance to meet all the people's needs.

Grounded Optimism

Virgo is a truly revolutionary sign of the zodiac, often unexpected and surprising, for her ideas challenge complacency and fatalism. She seldom gives up in any situation; however gloomy the outlook Virgo always sees something that might be done. Her optimism is based on an accurate estimation of what is feasible. Her ability to see how every situation might benefit from dedicated work makes Virgo a true healer – she brings 'medicine' in the widest sense of the word.

She has the dedication of the mediaeval alchemist, constantly seeking to refine gold from baser metals and, like the true alchemist, knows that the work cannot be perfected until the self has been refined. Virgo is committed to her own personal growth and is adventurous in her self-exploration. She is capable of great flexibility, prepared to change the framework of her ideas in order to view herself and her environment in an entirely new way. She needs time apart to analyse her experience and her reactions. It can be helpful for her to keep a journal or find some other way to record her process of self-refinement. Like the alchemist, she seeks for what is quintessential in her experience. When she is clear about what is essential to her, Virgo has courage in her convictions. Without melodrama she lives out her beliefs and shows the reality behind her words.

Virgoans need work to which they can dedicate themselves and through which their convictions can be expressed. Virgoan Nancy Prince was a black relief worker for destitute young people in nineteenth-century America, Margaret Sanger gave women more control over their bodies through family planning, while in Britain Annie Kenney dedicated her life to working for women's suffrage. A modern Virgoan is Margo St James who founded COYOTE (Call Off Your Old Tired Ethics), the self-help group campaigning for the rights of prostitutes. When Virgo is true to herself she feels no fear; Sofia Perovskaya, imprisoned for a successful assassination, wrote, 'I have lived as my convictions prompted me; I could not do otherwise; therefore I await what is in store for me with a clear conscience.'

Often Virgo works behind the scenes without recognition, for fame and gratitude are not the factors that motivate her. The important medical research of Irene Joliot-Curie has been overshadowed by her famous mother and also by her husband – as happens to many Virgoans. Virgo has an impulse to put all her skills into the service of her

beliefs, and she is not interested in the power she may derive from success. She does care about accuracy, however, and feels it keenly if her work is misunderstood. The impulse to serve may lead her to do all the work and have the credit taken by someone else. Virgo will work exhaustively to help someone if she can see that person would genuinely benefit from some practical assistance, but she will seldom give approval she does not feel. She keeps her own standards.

Separation and Relationships

The purity and integrity associated with Virgo is often expressed in the world of ideas. She can retain her own beliefs in spite of contact with an imperfect world about her. Sometimes, rather than compromise, however, she has to withdraw. The Greek Goddess Dike was said to have lost hope in humanity, but rather than sacrifice her ideals she left Earth to live in the heavens as the constellation Virgo. Her human Virgoan counterparts often crave seclusion and apartness. Virgo has a delight in her own company so she can be very self-reliant. She prefers to be alone rather than waste time with people who do not interest her. Her sense of separation from the world assists her dedication to cause or project, to her chosen work. Like the temple priestesses of the past she may live apart from the world in some way, perhaps accompanied only by her cat, for this self-sufficient and fastidious animal has many affinities with Virgo. In the twentieth century the archetype of the withdrawn Virgoan has been Greta Garbo who captured the public imagination by her desire to be alone. Yet Virgo thrives on interrelationships, for these allow her to express her concern and love for others. She may work as a counsellor using her considerable insight and sharp focus to help others to make their lives work better for them.

In loving relationships Virgo seeks a dependable partnership or a committed friendship that not only lives up to her high standards of personal behaviour but is also in tune with her commitment to a spiritual or idealistic purpose. She does not enter relationships lightly, and always keeps some part of herself separate and untouchable. Within the relationship she is always seeking for ways to improve and perfect both herself and the interaction with her partner.

Constant Refinement

The Virgoan addiction to perfection, to constant refinement, may be hard for others to take. Virgo tempers her love and compassion with discrimination. She retains her critical faculties and, unlike her opposite sign Pisces, she is never sentimental. This may serve the relationship. But the object of her scrutiny may feel unable to relax. Here Virgo can learn from Pisces to let things go at times, even when she feels she is 'right'. The Virgoan impulse to heal can be distorted into a need to fix and tidy everything up. She cannot bear other people's lives to be disorderly, and often has to restrain herself from interfering and correcting. Essential to the Virgoan spirit is the humility to accept other people's choices, but she may have to forcibly remind herself that people have a right to mess up their lives if they so choose. Her attention to detail can become pedantic and fussy, and her narrow focus seems constricting, far from the permissive and bountiful giving and forgiving nature of the Cornmother whose worship was once associated with Virgo. Her refusal to allow a little disorder, to be on nodding terms with ancient chaos, can be compulsive and lead to illness. Most of all, Virgo needs to forgive herself, to allow herself a few mistakes. When the Virgoan nature becomes cramped she needs to free herself from the pettiness that often goes with an underlying sense of inferiority.

At the heart of Virgo's perfectionism lies a lack of confidence about herself. She often feels rejected and longs to help others, so she can feel useful and necessary, to have a place. She feels a great deal of pain about rejection and often repeats a pattern of entering new situations where she will yet again be rejected. Essentially Virgo needs to find within herself the conviction that she is worthy and lovable without having to *do* anything, that 'as much as the trees and the stars she has a right to be here'. Once she has discovered this right she is able to feel accepted by others and her own critical nature can relax as her fears of loneliness and insecurity no longer control her.

A helpful image for Virgo is that of the oriental rug-maker who was always obliged to make one mistake in the rug. The imperfection was necessary for the pattern, lest humankind try to outdo the wisdom of divine nature which always makes some mistakes.

Wholeness

Virgo can find her purity in a sense of wholeness, instead of defining perfection as an absence of 'mistakes'. The wholeness is physical, emotional, mental and spiritual. It is reflected in Virgoan behaviour through integrity (a word meaning wholeness) and in Virgo's interest in health (which also means wholeness). Her own self-healing comes when she realises that, without constant striving, she *is* whole and perfect, as are all creatures.

The Virgoan instinct to understand detail is part of her desire for wholeness. Virgo breaks the world into parts so that she may better understand it. With her high standards she chooses to focus on the best she can find. Through her instinct to healing she brings back into the whole those parts that have been left out. Yet in her desire to understand truth in its completeness she is faced with a paradox, for everything cannot be understood in a universe which is infinite. The ancient concept of the Virgin Goddess included this paradox, and as Virgo seeks truth she discovers that it exists in the spaces between the things she can name.

> For I am the first and the last
> I am the honoured one and the scorned one
> I am the whore and the holy one
> I am the wife and the virgin . . .
> I am the silence that is incomprehensible
> I am the utterance of my name.
> (from Elaine Pagels *The Gnostic Gospels*)[6]

Background to the Sign

Libra is the only one of the twelve signs not symbolised by a person or animal; she is more concerned with abstract concepts than any other sign.

LIBRA

The Scales
The path of balance
Approach to life of **cardinal air**:
fair, loving, co-operative,
harmonising, enhancing,
acknowledging
Planetary ruler: Venus

The name Libra comes from the Libyan Goddess of Holy Law who carried the scales of judgement, and her counterpart in Egypt was Maat, the spirit of equilibrium, of justice, truth and rightness. She lived within a person and also existed outside and so was known as the 'double Maat', encompassing both individual and cosmic consciousness. After death the Egyptians believed that the heart was weighed against a feather in the scales of Maat. Maat was no dispenser of punishment, however; she was the personification of truth, the spirit that animates all living beings, both divine and human. If the heart were too heavy then, without blame or punishment, the soul would return to earth to reincarnate until light enough for final liberation. Maat had no temple because she could not be confined; she was the natural order itself. To be in accord with natural truth and justice creates harmony, and Maat symbolised this quality.

Desire for Balance

The scales of Maat are the most appropriate symbol for Librans, who are constantly balancing everything in their environment and recreating harmony around them. Being a cardinal sign, Libra takes initiatives to restore order, but unlike her opposite sign Aries she usually avoids direct confrontation. The Libran approach is like that of the Chinese concept of Yin – the gentle strength that circumvents obstacles.

Libra has a particular affinity with the far East and is drawn to societies such as the Japanese where aesthetics are highly valued. She is as much aware of the spaces around an object as the object itself, and considers the position and balance of factors in any situation as well as the nature of its components. The Chinese concept of the Tao,

the balance and interrelationship of Yin and Yang, is as Libran as the scales of Maat. In Chinese and Japanese cultures Libra finds recognition of her own values and she can relax in an oriental setting, which for her is more restful than any other. She does not enjoy a discordant, over-stimulating or loud environment, for she is always seeking beauty and needs to surround herself with it. She can make deft and minute changes within a room so that the harmony of its proportions are enhanced. Essentially she understands beauty as the outward manifestation of natural order. The concept of beauty is central in the culture of the Navajo people, who speak of 'walking the trail of beauty' to explain the way to co-operate with nature rather than to try to control her.

Librans are often artists, like French painter Suzanne Valadon who had Libra rising, for their desire for harmony is coupled with an ability to create it. It is often those who understand how to make beauty who have the confidence to make initiatives for peace. When she makes something which pleases her Libra becomes inspired with a desire for the harmony of the whole world. Her own creation makes her believe this is possible, for she has fashioned beauty out of raw materials. The Jicarilla Apache tell of the first woman, Wild Pony, who learned how to make bowls from clay and then made the sacred pipe of peace which she bequeathed to her people.

The Peacemaker

Very many Librans are drawn to the Peace Movement where they can use their cardinal sign initiative to try to redress the world's balance. Libra has the courage of the peacemaker who walks on to the battleground or sleeps near the nuclear missile. It is the philosophy of non-violence that attracts her.

Another symbol for Libra is the dove, the bird of peace sacred to Venus, whose planet has long been thought to rule this sign. The peacemaking instinct of Libra is the saving of many a violent confrontation. Libra has great skills of diplomacy and tact; she knows how to make a proposition acceptable and how to soothe ruffled feathers and injured pride. In contrast to her polar sign, Aries, whose direct and combative methods may stir up conflict, Libra always pours oil on troubled waters.

The Libran way of taking the initiative is often very subtle. She researches everyone's viewpoint, and then makes a suggestion calculated to be attractive even to the intransigent. Unobtrusively she is able to identify the exact changes or compromises to which each party would be open and uses her inspired diplomatic genius to work out a solution which will cause no loss of face.

Libra has poise and an easy manner and excels at bringing people together; the American feminist Perle Mesta, for example, was famous both as a political hostess and as a diplomat. Libra introduces people who subsequently have historic working relationships; her skills facilitate many social situations. Essentially her talent is her fairness, her ability to see everyone's point of view and to be interested in what they have to communicate.

Her methods do not make her popular with everyone, for those with a more blunt approach may distrust her. Libra often wants to be friends with everyone in a situation of conflict. She finds herself sitting on the fence because of her inability to be partisan; her scrupulous fairness can become wavering indecision at times when action is vital.

However there is a tendency in the West to idealise the activity of Aries and to dismiss the Libran methods as too refined or wishy-washy. It is often those with little power who use Libran methods of conciliation to protect themselves, to get their needs met and to achieve changes in the world. In most societies this has meant that women have taken the Libran role – as the hand that rocks the cradle and the power behind the throne. Mothers, wives, daughters, sisters, mistresses, concubines and courtesans have had far reaching effects on history by using Libran tactics, and prejudices against the sign are sometimes the result of misogyny in men or a lack of self-worth amongst women. It is the Libran impulse that inspires a woman to talk her way out of a dangerous situation, and this is as valuable a skill in the face of the rapist or murderer as prowess in physical self-defence.

New Understanding

Because the Libran approach to the world has been seen as an appropriately 'feminine' one in the past, there is an urgent need for the sign to be redefined without this assumption and indeed at the present

time both sexes are engaged in learning the skills that the other sex previously over-emphasised: men are learning Libran gentleness while women discover Arien directness. Even so, Libran women may still achieve fame for the 'acceptable' traits of the sign, while the other sides of their Libran nature remain less known. Brigitte Bardot, for instance, is well known for her appearance (a physical manifestation of Libran harmony) but it is her commitment to animal rights which expresses the Libran impulse towards justice.

Libran women often surprise the astrologer. Martina Navratilova, for instance, appears superficially to be more in tune with her Arien Moon than her Libran Sun, but this impression may well be due to the fact that we do not yet have a full understanding of the sign. Many Libran women have seen the need to work for justice without using the tactics of conciliation traditional to the sign. Christabel Pankhurst, for instance, chose the path of confrontation. Today, Librans can be inspired by Winnie Mandela who has the Sun in Libra. She also has Jupiter in the sign, showing the wider political understanding which accompanies her Libran courage and vision of peace and justice.

We are unlikely to be able to understand the sign thoroughly until there is a balanced sharing of power between men and women and between all peoples within world society. The paradox for Libra is the difficulty in establishing both peace and justice when faced with oppression. It is possible that very soon humankind will evolve a new understanding of the way harmony might be achieved, and Librans themselves will be both the changers and the changed. A breakthrough in possibilities for the creation of social justice and harmony could well occur around the time when astronomers are able to identify the planet Persephone, which is currently being sought beyond the orbit of Pluto (see p 267). Persephone may be found to be Libra's ruler rather than Venus, for Persephone was the Greek Goddess who represented the balance between the seasons and was associated with the spring and autumn Equinoxes, the times when the Sun is in Libra in the Southern and Northern hemispheres.

Finding Personal Balance

At the Equinox the days and nights are of equal length and one season turns into the next. It is a time of letting go of the passing season, of

acceptance. The Navajo Creator, Changing Woman, teaches of the cycles of summer and winter, seedtime and harvest, birth and death. Like Changing Woman Libra is concerned with the balance between the archetypal polarities, being born at a time when light is in balance with dark. The balance does not always come easily for many Librans. The idealism of Libra makes it very hard for her in the real world which is disappointingly far from the social harmony she envisages. People shock her by their aggression, intolerance and willingness to spoil the greater pattern of harmony for their selfish concerns, and she is equally pained by this behaviour if she finds it within herself.

Libra finds it hard to tolerate inequality in any relationship and yet dislikes expressing anger when she encounters unfairness. She hates quarrels and emotional storms which she regards as unproductive. Her vision of co-operation is an inspiring one, but it can lead to emotional repression, as Libra finds it hard to admit to emotions in herself which violate her ideals of behaviour: anger, resentment, jealousy or possessiveness. She also has difficulty coping with other people's anger towards her, because she sees herself as always well-intentioned and innocent. Denial of her own negative feelings and the fear of violent feelings in other people can make her ill, and she may benefit from personal therapy to help her recognise and transform the parts of her self that she has repressed.

Librans are often attracted to people who are strong and forthright rather than diplomatic and co-operative. What she sees as fascinating in others are her own qualities which have never been tapped. So long as Libra projects her own hidden strengths on to her friends she avoids meeting herself. By truly appreciating her own strength she is able to free herself from the need for social approval which can inhibit her personal expression. When Libra runs away from unpleasantness, pretending that the world is all sweetness, she finds a superficial rather than a natural harmony. If she compromises for 'peace at any price' she discovers that peace will not last if it is patched up, that bitterness is often the legacy of too easy a solution. She can learn from her polar sign Aries the value of confrontation, and also from her preceding sign, Virgo. It was the Greeks who believed it was the Virgin who held the scales of justice, and it is Virgo who subjects everything to fine analysis and will never run from truth.

Libra has her own internal balancing mechanism that will continually force her to face whatever it is she is avoiding until she finds a

place for this and allows balance again. Her instinctive tendency to avoid discord is strong, but her commitment to justice is stronger still. If others criticise her behaviour (rather than merely shouting at her) she will listen openly and fairly, and her desire for co-operation leads to many helpful discoveries and changes.

Libra appreciates the insights other people offer her, and has a deeper understanding of the value of personal interaction than any other sign of the zodiac. She brings her best energy to work in a partnership or a team and excels in collectives and co-operatives. Her ideals of co-operation are inspiring and necessary in an age which has romanticised rugged individualism.

The Idealist

Libra can express her need for harmony artistically or musically in order to express her idealistic vision and it is very likely she may inspire others. Libran Jenny Lind, the Swedish singer of the last century, had a tremendous effect on her contemporaries, not only because of her extraordinary voice, but because her ideals of social justice led her to give away thousands of pounds to the needy in the countries in which she performed.

Libran intellectual skills and openness to ideas often lead her to philosophy (as they did for Libran political theorist Hannah Arendt), for she loves to balance abstract concepts. Libra avoids making definitive or final statements, and remains an open rather than a decisive thinker.

Libran idealism extends to all relationships. She has a clear picture of what the relationship between sexual partners should be: a meeting of mutual respect, concern, caring, and committed love. She uses the balance that the other person provides to know herself better and be constructive in the world, for her lover's view of her gives her a mirror in which to see herself.

Libra loves courtship, its ceremony and stylised rituals, and will spend hours preparing a special dinner party or an elaborate present. To be on the receiving end of Libran appreciation can be a validating experience. She can see the inner beauty in another person, and make those she loves feel beautiful and worthy of her attention.

However, idealism about relationships can sometimes make her the

supreme romantic, in love with love itself, putting the relationship on a pedestal and failing to see her love as a whole person with her or his own conflicting needs. She may be engaged in a quest for the ideal partner, either seeking her or him out in the world or striving to educate her partner to become her ideal. Colette had her Ascendant in Libra and in her writing we see the Libran interest in love as an experience for its own sake.

The pursuit of love can distance Libra from the real world, just as she can become remote through an over-emphasis on art, beauty or abstract concepts. She is devastated if her ivory tower crumbles. Very often her beloved fails to behave in the way Libra expects and she then feels deeply wounded and let down. She is also caught between her desire to stay constantly in a relationship and her quest for the perfect rapport. Often she is engaged in serial monogamy, committed to one person totally until the relationships falters and then falling in love again and restarting the same process. At some point in her life Libra may have to examine such a pattern of events and decide whether to continue following it. She may need to take the path of celibacy for a while, or perhaps stay with an imperfect relationship to make it work, in a practical rather than idealistic fashion. When she is able to accept a relationship that seems less than ideal to her she often discovers that eventually it fulfils her expectations.

Libran Marie Stopes showed the positive focus of the sign on sexual relationships; her interest in contraception was inspired not only by a vision of justice for women, but also by concern for the quality of the relationship between women and their partners.

Bringing the Ideal to the World

Libra is very good working in one-to-one relationships and may become a skilled counsellor or therapist. She understands that personal interaction is the microcosm within the larger whole of societal, political and international relationships. She believes that personal interaction is the basis for all major advances, and that the power of love, in the widest sense of the word, can change the world.

Yoko Ono has Libra rising and in her life are the Libran themes of art, peace and a great love. For less famous Librans the inspiration of

the ideal and its joys and disappointments are depicted on a smaller canvas and in the gentle colours which are Libra's hues. The scales of Libra are the symbol of her instinct for harmony and equality. In all relationships Libra is sensitive to any power imbalance, any over-emphasis on one partner's experience. Her ideal is always before her, inspiring her to bring to the world a vision of perfect love.

In her maturity Libra's vision expands from her early romanticism to encompass a love so balanced that the beloved is not placed higher than the lover and selfish ego concerns do not motivate the relation-ship. Lover and beloved, friend and friend, are equal; their needs are not in conflict or bargained over but pooled and shared openly in Libran trust. Libra loves her friend as she loves her self, for she knows that the breath of Maat, the Cosmic Consciousness, flows equally through one as through the other.

Background to the Sign

The constellation of Scorpio is the only one that looks very much like its name, which may explain why it was called the Scorpion by the Central American civilisations as well as the Babylonians and Egyptians. Scorpions abound in ancient mythology, usually symbolising death or regenerative powers. Everywhere the Scorpion seems to have

SCORPIO

The scorpion
The path of involvement
Approach to life of **fixed water:**
*intense, perceptive, concentrated,
passionate, powerful, resourceful*
Planetary ruler: Pluto

had a connection with the land of the dead. The Babylonian Great Mother Tiamat made the Scorpion Women who guard the dark passage to the Underworld. Like all her creations they fought for mother rights against patriarchy.

The Egyptians were much impressed by the maternal qualities of the scorpion who liberates her young from the bag in which they are born and allows them to climb on her back. There they triple in volume by draining fluid from her body by osmosis. It is perhaps because of these associations with motherhood that seven scorpions attended Isis and the scorpion Goddess Selket guarded the infant Horus who was born to Isis. Selket, shown in some statues as a woman with a scorpion on her head, or as a scorpion with a woman's head, would meet the soul in the underworld. Sometimes she was shown with winged arms that protected the dead, and she carried the healing sign, the ankh. She was shown on the corners of sarcophagi and on the jars that contained the mummies' intestines. This association remains, for Scorpio rules the lower part of the colon and rectum of the living person.

Birth, Death and Regeneration

Throughout ancient myth and history we feel the scorpion's association with birth, death and healing. In this Scorpio is similar to Cancer, but Scorpio focuses far more on healing, death and regeneration. Birth for Scorpio is the end part of a process, the reincarnation that follows a previous death. Scorpio is the sign of all the ancient women's

mysteries, of the hidden and holy, such as the mysteries of Eleusis in Greece. Scorpio wants to understand the mysteries of birth, sexuality, death and the meaning of life. She instinctively recognises sexuality as both a holy and healing force and struggles to find a way she can express this in a world which often trivialises and sensationalises her perception. She also recognises power wherever she sees it, and does not naively assume that all power is bad; she looks to its use to assess it.

Scorpio rules surgery, the knife that heals if it is used in the right way at the right time. Scorpio knows that power can be used to hurt or to harm, and so looks deeper into the motivations of those who wield power. Her own intensity serves as a searchlight to illuminate the workings behind the scenes in every situation that she encounters, for she loves to seek out secrets. Scorpio is not a light sign, but the apparent heaviness is matched by an unparalleled courage. While Aries acts courageously on natural impulse, Scorpio has the more considered bravery to take on the most challenging confrontations and see them through. Scorpionic strength of will is shown in the life of the Chinese Empress Tzu Hsi, and determination in the life of Ghanaian Alice Appea who worked to create the Organisation for African Unity. In the literary world double Scorpio George Eliot had the courage for a life of social daring in her time, living 'in sin' with her lover, fortified by her will and creative ability. The poet Natalie Barney showed a similar disregard for convention by living openly as a lesbian.

Scorpio is the sign of perseverance and determination, the most fixed of the fixed signs when she has a deep purpose, a Watersign more enduring even than the Earthsigns, once her will is engaged. Scorpionic water is not the changing ocean of Cancer or the still, quiet pool of Pisces, rather it is the underground water that rushes into a chasm – direct and powerful. Scorpio has a driving need to explore the hidden areas of life and of the self; she must delve. She believes in her perceptions, and has the audacity to take the power to put her plans into practice. The strength of will in Scorpio can be inspiring to others, as can her courage. She has the self-confidence and faith in healing to push others through painful transformative changes they want to make, either through personal relationships or by working as a therapist or healer.

The alternative symbols for Scorpio are the snake and the eagle.

The snake has long been associated with healing power; with the poison which can bring death, or which, when given in exactly the right way, can bring healing. The eagle represents the soaring spirit of Scorpio that balances her desire to plumb the depths. She is strongly aware of the way good and evil may be polarised, though she does not equate the heights with goodness or the depths with evil.

The Journey to the Underworld

Scorpio can only learn by experience; second-hand information is no good to her and so she often enters into extraordinary experiences of spiritual heights and depths. She has a strong need for feeling; it is more dangerous for her to feel nothing than to feel painful extremes. On this path she encounters a great deal of trauma and tempestuous relationships; she faces the hidden things in the human personality; the abuse of power; destructive behaviour in herself and others. Sometimes she lives through the death of a loved person or has a close escape from death herself. While another person might be broken, Scorpio is strengthened and her wisdom grows by the transformative power of the pain she has experienced. She knows how to receive a gift from the claws of the most terrifying monster, how to go down into the Underworld and come back alive and regenerated. On the rare occasions when Scorpio does not return from thence she leaves a gift from her discoveries. Marie Curie's discovery of radium was the result of her Scorpionic perseverance and determination. In the end the Scorpion sting of the substance was too much for her.

Scorpio has the courage to look deep within herself, but does this in her own time. She is resistant to anyone else's pushing and she does not want to be dragged there. She has an instinct for what she should dig up, and when. For this reason she can be an excellent psychotherapist, for part of the skill of helping another delve into the unconscious is to know when the time is right to do so. Because of her concentration on the intense, the difficult and the painful she sometimes sees depths and heaviness in other people when they are not in fact there. But the knowledge she has from her own transformative experiences is of enormous value to others, once Scorpio learns how to share it without frightening or disturbing them.

When Scorpio looks deep into herself she does not find anything especially evil or dreadful; she is just more honest with herself about her negativity than most of us. She knows her own jealousy, possessiveness, resentment and hatred very well. This is because of Scorpio's intense will; she desires very strongly and so it is hard for her to let go. She is often very secretive, because she does not want everyone to become aware of these negative feelings with which she struggles. Scorpio's intense feeling of emotional vulnerability makes her very suspicious of other people's motives. She knows human nature from the inside, and she knows how deep a wound may go.

Learning Simplicity

Scorpio needs to learn to trust herself, which she can do using her knowledge of her innate goodness and her ability to survive whatever challenge comes her way. Once Scorpio has found faith in this most vulnerable part of herself she can open up to the world. Trust is not easy for her; she can always see the hidden depths, but sometimes cannot see the surface. She may need help from someone else to recognise and trust the obvious – simple affection and enjoyment and good intentions on the part of others, for her own pain may obscure these from her. It is from her opposite sign, Taurus, that she can learn to respect these less dramatic but stabilising aspects of interpersonal relationships. Her suspicion of hypocrisy and sham in others and her awareness of the dark undercurrents in herself make her paranoid at times.

To change this pattern Scorpio needs to really feel the value of a less exciting but more equable way of life. This is the more pedestrian approach that Scorpio most usually scorns, patronising those poor souls who tread such a boring path. Until she can find in herself respect for those who do not live through constant crises of destruction and regeneration, Scorpio exiles herself. She is left with a feeling of being apart, of being too intense or extreme for the rest of the world. While she feels this separation others will pick it up and project on to her whatever they find most fearful or unacceptable within themselves.

Scorpio in Society

The path for Scorpio is particularly hard to walk at the end of the twentieth century. Just as Hades or Pluto (the planet that rules Scorpio) was said to have raped Persephone as she wandered in a flowery field with her adolescent friends, so contemporary women often feel violated by their experience of Scorpionic mysteries. Birth no longer takes place in dark corners surrounded by healing wisewomen, but under the bright lights of technology. Sexuality is itemised and trivialised for pornographers' profit, and death and the dying are removed from the experience of most of the community. This is a situation of great imbalance, and Scorpio feels it at an unconscious level. She wants to take back the mystery, to reclaim the night, to accord respect to the hidden and the sacred in human experience. She may be involved in work to reclaim birth and make it safe not only physically but psychologically for mother and infant. She may work to draw attention to the dangers of pornography, to make healing spaces for those who have survived rape or incest. She may be concerned with the dying or the bereaved, trying to bring the experience of death back into the community as a whole. Another Scorpio journey travels into and through madness, and she may spend time with the mentally distressed or ill. Scorpio needs to beware of too much attachment to the difficult areas of human experience; she must be sure that she is as supportive of the life impulse in the very ill as of the dying process — as interested in health as in sickness.

Popular astrology columns usually fail to explain the depths of power and wisdom in this sign. We are told that Scorpio people are mysterious and sexy, with a brooding intensity, but not about the importance of mystery, sexuality and intensity in human experience. The meaning behind sexuality, behind life and death, can puzzle and frighten us. Darkness and depth are mistakenly equated with evil, and the Scorpionic woman finds herself in the middle of all these fears in a society that represses both the unconscious and the sublime.

Scorpio may respond to this situation by exercising her natural desire for power, even her desire to dominate others. She can use the power others give away to her, the charisma and magnetism accumulated from the projection on to her of the mystery and 'dark forces' that they fear. This is often Scorpio's technique for survival, but it increases her loneliness. When her friends are in awe of her, Scorpio

trades companionship for power or status, often feeling emptier for this exchange.

Transformation

Scorpio is particularly likely to be caught in this trap if she avoids looking into her own depths. What is unacknowledged by her seems to scream for attention by others. Her most intense feelings, however negative they might seem, are the raw material for transformation. The snake is famous not only for its poison but for its ability to shed its skin and be reborn with a new one that allows room for growth. This process of regeneration and transformation is Scorpio's great strength. While she holds on to her 'poison' she may become intoxicated with power, sick with bitterness or poisoned by self-hatred. She often hangs on to old feelings long after they are of any use to her in her growth process. Her desire for justice and reparation for hurts has an ancient and unforgiving quality, until, like the eagle, she learns to soar above her pain. Most important to her is the recognition of her own part in hurting herself, in holding on to pain and using wounds as a spur to her own progress. Taking responsibility for her own part is the beginning of her transformation. However badly Scorpio feels about herself she always has a new skin waiting underneath the old outgrown one. She needs only to slough off the old patterns.

In spite of her intensity, Scorpio often has the appearance of great calm and tremendous self-control. This calm may be one of her greatest assets. However, if Scorpio has not reached peace within herself, her calm may be that of the quiescent volcano, giving the misleading impression that the volcano Goddess Pele is absent rather than sleeping. Her true and deep calm assists her in a crisis, for she is not afraid to take control and become the leader or the healer. As she becomes more sure of her own inner strength Scorpio can let go of the need to manipulate or control every situation. As her belief in her own transformation grows, she trusts that she will be able to protect her vulnerability without lashing out with her scorpion tail. Her strong sense of purpose and will can take her through to the other side of her pride and obstinacy.

Magnetism and Passion

The effect of Scorpio on others can be arresting. In Bette Davies and Edith Piaf we see the magnetic quality of the Scorpio Ascendant; audiences are drawn and held captive by the Scorpio gaze which reminds them of the depths they dare not plumb themselves.

In relationships Scorpio demands and expects a great deal. She is extremely sensitive, making instant, deep connections with other people. She can have sudden and intense loves and hates and these may stem from knowledge she has gained unconsciously, with the natural psychic ability of the water sign. She longs for a profound, transformative and lasting union with another person, in which sexuality will express the deeper mysteries of their connection. When she finds such a relationship she values it highly and fights for it fiercely. Jealousy is a problem as long as she mistrusts others, and feels at the mercy of her own intense need for love and sexual expression. Scorpio's faithful nature is accompanied by an immense fear of betrayal, and she can make betrayal more likely by her own suspicious and paranoid behaviour. She is shocked by the casual hurts she sees those around her inflicting on those they love. Scorpio may wound but not casually; for her, sex is a great mystery and sexual connections sacred. Though passionate she is often reserved through fear of overwhelming with her intensity or of exposing her vulnerability too soon. She may choose celibacy and a spiritual path as a less threatening way to experience the intensity she desires.

Scorpio's passion may be for a cause or a belief as much as for a person or for the infinite. In spite of Scorpio's tendency to soar to the heights and plumb the depths, she also knows that these apparent polarities are an illusion. She does not truly believe in the split between the sexual and the spiritual – for her, sexual experience has the transformative power of religion, while spiritual experience has the intensity of desire and devotion to the act of love.

It is not always easy for Scorpio to accept her role and the Scorpionic nature may feel a very heavy burden. In statues of the Egyptian Goddess Selket, however, we see her hands spread out to the heavens, free of any load. Once Scorpio accepts her nature she can feel her power, as healer, as night-walker, as watcher of the unknown, and as the one who goes down into the depths and returns to act as a guide to transformation.

SAGITTARIUS

The centaur
The path of exploration
Approach to life of **mutable fire:**
*expansive, philosophical, wise,
optimistic, independent, questing*
Planetary ruler: Jupiter

Background to the Sign

The myth of the centaur comes from India and the Aegean, where creatures half-human and half-horse were reputed to interfere with weddings, carrying the bride away. They seem to have represented the freedom of spirit that women did not wish to relinquish in marriage. Centaurs were believed to be great wizards and expert healers. The most famous was Cheiron, the gentle and wise centaur-king who incurred an incurable wound whilst in the process of healing someone else and so became the 'wounded healer'. He was a famous teacher and many of the Greek heroes were educated by him; it is his role as teacher rather than as healer which seems most relevant to Sagittarius today. The wisdom of the centaurs derives from the fact that they span two realms – the human and the animal – and Sagittarius is the only one of the zodiac signs to have this breadth of perspective. Because centaurs are part horse, people may have believed they originated as the children of the Goddess in human form and of her consort god as stallion, for a ritual marriage between the two was once acted out annually in India. The horse was also a manifestation of the Great Goddess all over the ancient world. She was known as the White Mare Leukippe in Crete and as Saranyu the Mare-Mother in India.

Amongst the Celts the White Mare was called Epona, and her great image is carved in the chalk hillside at Uffington in England. The Mare Goddess culture was kept alive by the Amazons of the Black Sea area. They were said to be the first people to tame horses, and the Amazon was so much in tune with her steed that the two seemed to move as one being. The constellation was sometimes shown as a bow (in China) and as a horse (in India). It was also known as Diana's star in honour of the hunter Artemis/Diana who was the Moon Goddess of the Amazons.

Sagittarians have the Amazons' love for open spaces; they need room to move and space to gallop in, emotionally, mentally, and physically. Sagittarius enjoys sports and likes to live outside the city or to

make frequent journeys to explore the surrounding countryside. She hates to be hemmed in, for her mind ranges widely, her spirit has to be free and her eye needs a broad perspective to satisfy her.

The Explorer of the Wild

Sagittarius is always seeking something greater than herself – she wants to travel to find a wider scope, to challenge her philosophy with that of different peoples. A natural philosopher, she shrugs off difficulties she encounters and is versatile and adaptable, open-minded and scrupulous about truth. She always wants to see over the next hill, especially if she thinks it might give her a better vantage point. Instead of being interested in detail, like Gemini and Virgo, she wants to get everything into perspective. While she likes to soak up the cultural climate of a foreign country, she always retains a sense of how this particular culture compares with others. She has a memory of the past from whence she came and a sense of the future she is moving towards. Like all Firesigns her enthusiasm catches fire within the moment, but Sagittarius can always return to her broader perspective. This consciousness enables her to write about her travels; to make her perceptions accessible to an audience at home, as Sagittarians Dervla Murphy and Margaret Mead have done.

Sagittarians often settle in foreign surroundings, using the vantage point of other cultures to reflect on their own backgrounds in order to see the wood rather than the trees. Canadian artist Emily Carr lived in a forest with tame animals and in contact with native peoples. Her paintings reflect her very Sagittarian relationship with the wild. Sagittarians love huge canyons, waterfalls, majestic buildings and symphonic music, whatever nature or humankind has made that overawes with its scope, breadth and height. This awe with which she regards wild nature brings her to understand the spiritual and the religious, and this quest for something greater than the self is revealed in the poetry of Sagittarians Emily Dickinson and Christina Rosetti. Sagittarius may be profoundly unsatisfied by the religions she knows, but she has an instinct to worship and turns back to contemplate nature or consider abstract concepts that inspire her. She loves to gaze at the stars and think about how far away they are, to wrestle with ideas of infinity and relativity.

The Philosopher

Sagittarius always needs a goal to aspire to, for her spirit is like the arrow from the bow – if it is loosed aimlessly it may become lost. When she has a philosophy to believe in Sagittarius is the most optimistic of all the signs. In a crisis of faith she may become pessimistic and depressed, yet she is bound, sooner or later, to discover a new faith or cause, for Sagittarius is a true believer, and her natural optimism reasserts itself. At times she can have the enthusiasm and inflexibility of a new convert. She can become fanatical and zealous in her philosophy, politics or in her spiritual life, even judgemental or moralistic. However, when she recovers her flexibility, Sagittarius understands well the need to integrate the self into society. For herself she wants a socially useful role, and often finds this as advocate or as arbitrator. She excels in her understanding of the process of disputes and many Sagittarians make good lawyers. As a politician she is in her element because she enjoys debate and has the wide-ranging mind and confidence to express her ideas forcefully and with wit. Like her polar-sign Gemini, Sagittarius has a natural intuition which she uses when she speaks in public. She can change tack in mid-speech to adapt to the response she detects. Sagittarius is concerned with the established order within society, but is not inherently conservative as we see from the radical views of Sagittarian Shirley Chisholm in American politics. Sagittarius believes in the due process of law and government more than her fellow politician Aquarius. She identifies with society as a whole in her concern to find ethical and peaceful solutions to the political dilemmas she sees.

The archetype behind Sagittarius is that of the wise teacher and the perfectly fair judge, the spiritual leader or philosopher. She works in the tradition of Deborah and the other 'mothers of Israel' who were known as 'judges', meaning wise rulers. In Greece, few traces remain of the many women philosophers, such as Socrates' teacher Diotima, but the tradition of female wisdom survived. The gnostics in the first centuries CE described wisdom as the female divinity Sophia, who was later invoked by alchemists in mediaeval Europe. The tradition of the wisewoman as judge and teacher exists all over the world, and women still take on these roles in some tribal societies today. Like the wisewoman who has the good of the whole community at heart, Sagittarius is always seeking for a way to link each piece of knowledge

she acquires into a larger pattern, moving towards ever broader contexts of wholeness. From the community she considers the nation, and some Sagittarians may become stuck at this level because their impulse to grandeur makes them prey to sentimental patriotism. But the philosophical and ethical perspective of Sagittarius can lead on to an international vision, and the widest context of wholeness imaginable.

Sagittarius expresses this impulse towards wholeness in many ways – through study of subjects that have a wide and comparative scope such as philosophy, literature, world religions and the history of ideas. She may express herself through travel or through political or social work for a cause she believes in. The modern Sagittarius is drawn to the growth movement (for her ruling planet, Jupiter, is concerned with growth) and the idea of personal growth provides a model of the potential for society.

Because she thinks so much about society and the state of the world, Sagittarius needs an outlet for her ideas. She may perhaps be able to write but is as likely to excel as a teacher or as facilitator of other people's discussions. Although she is fiery and enthusiastic (never stolid) she is able to keep one eye on the shape of the whole lesson or debate. This gives her many skills as a leader in group work, and may free other people to become more involved in their own participation while she preserves the overall view. Sagittarius has the ability to perceive the fundamental themes of any debate or discussion and to develop them to their logical conclusions. She shoots the Sagittarian arrow to the heart of the matter. When she makes her points people listen to her seriously. At times, though, Sagittarius can become so tied up with the philosophical ramifications of the debate that she loses sight of the practical realities which call for action.

Purpose

The Sagittarian emphasis on growth, aspiration, purpose and meaning can put her in danger of becoming pompous. She impresses people and, if she can get away with it, she may set herself up as a guru. So long as no innocent child speaks up to remark on the Emperor's lack of new clothes, Sagittarius often manages to surround herself with

admiring seekers and pupils. But when she goes too far she becomes ridiculous, and her ideas suddenly seem to be grandiose or even trite. It is when Sagittarius finds that even her optimism and enthusiasm seem heavy to her audience that she can start to learn from her opposite sign Gemini about lightness of touch, about the deft suggestion rather than the heavy-handed attempt to extract the maximum in meaning from the slightest source.

When she has been the teacher for a long time it is useful for her to find someone else from whom *she* can learn, and so regain her sense of proportion. Usually, when Sagittarius begins to take herself and her ideas too seriously she can be laughed out of court because she is good-humoured and enjoys the contact with those around her.

The Optimist

Generally Sagittarius gets on well with people; her social ease and cheerful nature provide comfort for others. She may be a wit who appreciates the ironies and contrasts of life, pleasantly happy-go-lucky, always confident something will turn up, and a welcome, breezy influence on her less venturesome friends. Her enthusiasm is the motivating power for many schemes, and she believes in them all – so on a mundane level she can be a brilliant salesperson, never deliberately hoodwinking the public because she always has confidence in what she sells. Her enthusiasm is often verbal and not backed up with hard action; she sometimes moves on to a new project when the hard work materialises.

Sagittarius finds it easy to promise her time away, and often her desire to participate only leads to her disappointing others. She needs realistically to assess how much involvement she can have in any project before she lets her imagination run away with her. Without a sense of inspired purpose, however, she can waste herself in pipedreams and trivial socialising. She hangs out with the 'right' people waiting for a break and dropping the right names (for she can sometimes be a snob). If she cannot grow psychologically and spiritually she grows physically – by over-eating. She is drawn to excess: of parties, alcohol and drugs. Many a Sagittarian fantasy has been set up under the influence of drink or cannabis, only to crash down in the harsh reality of the 'real world'.

She can be drawn in pursuit of grandiose financial schemes and 'the good life' which wealth brings. Without a purposeful philosophy to guide her use of material resources she can fall into a hectic and hedonistic lifestyle, behind which lies deep disillusion and cynicism.

The outgoing Sagittarian nature is generous and she likes to spread her good fortune around her. The Sagittarian optimism is least helpfully expressed in the compulsive gambler who always believes in the coming lucky break, that the next horse will be *the* one (for the Mare Goddess still has her modern-day devotees). Luck does come to Sagittarius, perhaps because she has the wit to see opportunity when it presents itself, and is always willing to believe and be quick to respond.

The enthusiasm of Sagittarius can be too boisterous; when she is having a good time she tends not to notice other people's reactions, and can tread on people's toes. Loving honesty, she can be tactless, and then with her boundless optimism she always believes she can make it all right again later. She has a lot of charm, but should not rely on this quality; if she does she may get some nasty shocks.

Freedom and Growth

Sagittarius enjoys other people in a good hearted way. The freedom of the larger social group gives her a sense of security which she often lacks in a one-to-one relationship, where she may be dominated by her fear of being tied down. Within her closest relationship she can suffer from an obsession that the other person is scheming to trap her, when in fact this is all her own fantasy. It is her own need for love that makes her feel trapped, and she has a quite unrealistic goal of total independence. Wanting a close relationship can seem to her like an admission of failure, and it may take a long time for her to understand that her emotional needs are as important as the need for space and freedom.

What Sagittarius craves, and must have, is enough mental and emotional space to retain and develop the sense of herself in relation to the universe. If she is always gazing into the stars in her lover's eyes she does not have time to gaze up at the stars in the sky, and then she is starved of her input of immensity and infinity. When she has space for that sense of infinity she is an imaginative lover, exciting to be

with, and often a revitalising force in her partner's life. Her optimism and enthusiasm are supportive and healing qualities. Sexually she is passionate and energetic, and in discovering love she finds that rather than an exciting sport it can be a sharing of beliefs and ideas.

Sagittarius has a romantic vision of life, and often believes that if she travels far and wide enough she will find the perfect lover or teacher. This romanticism can become a form of escapism in day-to-day living, as the Sagittarian seeker neglects to value the relationships she has already found. Like the children in Maeterlinck's *Blue Bird* [7] she follows the blue bird of happiness all over the world, only to find that it was nesting in her own garden. Sagittarius gradually discovers the value of commitment in relationship. With maturity she stops projecting dependence on to her partners and starts to accept her own love needs. When she forges a relationship which suits her philosophical nature (one with an inbuilt sense of freedom and mutual respect which allows each partner her or his own dignity), Sagittarius is free, yet committed. The full potential of Sagittarius can only be realised once such an understanding of the value of commitment has been reached, whether commitment is expressed through a relationship, a philosophy, or a faith.

Released from the constant striving and seeking of her earlier years, Sagittarius develops the awareness of self in the context of the whole of creation. More conscious than the 'I am' of Aries, Sagittarius says 'I know that I am' or 'I discover myself'. Her greatest discovery is conscience, a word meaning 'knowing with' and not necessarily implying guilt or anxiety. In some languages it is translated by the same word as 'consciousness' and has a similar reflective quality of knowing the self. A Sagittarian Goddess is Iranian Anahita, the Mother of Wisdom, at whose shrine in Persepolis an eternal flame burned and the words 'I am the conscience of thine own self' were inscribed.

Background to the sign

CAPRICORN

The goat
The path of commitment
Aproach to life of **cardinal earth:**
motivated, responsible, experienced,
dedicated, authoritative, sensual
Planetary ruler: Saturn

The constellation of Capricorn was identified by the Babylonians, who saw it as the fish-goat who has a goat's head and front legs and a fish's tail. This image was associated with their God Ea 'the antelope of the subterranean ocean', and myths tell of the heroine or hero who appears out of the waters of Ea and brings the arts of civilisation to the shore: agriculture, astronomy, mathematics, reading and writing, architecture and medicine.

Early Babylonian images show the goat nibbling the leaves of the tree of life. A goat is portrayed in a prehistoric rock painting which appears to show ritual performed by priestesses, and the animal has long been regarded as holy. The Greeks told how Zeus placed the goat Amaltheia in the heavens as a reward for suckling him as an infant when he hid from his destructive father Chronos. Amaltheia was a wondrous goat who struck awe into the gods themselves, for she represented an earlier tribal goddess whom the Olympians replaced. Zeus' mother Rhea was associated with goats. European legends, too, tell of the Love Goddess, who appeared to her beloved wearing only a net and riding upon a goat. Goats were sacred to Celtic Blodeuwedd, and the Middle Eastern bearded Goddess Mylitta also appeared naked and riding upon a goat.

The Greeks represented Pan, the great god of wild and untamed nature, as having the legs and horns of a goat. In one story he is turned into a goat-fish like the Babylonian Ea. Pan survived in mediaeval Europe as the god of the witches and the consort of their Goddess.

The Church fathers turned the figure of Pan into the devil, and the cloven hoof, once the sign of the Goddess' lover, was regarded as sinister. The freedom and innocence of the life of goatherds in mountains and forests was forgotten and a part of the character of Capricorn has been obscured with this change. With the subjugation of nature and the loss of the wild places over which Pan ruled, it has become harder for Capricorn to discover the whole of her true nature.

The Romans associated their Goddess Vesta with the sign; she

guarded the hearth and the traditions of the family. It is this side of Capricorn that has become better known. Tradition, not necessarily connected with the family, is important to her, and she likes to feel she has a long inheritance of wisdom from the past.

The Builder and Mountain-Climber

The Capricornian urge is to gather this ancient wisdom, profit by all the experience of the past and construct a society that works. Capricorn reveres wisdom, but does not study it for its own sake like Sagittarius; she wants to see it put into practical use: out of the library and into the workshop. Sometimes she works with her hands as a builder or carpenter; sometimes her constructions are more metaphorical, but they are always designed for the real world. She works to establish organisations like, for example, Clara Barton who founded the Red Cross, or businesses like those of Helena Rubenstein and her rival Elizabeth Arden. Capricorn is neither daunted by hard work nor afraid to take responsibility.

A cardinal (initiating) sign and with, at the same time, an earthy practicality, Capricorn has the persistence to work for years for new initiatives, as we see from Capricornian Hyacinth Boothe, the Jamaican who was the first woman to be ordained in the Methodist Church in the Caribbean and the Americas.

Like the goat, Capricorn will tackle any height. She is ambitious, but her ambition is for progress of her schemes. She is not interested in power for its own sake, rather to establish her work more effectively and firmly. She needs a difficult ascent in front of her to reassure her of her place in the world.

Capricorn is an Earthsign and feels part of the Earth. When she climbs mountains she is not trying to conquer them or bend the natural world to her will. The higher she climbs the more she feels part of the rock she touches. The same process happens when tackling a difficult task; through metaphorical sweat and tears she and her challenge become united. On the summit of achievement she does not lose herself in euphoria but remembers every part of her ascent. Capricorn does not look for easy 'highs'; for her, difficulty is an essential part of the process. When she has achieved something seemingly impossible

she looks around for a new challenge, for she comes alive at the frontiers of possibility and it is there she learns to know herself. While Aries is typically the pioneer, Capricorn undertakes challenges that are less immediately newsworthy but have more lasting effects.

Usually she is pretty sure to find some responsibility she could take, some monumental project. Her unease without a project is partly because she does not know enough about her own inner life, and inactivity brings her closer to the unconscious. She feels frustrated if she is not taking on responsibility, for she feels that her path is out in the world, sometimes in the public eye. For although Capricorn does not have the same need for an audience that Leo has, she does want due recognition for the hard work she has put in. She is always trying to test her own endurance in the long haul and the perseverance of her vision. She has great stamina and, like the camel or the cactus, can survive in conditions that would defeat anyone else.

Capricorn rules the skeleton, the part of the body that endures longest and which provides the strength for the living organism. Her strength comes from within, in contrast to the apparent external strength of the hard-shelled Cancer. It manifests in all her projects — her colleagues see her as the backbone of the group or organisation. Her solidity and consistency outlast the enthusiasms and spontaneous contributions of the Fire- and Airsigns.

Maturity

Her good qualities are those of the Earth herself: endurance, resistance and constancy. The symbol of bountiful goodness of the Earth Goddess is the cornucopia, the horn of plenty that was borrowed from the goat Amaltheia, and it would be unwise to ignore the gifts that tumble from it. Without Capricorn's maturity of outlook nothing would last for very long, and society would have nothing to build on and no past to refer to. The maturity of Capricorn means that early in life she manifests a wise head on young shoulders. A miniature adult, she has a seriousness beyond her years and takes on responsibility within the family. She often finds it easier to be among older people than many of her peers. Many Capricornians work with old people, for they have a respect for the wisdom and experience of the old that

is not often found in Western cultures. Amongst non-industrialised peoples and in the Far East the Capricornian values are far more prevalent. In China the concept of filial piety and respect for ancestors and inheritance has meant that older people are cherished with the same tenderness Westerners usually only show children. This gentle approach to the old is typical of Capricorn.

The responsibility possible in young children is more often seen in pre-industrial societies where young goatherds guard the valuable family property. Yet they can still be seen skipping with their goats or playing on the reed pipes of Pan. The contemporary Capricornian child does not always play enough, and benefits from time in the countryside to release this side of her nature. Childhood and adolescence are not Capricorn's best time, and she becomes progressively happier as she ages.. In middle age many Capricornians are able to relax and let go of their drive to achieve and their strong sense of purpose, recovering some of the goatherd's freedom. Many continue to succeed, almost in spite of themselves, like Billie Jean King who kept on winning and has Capricorn Rising.

The Saturn Return, which occurs between the ages of 28 to 30 is of particular importance to Capricorn. This is the time when she faces crucial changes and choices, for Saturn, her ruling planet, has gone through one complete cycle of the zodiac. For many people this is a difficult time, but Capricorn often feels she is coming into her own. She usually emerges strengthened and validated with a clearer sense of her life path. If this opportunity is missed the second Saturn Return around the age of 58 gives her a later chance for consolidation.

Capricorn is only occasionally the rebel, rarely outrageous, and yet she may be a radical thinker. Like Simone de Beauvoir, the Capricornian radical will be cautious, consistent and considered in her politics. She weighs up ideas carefully and when she produces a revolutionary thought we may be sure the background to it has been thoroughly researched. In every sphere of life Capricorn is cautious and prudent and she finds it hard to trust to luck.

Past Hardships

Because of the responsibility she takes on, Capricorn can be grudging

to those who have not done the same amount of hard work as she has, for she lacks their *joie de vivre*. Her natural seriousness can lapse into gloom or depression and she can be profoundly pessimistic. She feels then that no one understands how truly helpless and thankless her struggle is. Despite all her emphasis on responsibility it can take Capricorn a long time to take responsibility for her own choices. If she overworks, gives up fun and spontaneity in favour of self-discipline and duty, the choice has been hers. She can learn tolerance of others that will free her from many of the internalised rules with which she oppresses herself.

This tendency to unrelenting hard work in Capricorn did not just develop out of the blue. At a very early age Capricorn has usually had an experience of deprivation, an encounter with intractable refusal. On a deep level she may feel rejected and unloved for this is the sign furthest away from the nurturing qualities of Cancer. There may have been difficulties with her mother, or her family may have been too worn down by circumstances to give her the welcome every new baby needs. Even when her parents have been deeply loving there is often some insecurity in Capricorn. She suspects that love is conditional, that it needs to be paid back, and that it depends upon right behaviour and achievement. Often her parents have felt the same in their own family situation and the sense of duty is passed from generation to generation. Capricorn's need to succeed and prove herself are part of her attempts to deal with her essential insecurity, to establish for herself a conviction that she is worthy of love. Parents who teach by strong reliance on blame and reward reinforce this insecurity, and Capricorn has often had to cope with a stern parent who has denied the value of emotion and intuition.

There is a very old pain within Capricorn, and she may go through times of depression or withdrawal that she does not herself understand. Part of her process of self-healing will be to discover the unloved child within herself which will lead her from the bleak world in which she lives to the abundance of the Capricornian cornucopia and the freedom of the mountain. She only believes that the world is a difficult place because that has been her own experience when she was first learning what to expect. The cornucopian vision is a very different one, for the Earth Mother pours her gifts from the horn of plenty on to the deserving and the undeserving alike.

Saturnalia

In agricultural societies there has always been the need to work hard,
even if the vision of a land flowing with milk and honey, the land of
the cornucopia, was there to sustain the people through lean times.
Abundance could only be achieved if people were bound by rules and
regulations – the seed corn could not be used for making bread or
there would be no harvest in the following year.

Yet once a year, when the sun was in Capricorn, the people celebrated a time of licence called Saturnalia. The spirit of this festival was
preserved in Britain in the tradition of the mumming plays at Winter
Solstice – an opportunity for chaotic merriment. We see this side of
Capricorn in her humour. Capricorn often has a self-deprecating manner which is extremely funny, a wry wit and a cynical acceptance of
the world. Her ironic jokes assume that we share her expectation that
everything will be hard, and she is able to laugh at herself for her own
pessimism. Her humour is the lever she can use to prise herself from
depression. It may be a practical form of joking, Earthsign as she is, and
she plays tricks on people like Puck or Robin Goodfellow. These gob-
lin creatures, mischievous yet hard-working, are typical of Capricorn
and traditionally wore her colours of dark green and dark brown. They
would help around the house, country people said, but if not recognised
and quietly rewarded they turned to destructive tricks.

Another way Capricorn breaks out of her serious mould is through
her sexuality. She is closely in touch with all her five senses and cele-
brates her delight in the body with her sexual partner, as a true Earth
sign. Pan represented to the Greek world the power of physical enjoyment, sex as an elemental force in nature and lust in its original meaning of pleasure. We see the lusty, pleasure-loving Capricornian in
Janis Joplin who seemed to live in a long Saturnalia, in spite of having
the qualities of hard-working endurance typical of her Sunsign. The
physical nature of the sign is emphasised by Anais Nin in her erotic
writing, and the Capricornian nature of her Moon is apparent.

The fires lit at winter Solstice, the first day of Capricorn and the
darkest time of the year in the Northern hemisphere, remind us of the
fire of sexual pleasure or the spark of humour in the midst of the cold
earth of duty and hard work. Through sexual expression, usually in a
committed and loving relationship, Capricorn recovers the lost
aspects of her personality, the freedom of mountain and woodland.

Capricorn receives the gifts of civilisation, a heritage on which to build and a sense of duty to those who have gone before. These gifts may inhibit spontaneous action, and in accepting them she needs to remember the importance of Capricornian humour and earthy sexuality.

Emotional Consistency

In personal relationships Capricorn is protective to those she loves. She wants to use whatever she has achieved herself to help the person she loves. For herself, it may be hard to accept help as she is proud, fearing weakness and dependence. Yet she needs consistent and ordered relationships on which she can depend. She is very private about her emotional life and concerned that her relationships should appear well from the outside, for her dignity is easily hurt.

Her perseverance means that she gives any relationship a good chance to succeed. A typical life-long friendship was between French painter Rosa Bonheur and her friend Nathalie Micas. Bonheur had Moon in Capricorn and she achieved both wealth and fame over a long life of hard work as a painter of animals. Her Capricornian persistence is shown by the fact that she studied animal anatomy in abattoirs for years, and was not sentimentally deterred from doing this by her great love of living creatures.

Wisdom of Earth

There is some mystery in Capricorn that is not readily understood and this is shown by the most ancient image of the unicorn, which was originally a goat. It is interesting that the Chinese name the sign the Dolphin, for we cannot know what these intelligent creatures are thinking. Capricorn has a profound wisdom, born from her deep relationship with the Earth. Years of self-discipline open the way to spiritual understanding. After Capricorn has established herself in the world she may well turn to the spiritual or the occult, and the Platonists called this sign the Gate of Souls through which the other world was attained. But Capricorn keeps returning to the earthly level; she

believes enlightenment should have a practical use and uses her spiritual understanding to teach or to heal.

There are surprises within Capricorn, the most apparently conventional of signs, and while these seem to be contradictions they are not truly so, but part of the dual nature of a sign that is part-goat part-fish, which spans two worlds. The fish part of her nature is hidden, for usually Capricorn has forgotten how she emerged from the waters of the unconscious. She not only believes herself to be a land creature, but one who reaches higher than any other, a mountain-dweller on the peaks of achievement. She sees her opposite sign, Cancer, swimming in seas of emotion and intuitive experience, while she herself keeps her emotional life in its 'proper' place. Yet she needs at some time to recognise her hidden side and to know the depths. When she has done this Capricorn is more free to pursue the path to the mountain peak.

At the summit Capricorn turns round to survey all she has built and made on her way and is satisfied with her achievement. She knows that what she makes is solid and lasting, because she has put into it so much patient labour. When she reaches this point she is able to see that she could have taken an easier way, that her self-discipline need not have been so stringent and that she could have been easier on herself. Yet by her efforts she has gained a wider and greater perspective, and gained it in fact, not in vision or imagination as other signs may have done. Around her blow the four winds, but beneath her feet she feels the solid Earth reaching down for thousands of feet into its roots.

Background to the sign

The sign of Aquarius has been associated with a water jar from very early times. In Sumer the jar was carried by the Goddess Gula of healing and childbirth whose urn of fecundity symbolised the pregnant womb. The Egyptian Goddess Nut was shown in the sky with milk pouring from her breasts and the waters from her womb, and the

AQUARIUS
The water-carrier
The path of idealism
Aproach to life of **fixed air:**
visionary, prophetic, revolutionary,
far-reaching, detached, eccentric
Planetary ruler: Uranus

hieroglyph for her name was a rounded vase. In Hebrew, Aquarius is DLY or Delilah, whose name means 'her water-pitcher'. (see p 21)

In earliest times, the Celestial Waterer was always associated with female sexuality and fecundity; the Akkadian name for Aquarius was 'Seat of the Flowing Waters'. In later times Aquarius was shown as a young man – in Egypt as Hapi the Nile God who poured out the waters of the inundation when the Moon rose full in Aquarius. The Greek story of Hebe and Ganymede explains in part the shift away from the female image of Aquarius. Hebe was the cup-bearer to the gods and goddesses, refreshing them with the liquid of eternal youth. One day she slipped over and fell, exposing her genitals. Such an exposure might once have been sacred, for earlier legends from Egypt and Sumer tell how the sick were healed by the power of the sacred genitals of the Goddesses Hathor and Ninhursag. But in the Greek story the gods were embarrassed by Hebe's exposure. She was banished and in her place came Ganymede, androgynous boy-lover of Zeus.

The Visionary

The modern Aquarius often feels embarrassed when faced with the earthly passions and emotional complications of human life; the early associations of the sign long forgotten. But she has retained and developed a connection with prophecy and the future. Aquarius is the sign of times to come, symbolised by the unborn child floating in waters of the 'urn'-like womb. The Aquarian urn is also associated

with the cauldron of the Celtic Goddess Cerridwen, one sip from which conferred infinite knowledge and the power of prophecy.

In spite of Aquarius' title of Celestial Waterer we now see her as an Airsign, for she sits in the rain-carrying clouds above the flow from her urn. She has the Airsign concentration on ideas and ideals, and she is a visionary living in the world of tomorrow. Like the rounded vase her vision overflows (with plans for the future) and from her vantage point in the clouds she has a broad view encompassing the whole of humankind. Like Libra she yearns for a social order that embodies her ideals, and she is strongly convinced that it can be achieved. Aquarius has the inspiration of her prophetic sense that tells her not only that it ought to be so but that it will be. Aquarius has seen the future and she knows it works. She may write of her vision and often she is a radical like British socialist Beatrice Webb, or Indian feminist and novelist Sarojini Naidu who worked with Gandhi. She may be a revolutionary like double Aquarius Angela Davis or like nineteenth-century Russian Vera Figner. When she excels in another field altogether like singer Leontyne Price (who has Moon in Aquarius) she shows her loyalty to her politics publicly.

Aquarius respects movements which avoid personality cults and try to share leadership. She is drawn to feminism because it is egalitarian and progressive, and because the notion of sisterhood, bonds formed by common experience, is inspiring to her. Double Aquarius Germaine Greer is typical for her outspoken eccentricity and, a true Airsign, she will discuss anything. There are also many Aquarians who are radical thinkers but who do not fit into the contemporary political scene. In her book *The Aquarian Conspiracy*, Marilyn Ferguson[8] writes not of actual Aquarians but of the Aquarian impulse. She describes a leaderless network, 'working to create a different kind of society based on a vastly enlarged concept of human potential'. Aquarius thinks far more about the organisation of society as a whole than of the individuals within it, though deeply committed to the rights and concept of the individual. She loves humanity, but finds people difficult. While she champions the cause of individual freedom, protecting the underdog and fighting for everyone's rights, she can become involved in rigid and restrictive groups or ideologies. Temperamentally she is an anarchist, but her concern for the welfare of society as a whole can lead her into narrow 'party lines', not only within politics but in any other field where there is a strong idea holding the group

together. Aquarius can also be the rebel, in spite of her strong need for an affinity group. She is a compulsive 'outsider' who is driven to break away as much as she is instinctively loyal, for Aquarius is ruled by the rebellious planet Uranus as well as being a fixed sign.

Fixedly faithful to her ideals and ideas she defies the institutions, groups and people she sees as standing in the way of progress. She feels so identified with her ideals that, if a time comes when they no longer have meaning for her, Aquarius passes through the dark night of the soul. In deepest despair, she goes through a crisis of meaning in her life, bereft of her usual sense of purpose and prophetic vision. At such a time it is important for her to realise that this breakdown of her old methods of operating is, in fact, a break-through, painful and disillusioning through it is. The breakdown of the old is necessary before new forms can arise, and Aquarius may emerge from the desert with a new sense of self. She may also discover, through her time of meaninglessness, that life does not have to be lived by constantly striving after a goal or being inspired by a sense of purpose. From her opposite sign Leo she can learn of the possibility of joy and acceptance of what is, to relate to the present, to 'be here now'.

Companionship

Friendship is the Aquarian solace and, unlike Sagittarius or Pisces, she does not seek a teacher or guide in her transitional times but looks for a community of equals. Old friends mean a great deal to her, especially friendships which have survived the abrupt breaks she often makes over matters of principle. Though fiercely loyal, she can simultaneously be rude or bizarre in behaviour. She expects this to be understood as superficial and unimportant, and sees courtesy not as a form of respect but as a stultifying convention. She makes new friends easily, drawn to them more by interest and curiosity than a sense of emotional need. Her friends are from wide and varying backgrounds. She is stimulated by cultural differences, but she can also spot and cultivate original thinkers in even the most conventional setting.

It is Aquarius who keeps society growing by insisting that room is kept for the outsider, for the bizarre visionary, for the apparent lunatic who speaks truth amongst garbled ideas. She often idealises these

people and would rather meet a tramp than a cabinet minister. Her reversals of social norms and expectations give her personal satisfaction, but they can cut her off from her fellows, and there may come a time when she realises this. If she wants to change her sense of loneliness, of being a prophet crying in the wilderness unheeded, Aquarius may have to give up some of her sense of herself as special, as marked out by her vision. Aquarius is happiest when she meets her need for companionship as well as her need for ideals. When she lets go of her tendency to arrogance and her dogged determination to be an outcast she finds the world contains many people with a similar vision to her own.

Whether she is going through a time of change or is in the thick of group involvement, Aquarius will usually share her experience honestly and straightforwardly with others. She is uneasy talking about her emotional experience but will discuss changes in orientation. She has nothing consciously to hide, and is prepared to be quite open about much that others would keep hidden. She has little consciousness of norms of behaviour, and often breaks rules inadvertently because she never knew they existed. She may make astonishing gaffes through her naivety, and if a spokesperson for an organisation or movement she needs to be well briefed by someone more worldly wise.

Liberating Potential

Aquarius has a very direct awareness of her special and unique nature. This vivid individuality is something that all people have but it is the strongly Aquarian types who are aware of this characteristic.

Aquarian consciousness is always moving between individuality (with its possibility of isolation) and inclusion in a group or in society, or is making the journey from the group consciousness back to her unique viewpoint. It is from the preceding sign, Capricorn, that she inherits her concern with the organisation of society, but unlike Capricorn Aquarius is impatient with the forms that presently exist. All Airsigns search for the perfect and the ideal and it is Aquarius who makes expansive plans for the human potential, or who liberates it by scientific invention. Like Aquarian Elizabeth Blackwell, the first woman doctor to qualify, she is often a medical pioneer. In the last 15 years many

Aquarians have become disillusioned with the frontiers of traditional science in medicine; their flashes of insight light up for them the path to the 'fringe'. Aquarius investigates alternative medicines, especially those that acknowledge vital energy – homeopathy, acupuncture, radionics and cranial osteopathy. Often she trains successfully to practise one of these disciplines, her only limitation being her over-emphasis on the technical correctness of the treatment rather than a trust of her own healing ability.

Aquarius has long been associated with the practice of astrology. The subject attracts Aquarians more than other forms of character analysis and prediction, because it combines the intuitive element with the scientific and technical. Aquarius does not like her information to have fuzzy edges. Many Aquarians find that science alone provides them with a vision of the future, enough scope for awe as the workings of the natural world are unravelled in minute detail. Others take their questioning unorthodoxy to the frontiers of science, and come to believe that science and technology will not be enough without further development of the human being. Then Aquarius turns her attention and her idealism to the potential of human consciousness.

Clarity

Aquarian visionaries can be found throughout history. Often they have worked for human rights. Strong and impressive Aquarian visionaries have arisen through the Black church in the United States. In the last century Jarena Lee was one such who preached many inspiring sermons each year, while Amanda Berry Smith, an itinerant preacher with a compelling voice, visited India and Africa and was said to possess 'an unequalled clearness of vision'. Aquarius impresses us by this clarity, for she sees in greater contrast than her fellows. Her perception is often in extremes of contrasting colour, not because she is a simplistic thinker but because she is a visionary for whom the lightning flash of Uranian intuition has lit up the world, lending it stark rather than subtle tones. Electricity and lightning are symbols with which Aquarius has a strong connection. The colours she is most drawn to are 'electrical' colours – the acid greens, blues and yellows that are seen before a storm; they seem to be unearthly and outside

nature. The Aquarian visionary world is *totally* 'other', futuristic and like nothing we have ever known, while the Piscean magical world has the familiarity of dream and trance which is inside us waiting to be discovered. Aquarian visions lead us to expect the appearance of something alien; extra-terrestrial visitors or a fifth dimension.

Room to Move

Aquarius seeks surroundings that are completely different from those she was familiar with when young. Unless she was born there she often gravitates towards the anarchic inner city. She is not concerned with having comfortable surroundings (though she may be attracted by high-tech furnishings). She prefers the company of the poor and the alienated to the hypocrisy of the rich, and seeks out the most eccentric of companions, the outcasts, the weird and bohemian. Aquarius does not believe in norms; two lesbian Aquarians who disregarded sexual convention were Colette and Gertrude Stein. Aquarius identifies with 'difference' and because she is born before her time she has often felt a misfit all her life. She is more comfortable at the margins of society than at its centre. (Aquarius rules the circulation of the blood around the periphery of the body.)

Aquarius keeps a distance from emotional storm centres, too. She is very ill at ease when she encounters violent behaviour, jealousy, possessiveness and revenge, though she strives to understand how the pain people have experienced could have produced this reaction. She avoids close personal involvement with those she helps and her concern for equality leads her to treat all her friends alike with scrupulous tolerance and fairness.

Aquarius sees the spark of individuality in each person and her interactions are inspired by a respect for every person's worth. Her integrity in personal dealings is striking and memorable, and she is often much loved in her community. Her instinct is to transcend the selfish motivations and distorting needs of human emotion. She seeks a way to express love rightly and yet not to bind herself or another being. She hates to be trapped and needs a lot of space and independence; like Aquarian Virginia Woolf she knows the value of keeping a room of her own. She is happiest when her love relationship centres on friendship rather

than on passion. Her love is deeply felt and loyal but she views anything romantic as sentimental. She wants a companion, someone who shares her commitments, with whom she can gaze towards the same distant goal rather than into each other's eyes. Like Libra, her ideals of human interaction are very high and she often prefers to relate to a group when one-to-one relationships have disappointed her.

Inclusion

Aquarius will often rationalise her own feelings and use language that depersonalises her actions; 'it was felt better to change plans' rather than 'I changed'. Before her visions can become real she needs to see the value as well as the dangers of the passionate intensity she wishes humanity to transcend. So long as Aquarius shies away from feeling she is avoiding a deeper knowledge of herself. Committed to truth in all personal interactions, she can be inadvertently untruthful because she will not look deep enough to discover and include her own passionate longings and needs. Often she has felt hurt or rejected when young and has focused all her attention on her ideas and ideals to prevent this pain ever happening to her again. But until she faces her own vulnerability even her closest friends will feel they can never truly reach her, and are hurt by her off-hand approach to matters of great emotional importance to themselves. She risks carrying her loneliness with her and remaining the eternal outsider.

There is a way for Aquarius to bring into her airy environment the life of the heart which is the natural habitat of her opposite sign, Leo. If people push her to recognise her own feelings, she will back away, but she will respond to honest and undramatic explanation of the hurt she can unwittingly cause. Though she focuses naturally on her difference from her friends, it is by understanding her essential similarity with them (that she, too, has been hurt) whereby she can make deeper connections.

Through recognition and acceptance of strong feeling in her self or others Aquarius reaches a deeper serenity, for she no longer has to expend so much energy running away. By acceptance of human passions, Aquarius finds metaphors for the deeply passionate love she has for humanity and for the universe. She discovers that her emphasis

on the power and value of friendship comes from the strength of her own emotions.

The Age of Aquarius

We live at the end of a time when Ganymede has taken over from Hebe, and the waters of Aquarius are full of the accumulated wisdom of human ideas and ideals, but they seem to contain too little acknowledgement of human joys and sorrows. The modern Aquarius brings a cup that brims with waters from an ancient spring, effervescent with the new ideas of an Airsign. Drinking from it herself she gains more of the prophetic insight which inspires her. She speaks to us of needs that we did not know we had, of the frontiers of possibility. We cannot know what she will bring, for the ideas animating her vision are still being formed. Yet the cup she bears will quench a long, unnamed thirst.

Background to the sign

PISCES

The fishes
The path of understanding
Aproach to life of **mutable water:**
compassionate, imaginative,
impressionable, meditative, mystical
Planetary ruler: Neptune

The symbol of the fish has been important all over the ancient world, because civilisations emerged on the banks of rivers, lakes and seashores. Waterways were routes for communication long before roads existed. The fish was a staple food and by sharing its habitat different peoples met and their cultures mingled.

The fish swims in the past of humankind, and also in the past of each individual, for the child in the womb passes through a fish-like stage of development. Although Pisces is the last sign of the zodiac, it is also the one before the first, Aries, for the zodiac is a circle. Pisces symbolises the pre-birth era, and precedes the Arien impulse to birth.

The Goddess Aphrodite was shown with a fish-amulet over her genitals, and fishes were sacred by this association. The most ancient goddesses of the Middle East swam in the waters of chaos; the Great Mother of the Deep was the fish Abtu and the whale Derceto. The worshippers of the fish-tailed Goddess Atargatis found peace and respite from the world in their cool, quiet sanctuaries where fish were kept in ponds and their movements interpreted as oracles. Many others have found that keeping fish has helped towards a meditative life. The Chinese cultivated goldfish and the Christian nuns and monks stocked their ponds well to feed them on Fridays, the day originally sacred to Aphrodite whose love feast continued to be eaten, through with a different meaning given to the feast.

The two fishes of Pisces have been identified in the sky from an early time in astrology's history, and myths were elaborated to explain them. For the Romans they represented Venus and Cupid, turned to fishes to escape the monster Typhon.

The Intuitive

Salmon were particularly revered by the Celts, who thought they had

powers of prophecy. Pisces is a prophetic and intuitive sign like Aquarius, but the ways in which her powers are manifested are very different. While Aquarius is an airy or intellectual sign in whom intuition bursts through in lightning flashes, Pisces drifts in the waters of intuitive perception, in her own element.

Just as Venus and Cupid were able to escape as fishes, so Pisces' access to the unconscious gives her a great resourcefulness, but it is not of a kind that the world usually recognises. The sea of the unconscious in which Pisces swims gives her a deeper knowledge than she can explain or justify. She understands with her feelings and her intuition, not with her mind. She cannot tell how she knows something, for the Piscean memory is not like the more conscious ability to recall and recollect of Cancer. The past Pisces remembers may not be her own, for intuitive knowledge seeps into her from the past and from those around. She soaks up atmosphere and emotions like blotting-paper. If there is fear in the air she will probably be affected by it; if there is joy she will feel an unaccountable sense of happiness.

Pisces receives impressions in a way that most of humankind has forgotten. Originally the shaman in every tribe had the ability to sense where they should make camp; when they should leave; what they could eat and drink safely. This sixth sense is still within us, undeveloped in most human beings. Pisces may not know what is affecting her, but feels an unconscious pull, just as the fish are moved by currents of the sea, whose source they do not understand. The strong Piscean intuition enables her to enter into the experiences of others, and so learn far more than most people in one lifetime. From her intuitive understanding she develops wisdom. Often she cannot explain all her ideas to others, but they are usually aware of the insights that come from her sensitivity.

It may help Pisces to learn how to understand more about this faculty she has inherited. She may be able to learn to see auras, or to use a pendulum or Tarot cards so that she can translate the unconscious information to the conscious mind. Formal education is often irrelevant to Pisces for she learns most by empathy with the creatures around her.

The distinction between empathy and sympathy is an important one. While sympathy may patronise or devolve into pity, Pisces can develop a true compassion which is based on em-pathy – feeling *inside* another being rather than feeling *with*. Pisces feels the suffering of others as though it were her own.

Compassion

Through history there have been many archetypes of this sensitivity and compassion, figures to whom people have turned in prayer or in imagination. In China people revered Kwan Yin, the Spirit of Infinite Compassion, who rode on the back of a dolphin, and Nu Kwa, the fish-tailed Goddess who repaired the chaotic world and restored order to it. In Egypt Isis was addressed as the Mother of Compassion, for her tears filled the Nile annually as she wept for the death of murdered Osiris. People yearned for a deity who understood their sorrows and who felt for them.

For later peoples the Virgin Mary, Lady of Sorrows, became a necessary part of the Catholic religion. It is Christianity that has been most commonly associated with the Piscean Age, dating so accurately with the changeover of the Great Ages to Pisces around CE 0. But many other world religions have strongly Piscean features, particularly Buddhism, and the pagan religions of the dying god and sorrowing Goddess that were replaced by Christianity.

Amongst the pre-Christian Celts the Goddesses Bridget and Rhiannon were renowned for their compassionate love for all creatures. It could be dangerous to kill an animal, because the Goddess herself or one of her priestesses might have taken its form. This vivid metaphor for the interconnection of all life was a marked feature of Celtic mythology. Shape-shifting into a succession of animals happens so frequently that the tales take on some of the feeling of drug-induced trance.

Pisces' empathy means that she cannot blame others, for she feels that she cannot judge until she has 'walked a mile in the other person's moccasins'. Her tolerance can be an inspiration to other people, and often she is looked to within her community for guidance when decisions have to be made affecting the welfare of others. Pisces accepts other people, however difficult they might be, for she has a deep understanding of the pain that is likely to underlie anger or resentment. She refuses to over-react and is seldom shocked, whatever confidences are shared with her, and so finds herself in a special place in many people's lives as the only person they can turn to in a crisis.

This can put a strain on her, but at the same time Pisces is herself helped and regenerated by the work she does in understanding others;

it allows her to express the qualities in the world that she most deeply believes in.

She is often ambivalent about her own limitations; Piscean fish swim in two different directions. Her identity as a compassionate person is central to her, and she often fears that to say no means being hard and cruel. She can benefit from work on self-assertion, for Pisces does not battle for her own needs with any conviction.

Dealing with Pain

The instinct to sacrifice herself is deep within the Piscean urge, coming not only from her empathy but from a sense of sadness about the wrongs that have been committed by human beings. She is sensitive to all the cruelty in the world: to war, torture, rape and famine. She identifies with the victims, but also feels she cannot totally separate herself from the aggressors, for they, too, are part of the human race. Pisces feels the oneness of all existence, and this is not always easy for her. Sometimes she reacts by distancing herself from other people in order to feel more sure of her own identity and boundaries, and represses her own imagination and empathy.

Pisces may be drawn deeper into her dream world by dependence on drugs or drink, attracted to these because they enhance her shifting perceptions. She seeks to put whatever boundaries she can between herself and the painful world. When she feels unable to deal with it she may depend on others for practical matters.

More often it is Pisces who finds others depending on her for emotional support, for she can make great voluntary sacrifices for those she loves and can be a wonderfully loving friend. Only when she is hurt and frustrated will she feel a martyr burdened with the weight of all she has taken on. She needs to keep a humorous approach and not become too serious about her mission in life. She is particularly prone to trying to 'save' her lovers, attracted to those who feel themselves to be victims, and this may set her on a succession of unequal relationships. Yet whether she is trying to 'save' a lover, a friend, or someone in her working life, her impulse comes from her compassionate love.

When she finds it hard to separate from the suffering from others she needs to ask herself whether she is dealing with her own pain

indirectly by being attracted to other people's. At these times it is important for her to realise that while she feels other people's pain, the tears she weeps are her own, and that she is crying for herself, too. She is the wounded healer who heals herself while she helps others, but at some point she needs time to focus directly on her own healing.

The Healing Journey

These are the times when she can benefit from a sanctuary; for when Pisces looks for time apart to heal herself she is no longer escaping. When she is ill or unable to continue for other reasons she can create a new relationship with the physical world around her. She needs the solid earth, the island in the midst of the shifting waters, and benefits from work with a guide who can help her to get there: a therapist or healer. Her strong imagination is her greatest resource to help her in her journey.

The salmon swim upstream once a year to spawn and to die in the place where they were born. This journey back to the beginning symbolises the process whereby Pisces enters into her past to know herself better, to allow old and unwanted parts of herself to die and to allow new parts to be created. Pisces has an ability, paralleled only by Scorpio, to recreate her own life. She is open to many sources of healing, and this openness is ultimately the way for her to reach a place of even deeper wisdom and understanding than she knew before.

Pisces discovers, through her imagination and her mystical streak, that it is not only the pain of the whole world that she can share, but also the joy of all creatures. Many things can bring her happiness that would not even be noticed by other people. She can find within herself the ability to live within the moment, and to look with a gentle and amused tolerance at the intensities of feeling experienced in the past. She does not turn her back on feelings or repress them, but develops a sense of compassionate detachment so that she is no longer at the mercy of constant change.

More than any other sign, she has the ability to forgive herself for her mistakes. Her potential to pass through to the other side of guilt and self-reproach to self-forgiveness gives her great skills to help others on the same journey.

The Healer

Once she has made her journey of self-healing Pisces can become an effective helper and healer for others, no longer trying to save them, but using her empathy wisely and compassionately. She often works in institutions: with prisoners, in hospitals, with children or adults who have special needs. Her imagination and empathy prevent her from becoming patronising; because she has recognised her own pain she works from a place of true fellow feeling with those who are unhappy. She will not see those she works with as victims, for it is no longer their suffering that attracts her but their life and vitality, and the uniqueness of perception that is found in those whose experience has been different from that of the majority.

It is those Pisceans whose own paths have been hard who most widely extend their compassionate interest. Helen Keller had Moon in Pisces, and wrote not only about disability but about the needs of working-class people and the dangers of militarism for the world.

Pisces needs companionship and a sense that there are others following the same path. The structure and discipline of an organisation that can provide her with support or sanctuary in which to work is very useful to her, and rules (if they are not rigid) can protect her from taking on too much. She is often drawn to oriental religions which teach meditation, for she needs to focus and still her emotions.

The Creative Dreamer

Pisces always needs time for reflection, to consider her dreams, be still with herself and her imagination. Often she likes to read poetry or mythology, the folk-tales of many cultures, featuring mermaids, fairies, changelings, spirits, and magical islands that disappear and reappear. She is particularly attracted to the legends of peoples who live close to the sea, whether in the Mediterranean, amongst the Scottish islands or in the Pacific.

Others may find such stories an escape from the real world, but Pisces knows the importance of these messages from the waters of the unconscious, and the world of the imagination is just as real to her as the 'real' world.

The Piscean world is fluid and shifting so that everything appears like a dream. Semblance is not reality. Pisces herself often seems to move in a trance, alive only to her inner world. Her fantasy life is a useful protective device between her and her surroundings. She needs the space to be a dreamer or else she feels she could not survive, and her friends have to respect these needs.

From this process of imaginative reflection emerges the Piscean creativity. Many Pisceans have been poets. Native Canadian poet Pauline Johnson-Tekahionwake wrote romantic and evocative poems telling of the rivers, mountains and life of her people in the last century. Elizabeth Barrett-Browning also wrote in the Piscean tradition (and found a way to heal herself from long illness). Edna St Vincent Millay wrote of her sense of exile when away from the sea, and compared her broken heart to a drying tidal pool. Pisceans often express their compassionate understanding as novelists, like Carson McCullers who achieved fame at an early age for her insight into the lives of the estranged and alienated. Her imagination was her greatest resource in an unhappy marriage and in her bouts of recurrent rheumatic fever. Photography is ruled by Pisces' planet Neptune, and the work of the photographer Diane Arbus shows her Piscean identification with those whose lives were very different from her own. Singer Joni Mitchell has Moon in Pisces, and many of her songs evoke the lives of the lonely who sit in more modern versions of Carson McCullers' sad cafés. Drama also attracts Pisces, for it gives her an opportunity to use her empathic understanding, to become her roles. Rita Tushingham's performances in films during the 1960s made her a symbol of the fragile impressionability of her Sunsign, and suggested the dignity and paradoxical toughness that can accompany these qualities. Music and dance could equally well be creative outlets for Pisces, but they must be flowing rather than frenetic, with the gentle watery quality of the sea.

Pisces is the sign of dissolution. Through her understanding of others Pisces brings together the experience of the whole zodiac. Through the changes experienced she is dissolved, like minerals by the changing sea; broken down so that a new cycle can start with oncoming Aries. This process is continuous within the Piscean psyche, and she needs a creative expression to emerge from the welter of impressions absorbed. Self-expression through the arts provides her with a decisive way to take control of and use her impressionability.

Pisceans may not be poets, writers, musicians or actors, any more than they will necessarily work as healers. Yet most Pisceans seem to have a strong need for imaginative stimulus and an opportunity to feel empathy with the experience of others. Film, theatre and television offer the Piscean a world of the imagination where crisis and resolution can be acted out by the protagonists with whom Pisces vividly identifies.

Sharing the Dream World

Pisces is a sensitive companion and an imaginative lover. Often a very private person, she allows only those she loves to hear of her dream world and be enriched by it.

When she is no longer seeking to save or rescue, her compassion and empathy can play a role in the changing of someone else's life, for she has the loving will to allow miracles to happen. She looks for a deep and mystical connection with her partner or friend. At the same time she seeks acceptance of her desire to be intermittently alone, for without this she may lose herself in the relationship.

She seldom feels angry, forgiving readily. This may not always serve the relationship (for sometimes things need to be brought into the open), and it can help her to be involved with someone more down to earth, both emotionally and in the material world.

The Watcher by the Pool

When Pisces feels drained or turbulent, time for reflection allows her imagination to replenish her and her emotions to recover their tranquillity. In the centre of Piscean consciousness there is a still pool to which she can turn her inner gaze. Letting the waves die down from her own and other people's tempestuous feelings, she can recover the stillness of this quiet and tideless pool. In the pool she watches a sea anemone and sees how the creature spreads its flowerlike tentacles widely when all is still, but when the shadow of an observer falls across the pool the tentacles are withdrawn and the anemone closes.

In a similar way Pisces can learn to regulate the degree of her openness to her environment and still feel the compassionate impulse that animates her. Through recognition of her own separateness, her ability to close off when she needs to, she realises her deepest understanding: that all life is one.

References

1   In delineation of the signs of the zodiac we have drawn on many sources, ranging from astrological writings, religious works, mythology and biography. In the Bibliography at the end of this book the books we have used are listed under these sections.
2   Lao Tsu, *Tao Te Ching*, translated by Gia-Fu Feng and Jane English, Random House, 1972. (Chapter 16).
3   Graves, Robert, *The White Goddess*, Farrar, Straus & Giroux, 1966, p 420.
4   Gilman, Charlotte Perkins, *The Yellow Wallpaper*, in *The Charlotte Perkins Gilman Reader*, edited by Anne J. Lane, The Women's Press, London, 1981.
5   See Walker, Alice, *In Search of Our Mothers' Gardens*, Harcourt, Brace, Jovanovich, 1984. It is particularly Black and working-class women who have had to find their artistic expression through forms that are not accepted as Fine Arts.
6   Pagels, Elaine, *The Gnostic Gospels*, Random House, 1981. See also Greene, Liz, *The Astrology of Fate*, Samuel Weiser, 1984, for an in-depth examination of the paradoxical nature of Virgo.
7   Maeterlinck, Maurice, *The Blue Bird*, Methuen, 1949.
8   Ferguson, Marilyn, *The Aquarian Conspiracy*, J P Tarcher, 1981.

7
Coming Down to Earth
The Twelve Houses

The houses of the horoscope show the different areas in our lives through which we are able to express ourselves. Each house has a particular theme (see Figure 7.1).

Each house has a natural affinity with a sign (the First House with Aries, the first sign, the Second House with Taurus the second sign, etc). However, only those with an Aries Ascendant will have their signs synchronised with the associated houses in their horoscopes.

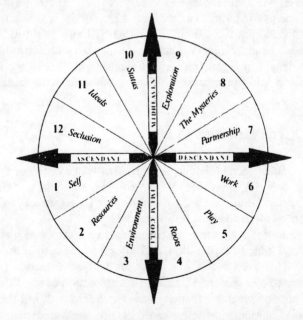

Figure 7.1 *The houses and their themes*

222 The Knot of Time

For these people the first sign (Aries) coincides with the First House. For the rest of us, the houses overlap with the signs in various ways, depending on the time and place of birth. (See Figure 3.4 on p 60 for the houses in a chart with a 7° Aquarius Ascendant, for instance). We can understand the way each house is approached by considering the signs that fall on each house's *cusp* or beginning point, and the planets that appear within each house.

The Planets in the Houses

Just as the planets are modified by the signs in which they appear, so their house position tells us the *area* of life in which a planet expresses its energy. For instance, Uranus in the Sixth House shows that the person's sense of her individuality is best expressed in her work.

We also take account of the sign the planet is placed in, as explained in Chapter 3. The combination of house and sign placements of the planets gives us a more complex and personal picture of the way the planetary energy is expressed and the area where it finds the greatest ease of expression. Uranus in Gemini in the Sixth House might indicate a person whose individuality (Uranus) is expressed with versatility and with a delight in communication (Gemini) in her life of work. She might be a writer or speaker with unorthodox views, for instance.

The Sign on the House Cusp

In the chart of each individual some houses will be empty of planets, but this does not mean that this part of life is empty of meaning for her. The sign falling on the cusp of the house shows the way in which this part of life is likely to be approached.

For instance, in a given horoscope there happen to be no planets in the Ninth House of exploration, and Aries is on the cusp of the Ninth House. This person has a courageous and adventurous (Arien) approach to overseas travel, and to the exploration of ideas through study, both of which are themes of the Ninth House. While there are no planets emphasising these areas of her life, she is able to approach travel and study in a relatively straightforward manner.

The Themes of the Houses

Each house tells us about several different areas of our lives which are united by a particular theme. The Sixth House of Work, for instance, also gives us information about the person's health. Her efficiency in her work life will be affected by the efficiency of her body.

The Opposite House

Each house has a particular connection with the one diametrically opposite (see Figure 7.1). To explore one house it is often necessary to consider the themes of its opposite and complementary house.

Note on House Systems
There are various ways that astrologers use to divide the horoscope into houses. The subject is complex; more information can be found in the books listed at the end of Chapter 9.

The First House:

House of the Self

appearance; first impressions of the personality; self-oriented interests; major preoccupations

Associated with Aries and Mars

The First House represents the part of the character which makes a first impression on others, so the sign and any planets here affect not only how we see ourselves but also how others see us.

Traditionally, the First House is said to govern the person's appearance, and it can be impressive to see the astrological correlations with appearance that are sometimes evident, Mercury in the First House accompanying an unusually youthful appearance in an older person, for instance. (There are also various other factors – Sunsign and Moonsign in particular – in the horoscope that may be said to relate to appearance.) While such correlations can be interesting for students of astrology, the deeper meanings of the First House are of greater importance to the person involved. With Mercury in the First House we could say that it is the importance of youthful Mercury in the person's chart, telling us about her open and enquiring attitude to life, which has led to her Mercurial appearance in maturity.

The sign on the First House cusp is the rising sign or Ascendant, and the approach to life that the sign has will be an important factor in the person's life, allowing her to express her very personal interests. With a Libran First House, for instance, an interest in art may be the way that this person first distinguishes herself from her sisters, brothers or schoolfriends. Art becomes uniquely 'hers' in her perception, bound up with her personality and identity. When she grows up it is important for her to maintain and feed this 'self-oriented' interest, for so she maintains and feeds her sense of self in the world.

The main effect of the First House in the horoscope is to magnify the importance of any planets that are placed in it, and the aspects that are made to them.

Any planets within the First House have a strong influence on the personality, rivalling the Sunsign and Ascendant for dominance of the chart. A person with Leo Sun, Libra Ascendant and Saturn in the First House will have many Saturnian qualities, along with her Leonine and Libran personality. The Saturnian qualities may well be the most obvious, for planets in the First House give a strong and definite

personality, one that attracts attention and makes a mark in the world. Those with a planet in the First House can put over strongly the positive qualities of that planet. For instance, with Mars in the First House the person can make her dynamic energy and courage obvious to those around her.

The First House is *self*-centred. It governs everything that we do entirely for ourselves, and tells us how we feel about ourselves as personalities. Planets in this house can also indicate problems, demonstrating a poor self-image when they receive challenging aspects from other planets in the horoscope. The situation is not static, or preordained, however, for the person can work towards a positive understanding of the value of the part of the psyche the planet represents, and so recover her sense of self-worth. For instance, with the Moon in the First House receiving challenging aspects from other planets a person may well be criticised for her apparently incomprehensible moods. Part of the process of transforming the difficult side of her lunar nature, to make contact with other people more easily, will be for her to discover the positive sides of the Moon. By realising her qualities of imagination, responsiveness, and her great emotional range she can accept a better image of herself. This will inevitably change the way others see her and improve all interactions with other people.

Those who have the First House emphasised by more than one planet tend to have a very strong effect on other people, and often become well-known. They are usually very involved in their own experience and actions, with some of the innocence and surprise of the small child that most of us have lost.

One way that all of us can look after ourselves and take care of the First House area in our lives is to have at least one activity, for the self alone, that is, where we can be self-centred without guilt or embarrassment. This allows the healthy selfishness of the child to be reestablished amidst the anxieties and responsibilities of adult life.

The Second House:

House of Resources

background; possessions; property; money; income; values; relationship with the body; comfort; physical experience; appreciation of beauty

Associated with Taurus and Venus

This is the house that tells us about the resources available to us. For example, a well aspected Jupiter in the Second House might indicate a comfortable or even wealthy background with a generous family, and /or great luck with money, and the ability to seize opportunities.

The Second House shows, by the sign on its cusp and any planets placed within it, the way money is handled. It describes how effective a person can be in the practical world, and suggests ways she may earn her living. The Second House can indicate the acquisition of possessions and property. When the Second House is emphasised in the chart it can show the importance of economic factors in determining the person's experience of life. It can also show a preoccupation with values. In dreams our values are often represented by precious objects or money, and in waking life the way we spend money demonstrates our priorities. For instance, Leo on the Second House might suggest an extravagant and generous attitude to money, possibly the ability to make one's living by a performing art. This person's values would be based above all on a respect for creativity, and the recognition of warmth of heart as the most important virtue.

When there are several planets in the Second House the person is likely to be strongly involved in trying to create an environment around herself which expresses her values, or in setting projects in motion which express them.

The Second House also shows the ways we meet our own physical needs. Money and resources can help with this, but our greatest resource is our own bodies. The Second House shows whether we feel beautiful, and comfortable with ourselves, and how we express warmth and sensuality with others. The opposite house from the Second is the Eighth which relates to sexuality, and the foundations for sexual expression are laid down by the Second House experiences of comfort and sensual enjoyment.

For instance, someone with a strongly aspected Neptune in Libra in the Second House might show this energy by the imaginative creation of a fairy tale atmosphere in which to share physical pleasures with

her friends. The clothes she wears express her dreamy Neptunian sense of delight in her own body. It is not immediately apparent that she is direct, impulsive and a dynamic initiator in her sexual relationships. Yet she has Aries on the opposite, Eighth House, and the fantasy world she creates allows her to feel free and spontaneous in an Arien way.

We experience the Second House part of our lives when we are able to pamper ourselves and enjoy our surroundings. We can learn to value ourselves by feeling pride in our ability to earn our own living. When we are not able to do so, and have few material resources, it is all the more important to find ways to give ourselves pleasure and recognise that we deserve this. The appreciation of nature and physical beauty of our friends, children and other relatives is also a self-nourishing part of the Second House area of our lives.

The Third House:

House of Environment

siblings; schoolfriends; neighbours;
school-life; learning;
communications; short journeys;
transport; daily routine; mobility

Associated with Gemini and
Mercury

The uniting theme of the Third House is communication with the environment. While the Second House represents the immediate resources the child finds around her, the Third House represents the less tangible resources of the community in which she arrives, and the possibilities it offers of stimulus and interaction.

With this house the newborn child inherits a network of relationships with her peers; brothers, sisters, cousins and other children in shared households (or her lack of them if she is raised alone). Third House relationships are not with those we seek out but with those we find around us. Cancer on the Third House cusp, for instance, might demonstrate an affectionate, even clinging, relationship with siblings; more positively it might demonstrate a protective and nurturing relationship. In adult life this person might take a similar protective role towards her neighbours.

The sign on the house cusp and any planets within the house show how we interact with the environment. If the Third House is emphasised by the Sun, Moon or a cluster of planets this gives a lively, stimulating approach, of curiosity and openness, and a desire both to keep up with the news and continue to learn. It indicates the ways we make casual relationships with our peers. Capricorn on the Third House might be expressed by a committed approach to the needs of the community, which brings the person concerned many new acquaintances through her attendance at meetings and on committees. The Third House also represents the places where we encounter our neighbours: local shops and markets, the pub or cafe as social centres, the evening class.

This house in the horoscope shows the way learning is approached, and it can tell us about success or difficulties in schooling. With Mars in the Third House, for instance, there would be much dynamic energy expressed by the child's enthusiasm to learn, but she could be so assertive in class that she might become involved in arguments with other pupils. With an emphasis on the Third House there is usually a high priority on the acquisition of new skills, continued learning, and on

communication in the person's life. She may excel as a public speaker or as a journalist, or work with books as bookseller, editor or librarian. Third House Sun, Moon, Mercury, or Uranus in particular, may be the mark of the writer.

Mobility is a major theme of the house, and it can show by the planets and signs associated with it in the chart the importance of daily routine in our lives; the journeys we take to work or shop, our relationship with cars, buses, bicycles, trains. All Third House matters greatly influence our experience and mood, as we only realise to the full when their functioning becomes problematic. Those with planets in the Third House which form challenging aspects with planets in other parts of the chart often encounter difficulties with communication or mobility. The house is of special importance in the charts of disabled people; when mobility or communication are impaired it becomes imperative to ensure that Third House needs for stimulation and interaction are being met.

The Third House part of our lives gives us a feeling of being part of a network of other lives. A sense of sisterhood or brotherhood or community can nurture us when our closest one-to-one relationships are in trouble. By attending to this area in our lives we keep our minds active, exercise social skills, and avoid the pain of loneliness and the inertia of boredom.

The Fourth House:

House of Roots

infancy; childhood; the home; parents (especially the mother); housing; land; domestic life; ethnic identity; inner life

Associated with Cancer and the Moon

The Fourth House represents parts of our lives associated with the deepest part of the psyche, the most unconscious needs and desires. These needs are bound up with security, and refer back to our relationship with our mothers. The Fourth House often describes, by the planets placed in it and the sign on its cusp, the relationship the person experienced with her mother as an infant, her early home life, and the sense she has of her family and its importance in her life. If planets in the Fourth House of the chart are under stress (see Chapter 8) there is usually a particularly difficult relationship with the family.

The house shows the ways we are able to accept nurturing and the quality of the relationships we have with either parent, or with other close nurturers. Someone who has Virgo on the Fourth House, for instance, may be reserved but rather critical of others, having secretly high expectations of support and caring. At the same time this person may find it hard to express the Virgoan part of herself because it is buried in the unconscious.

The Fourth House shows an area in the chart which may be prospected for 'buried treasure'. For instance, someone with Uranus in the Fourth House may have had a disrupted family life, or a parent who seemed like an outcast from society which caused the child much suffering. Buried in the unconscious is the person's own Uranus, her ability to be inventive, brilliantly eccentric, an inspired outsider to the conventional viewpoint. By working on ways to accept support from others, and learn how to nurture ourselves, the 'buried' areas of the psyche are better able to be expressed.

Psychotherapy and other work with the unconscious – such as art therapy or creative visualisation – may be used to resolve past trauma and to discover Fourth House treasures. This is especially important for those whose Fourth House is emphasised. Such work may not always be possible, but a great deal of healing and resolution also takes place in the unconscious through dreaming.

The sign on the cusp of the Fourth House can show how the person experiences her mother, rather than indicating what the mother is

actually like. For instance, a Geminian mother may be very interested in ideas and respond with interest to what her child tells her from learning at school. The child has a difficultly placed Mars in Capricorn in the Fourth House, and experiences the mother's interest as pressure on her to be successful, though this may not be the mother's intention or motive. Resolution of this problem at a later date might involve the discovery by the daughter of her own strong ambition 'buried' in the Fourth House.

Often in her adult life a person will embark on a search to discover her ancestral roots when a slow moving planet moves through her Fourth House. Planets in the Fourth House at birth indicate some of the ways we relate to our ethnic identity as well as to our family background. Venus here, for instance, might indicate not only an emotional and affectionate relationship with the family, but a strong desire to create art-forms from the culture which has been inherited.

The Fourth House also tells about the homes we make for ourselves. Through providing ourselves with homes we create bases for the rest of our lives. The nature of the home sought is often indicated by planets in the house and the sign on the cusp. For instance, with Mercury in Aries in the Fourth House the home would be streamlined for maximum efficiency.

Because the Fourth House speaks of such old and deep needs, it is an important part of the chart to consider in a close relationship, by looking at the planets and signs involved for each person. It is also of great importance in understanding our relationships with housemates and in communal settings.

The Fourth House tells of the inner life: of the unconscious and of the home. It contrasts sharply with the outer life of the Tenth House and is the basis from which we go out into the world. Those with the Fourth House more emphasised than the Tenth are often 'inner world' people, functioning in the imagination better than in the 'real world'. Closer to the unconscious, they often express this as artists, musicians and poets.

Whatever placements we have in the Fourth House, or sign on its cusp, we all need to build a firm base, by creating security and nurturing ourselves.

The Fifth House:

House of Play

recreation; fun; entertainment; creativity; holidays; sports; games; love affairs; children

Associated with Leo and the Sun

After the young child has shown interest in her physical comfort (Second House) her environment (Third) and her relationship with her parents (Fourth), she starts to develop her creativity more deliberately in her play. The Fifth House is the area of the horoscope that relates to fun and to joy, and describes the capacity for spontaneity and creative play. For the adult the Fifth House describes sexual relationships in their playful and fun aspects, contrasting with the Eighth House which is associated with sex as a much deeper and more elemental force. Fifth House relationships are full of romance and flirtation. 'Love affairs' are ruled by this house, while the Seventh House describes the more serious business of partnership.

The Fifth House is opposite to the Eleventh, the house of idealism, and Fifth House concerns are those that are not too weighty with purpose and intensity. The sign of the Fifth House cusp and any planets within the house show something of the person's ability to relax, to be silly, to be entertained. While some disdain Fifth House pursuits as trivial, the need to let go of seriousness is a strong one and we are revitalised by laughter, by a stretch of time in which few demands are made. Sport is a Fifth House expression, and though there are demands made on the amateur sportsperson these are different from those in her working life. Sports, games and hobbies are psychologically helpful because they offer a temporarily closed world where the rules are clear, where success, failure and competition can be ritualised and satisfaction gained. Games can also consist of spontaneous, non-competitive play. Adults often have to work hard to recover the ability to play, and sometimes can only manage this when involved in a love affair or by spending time with animals or children.

Traditionally the astrologer looks to the Fifth House to see how children feature in the client's life and how she relates to them. Sagittarius on the Fifth House cusp, for instance, would encourage the adult to take on a teacher's role, perhaps sharing outdoor pursuits with her own children, or as a youth leader. With Saturn in the Fifth House there might be some inhibiting factors with regard to children,

and even a difficulty in conceiving, but this is by no means a fatalistic prognosis. The same position of Saturn could be expressed positively by a serious approach to sport or outdoor pursuits, and by commitment to children.

The Fifth House also shows the need for personal creative expression. The same house tells us about both artistic creativity and physical reproduction. The sign on the cusp and planets here can tell us about the children we will have and/or the creative works we will give birth to. A well-aspected Mercury in the Fifth House would suggest creative writing, for Mercury rules communication. At the same time a Mercurial relationship with children is suggested, the individual concerned having a Peter Pan quality and relating to children as a child herself.

Problems can arise if planets in the Fifth House receive difficult aspects; the person concerned may tend to rely heavily on luck or depend on spontaneous self-expression in games, entertainments or love affairs in order to avoid responsibility. Even so, we need Fifth House interests to allow us to be entertained, to create, to relax and to have fun. We can fulfil this part of life by making sure we have time to play.

The Sixth House:

House of Work

working life; workmates and colleagues; the workplace; efficiency; health; diet; exercise

Associated with Virgo and Mercury

After the young child has learned a great deal through spontaneous play, she starts to want to plan games and build constructive toys that require forethought and may not always give immediate gratification. She has discovered purpose and the ability to act in the present for a future reward; she has started to work.

Planets in this house and the sign on its cusp show the nature of the joy and satisfaction we can derive from doing something well. As we do something competently and confidently we feel a sense of power and exhilaration. The Sixth House, too, can show the problems we have with routine tasks, the boredom of work that does not stretch us, and the sign on the cusp often gives clues to another kind of work that would suit better. With Libra on the Sixth House, for instance, work might be with people – in personnel, liaison or counselling. It could be connected with art or design. This person would need a gentle and co-operative interaction with colleagues, and would benefit from a team or partnership.

The Sixth House describes the role of work within our lives, and the need we have for workmates and colleagues as well as the importance and nature of our relationships with them. There can be problems with an emphasised Sixth House when the person so strongly identifies with her work that leaving it for motherhood, redundancy or retirement gives her a temporary loss of identity. Yet with this house emphasised in the chart work will be fulfilling, in spite of a tendency to over-commitment.

While the Sixth House can indicate great concern with efficient functioning in the workplace, it is also associated with the healthy working of a fit body. To be in balance we need to harmonise the needs for work and play. Often ill-health goes along with a lack of purposeful work, of motivation, or a sense of self worth. Healing will then be bound up with discovering a sense of personal value and a vision of the self as creative and useful. Traditionally planets in the Sixth House show the kinds of disease and ill-health the person is likely to suffer – Mars in the Sixth, for instance, might indicate accidents at

work or frequent fevers (Mars being the fiery-red planet). At the same time the planets in the Sixth House and the sign on its cusp can give us glimpses of what is to be learned from an illness. Sometimes the message is clear – 'cigarettes exacerbate bronchitis' but the causes can be remote. We may be able to discover from the Sixth House the emotional habits that have impaired health – Saturn here opposite to the Moon in the Twelfth House could indicate the suppression of grief, for example. When the causes of illness are buried deep in the family background, in the genes and psychic atmosphere inherited from previous generations, it may be best to work with psychic healing or with deep-acting systems of medicine such as homeopathy to reclaim the healthy body.

We fulfil the Sixth House part of our lives by finding the right work and colleagues, and by disciplining ourselves to work well. At the same time we need to take care of our bodies so they function at their best.

The Seventh House:

House of Partnership

one-to-one relationships; committed relationships; domestic or business partnerships; rivalry; counselling

Associated with Libra and Venus

The cusp of the Seventh House is the Descendant, the degree of the zodiac *setting* at birth. The sun crosses the Descendant as it sets each day, and the hours of sunset are often experienced as 'romantic', associated with love and intimate relationships.

This house shows by the sign 'descending', and any planets in the house, how the closest relationships are approached, and the ability to share and to be intimate. Although this need for intimacy is strong in most people, it need not be automatically associated with sexual sharing. The partnership may well be a platonic or working relationship. Through this house we learn how to relate to others, often by connections with people who were born with Sun or Moon in our descending signs. For instance, someone with Jupiter in the Seventh House in Cancer (the descending sign) will have an instinct to generous sharing with her partner, and a need to use the benefits of the partnership (Cancerian security) as a base from which to expand, perhaps socially, by entertaining other people in the home. This person may be irresistibly attracted to Cancerians. Equally, the descending sign may be experienced as repellent, and some people try to avoid people with the Sun in that sign. In either case the owner of the horoscope is projecting on to people of that sign her own undeveloped side.

By looking at the Seventh House we can tell what qualities the person has repressed and discarded in herself. When the descending sign attracts it is because we project our own undeveloped positive traits, often compulsively falling in love with our 'opposite' or complement. When it repels we are horrified by someone who reminds us of the unacknowledged parts of ourselves. The disowned part often reappears to haunt us, and we keep meeting people with this sign strong in their charts. The disowned self can manifest as a recurrent rival or enemy, turning up in every workplace, every group joined, with a new name and face but sharing the same characteristics. A person with Aries rising, for instance, projects herself with vigour and courage towards the world. Part of her, however, is not so assertive. She does

not express her indecision, her tendency to compromise, or her fear of conflict, traits that the Aries self often despises. Within the same repressed part of her personality are positive traits such as consideration of people's feelings and a love of harmony, shown in the chart by the Descendant in Libra. When she meets Librans, or those with a strong Venus (Libra's ruler) she might either conflict with them (negative projection) or fall desperately in love with them (positive projection).

The situation is more complex for those with Sun or Moon in the descending sign. In this case it gives her a focus on relationships, a particular need to learn through partnership. Many planets in the Seventh House usually indicate a person who has a co-operative nature, preferring to respond to other people's initiatives in creative collaboration. This would be changed by the presence of particular planets in the Seventh House. The presence of Mars, for instance, might indicate a need to fight through to a creative resolution with the partner.

As present-day planets move through the Seventh House they indicate an awakening to new issues in one-to-one relationships. The transit of Venus through the Seventh House once or twice a year is often associated with a particularly helpful and loving time.

The Seventh House in the chart helps us to elucidate what our closest relationships mean; to understand the patterns we repeat. When it is emphasised by many or important planets the person concerned often passes on her own insights in one-to-one relationships by working as a counsellor.

We can pay attention to the Seventh House part of our lives by recognising the need for intimacy and sharing. This can be expressed by making space for close personal interaction, by valuing intimate friendships, and by allowing ourselves both to love and to receive love.

The Eighth House:

House of the Mysteries

sexuality and its deeper meaning; death; the after life; secrets; the occult; psychic development; inherited money

Associated with Scorpio and Pluto

While the Second House relates to pleasure and touch, the Eighth House is associated with sexuality and the deeper meaning of sexual experience. The sign on the cusp of the Eighth House and planets in the house show a person's approach to sexuality. For instance, with Neptune in Leo in the Eighth House, sexual experience might become an arena in which to enact romantic and mystical dramas. With Mars in Gemini in the Eighth House the person concerned would be likely to experience a compulsive drive towards sexuality as a means of increasing her knowledge of the world and its people.

The Eighth House extends into a wider context. It represents the nature of the individual's search to understand her life, to face death and the meaning of the cycle of birth and death, to consider all the mysteries that are not addressed in the practical world of day-to-day living. Sexuality is one part of these mysteries and the individual often senses ancient forces working within her or him, so that sexual expression seems to contain more than could be explained by the sharing of pleasure, the release of tension and desire, or even the enactment of love. Sex raises challenging questions about the ways in which a person can or cannot let go of inhibition, achieve intimacy or experience fusion with another person. It raises fear of one's own intensity and emotional power, and asks what one is prepared to exchange or give up in order to experience intimacy.

When the Eighth House is emphasised in the chart the person is likely to respect the power of sexuality, and will seldom trivialise or ridicule it. She is also likely to devote time to considering the mysteries of existence and when the deeper spiritual needs of this house are met it is not always necessary to find sexual expression.

The relationship of the Second House with the Eighth is shown by the Eighth House emphasis on psychic development. The practical Second House concerns with money and comfort need to be attended to before the uncharted territory of the psyche is explored. In this way we can develop psychic skills without becoming ungrounded.

In any chart there will be a focus on hidden things when an outer

planet moves through the Eighth House. Modern psychology has expanded our understanding of the hidden things to include exploration of the unconscious, the part of the psyche hidden from view.

The Eighth House has traditionally been associated with death; as in the Tarot, Death usually stands not for literal death but for separation from the old and spiritual renewal. In a more literal sense, the death of relatives sometimes brings inheritance with it, and planets transiting through the house may indicate a gift of money. While the Second House focuses on income to provide for bodily needs, the Eighth House deals with the wider issues of money as a force in society and as a source of power in the individual's life. When the spiritual and sexual needs of this house are not expressed the desire for power or money may replace them.

We can fulfil the Eighth House part of our lives by allowing ourselves space to consider the mysteries of life and respecting the power of sexuality.

The Ninth House:

House of Exploration

travel; contact with foreign countries and cultures; study; further education; philosophy; belief systems; religion

Associated with Sagittarius and Jupiter

The Ninth House shows the areas of life where we can develop a broader perspective. This can be through study, through spiritual experience, through the development of a philosophy or belief system, or more literally through foreign travel or contacts with other cultures. Being opposite to the Third House of the Environment, the Ninth House develops experience of the environment into a meaningful philosophy and draws conclusions from what has been learned.

By looking at the sign on the house cusp and any planets in the house we see how a person reaches out for something greater than herself. For instance, with Taurus on the Ninth House cusp, the individual would experience a sense of awe and wonder through the appreciation of landscape, while someone with Aquarius here would be more immediately inspired by the vastness of space and the night sky. With Venus in the Ninth, beauty, harmony and aesthetics would be an essential part of the individual's philosophy, and she would be strongly attracted to foreign countries and foreign people. Involvement in politics is also shown by the Ninth House. Just as the Third House represents the community, so the Ninth House stands for a wider community and processes of government and law which hold that community together. Emphasis on the house could indicate self-expression through politics or law, while transits of present-day planets through the house often coincide with court cases. With Pluto transiting through the Ninth, for instance, a person might go through a process of self-confrontation and transformation initiated by her involvement in a long legal battle. With Sun, Jupiter, Mercury or Saturn in the Ninth it is likely the person concerned will be involved in the academic world. With Mars in the Ninth at birth she may feel impelled by a spirit of adventure towards foreign countries, or to explore world philosophy or religion.

Transits of the house can indicate the undertaking of higher education, private study, or foreign travel. For some people travel is combined with a quest for meaning and enlightenment, and the discovery

of a teacher or a guru. Emphasis on the house suggests that the person may learn best by becoming a disciple or apprentice to a learned and wise teacher. Equally, a strong Ninth House may indicate that she herself will become a teacher of these wider issues. Discoveries about life, death, mystery and meaning in the Eighth House, essentially private and secret in nature, are made public in the Ninth. For instance, with Leo on the Ninth House cusp the teacher of these discoveries would have dramatic flair and attract a wide following. In contrast, Virgo on the Ninth would indicate someone dedicated to truth whose humility led her to avoid the limelight.

The Ninth House is associated with human attempts to describe the indescribable, to create ritual and ceremony that preserve flashes and echoes of the inspiration behind them. It tells about the part of our lives where we have freedom to develop our own philosophy.

The Tenth House:

House of Status

public life; status in the community; the world outside the home; career, success and failure; public standing; reputation; ambitions

Associated with Capricorn and Saturn

The cusp of the Tenth House is the Midheaven by most systems of house division, the part of the zodiac highest in the sky at the time of birth. Those born at noon have the Sun at the Midheaven, and they usually become well-known, for the Sun, which represents their personal identity, is shining high overhead. While the First House and the Ascendant represent parts of the self we show on the outside as 'personality', the Tenth House and Midheaven represent a more deliberately chosen, more formal, public image. The sign on the Tenth House cusp shows how we would like to be seen, the role we would like to take in the community. Sometimes the combination of Tenth House with Sunsign and Ascendant can be surprising. A very sensitive and withdrawn Sun-Piscean, for instance, whose Cancer Ascendant reinforces her emotional receptivity and compassion, happens to have Midheaven and Tenth House in Aries. She teaches martial arts and is seen publicly as a tough and resourceful pioneer type, though all her friends know her softer, watery nature and personality. and she is able to express her compassion in her work with students. People often take up a career associated with the sign of the Tenth House, because that is a way for them to become more like the image they want for themselves. For instance, with Virgo at the Midheaven a person may take up nursing and through the nature of the work discover Virgoan healing skills within herself.

Planets in the Tenth House tell us about desire for recognition and the likely achievements. With many planets in the Tenth the person concerned will be known beyond her immediate circle of acquaintances; she will achieve some kind of fame or success. With Mercury here, for instance, the person may become known for writing; with Venus in the Tenth for her art (or her beauty).

Difficulties in the Tenth House are shown by challenging aspects to planets situated there, and they are associated with problems with one's public image. Sometimes the person has difficulties in her career; sometimes she suffers anxieties about her professional or social reputation. Yet challenges to the Tenth House have their benefits

strengthening the will and reaffirming purpose. Often a 'difficult' Tenth House is found in the chart of someone widely recognised for notable achievement.

The Tenth House contrasts with its opposite, the Fourth. While the Fourth House is connected with the most private aspects of our lives, and represents home life, the Tenth is the most public, representing the world outside. As a present-day planet moves through someone's Tenth House she often experiences the need to bring a part of herself out into the world; with Uranus transiting the Tenth she might become known for her unconventional political views, for instance. The two houses together, Fourth and Tenth, tell us about the parental expectations of the child. If there are many planets in the Tenth it is likely that one or both parents have exerted a pressure towards success.

The people we admire and are influenced by may have some connection with the Tenth House in our charts. If Leo is on the Tenth House, for instance, Leonians often have an impressive or formative effect. Unconsciously the person concerned allows them to become role models as if they were more 'adult' than her. For similar reasons the Tenth House indicates something of the relationship with authority – difficulties here could mean compulsive rebellion or an intimidated kowtowing. The Tenth House shows the need that everyone has for acceptance of her worth by the community. It describes the strong need for a sense of purpose and meaningful work that is in tune with the individual's sense of herself. Emotional problems stemming from unemployment, from compulsory retirement or redundancy show how important it is for the individual to feel purposeful and worthy of status and respect. We can fulfil the Tenth House part of our lives best by learning to accept praise and compliments, and by taking seriously our need for a sense of purpose and desire for just recognition.

The Eleventh House:

House of Ideals

shared pleasures; hobbies; interests; comradeship; futuristic visions and dreams; causes; communal experiments; movements; sisterhood

Associated with Aquarius and Uranus

This house shows the part played in life by the inspiration of an ideal. While the Fifth House (opposite to the Eleventh) points to individual fulfilment and creativity, the Eleventh focuses on what is shared with a group. When the Eleventh House is emphasised in a chart by several planets it is likely that communal experiences will be very important in the person's life. She may spend much of her time seeking the right group of kindred spirits who share her inspiration. Even when there are no planets in the Eleventh, the sign on the house cusp shows the way such a group is approached. For instance, Gemini on the Eleventh House might show a very lively need for the stimulation a group provides, while Cancer on the Eleventh would indicate a more emotional investment in the group. The 'group' associated with the Eleventh House is different from either the family or the community of neighbours in which a person finds herself.

Eleventh House associations are chosen because of the shared dedication to a common cause or a common interest. This might be a hobby or leisure activity; Venus in Taurus in the Eleventh could indicate involvement in a choir or other singing group – not professionally but as a leisure interest. The common cause that brings people together may be dedication to an ideal or political commitment. When the house is emphasised it is very important to the person concerned that she finds those who share her dreams about the future, her commitment to an ideal. She may engage in numerous attempts to find or found the perfect community, experiment with communal living, alternatives in education or social organisation, or with co-operatives. The sense of sisterhood within women's organisations, of comradeship in the co-operative and socialist movements and of fellowship in religious communities are all Eleventh House themes. The need of the Eleventh House is to find others with whom to share hope and a vision which the rest of the world seems not to understand. Often those with the house emphasised have felt excluded by society as outsiders or have chosen to exclude themselves, while they feel a sense of kinship with the whole world. The individual solutions of the Fifth House are

not possible for them and they keep seeking until they find the circle of friends who share their vision.

We can attend to the Eleventh House part of our lives by making space for friendships that come from a shared interest. Eleventh House relationships have a sense of freedom about them, because they are chosen (rather than inherited) and yet not bound by the ties of sexual and intimate relationship or the responsibilities and conflicts of partnership in working life. Eleventh House friends may work together for a cause, however it is the cause that animates rather than the work itself, and it gives a greater context to their interaction. It is with this inspiration of communal purpose that Eleventh House friendships are able to survive their internal problems and competition with other strong relationships in the person's life. The sense of companionship, of being shoulder-to-shoulder working for an ideal, can be very precious. Often these friendships last for years, outliving the different causes to which the friends have been committed, for it is the underlying idealism that brings them together.

The Twelfth House:

House of Seclusion

solitude; retreat and withdrawal;
reflection; sanctuaries; healing;
illness; drugs and addiction;
resolutions and endings; meditation;
mysticism; the spiritual life

Associated with Pisces and Neptune

The Twelfth House is the part of the horoscope that shows the areas where we withdraw, retreat and focus inward. Because the horoscope is a circle, the Twelfth House brings us back to the First, just as retreat and solitude allow a process of renewal to take place. The Twelfth House is opposite to the Sixth with its focus on health and work in the world. It emphasises the spiritual aspects of healing and work behind the scenes.

When someone has a strong emphasis on the Twelfth House she may live or work in a secluded setting. She will be drawn to people with special needs who require sanctuary and a protected environment.

Emphasis on the Twelfth House by Sun, Moon or many planets often shows a great gift as a healer or psychic, or as a worker in any area where suffering is encountered.

The Twelfth House (with the Fourth and the Eighth) is one of the gates to the unconscious, to the world of sleep and dreams, where we are able to retreat and renew our energy.

The Twelfth House also shows ways of escape that are not helpful to us; this may be through use and abuse of alcohol or drugs, for instance. In coming to terms with the Twelfth House in our charts we often have to face the instinct to sabotage ourselves, the enemy inside who criticises and tears apart all our achievements. Doris Lessing named this inner critic the 'self-hater' and in *The Four-Gated City* her heroine takes a path through madness to face the enemy within. It is the self-hater in the unconscious that is often behind a feeling we are being attacked by unknown enemies. By consideration of the Twelfth House in our charts we may be able to understand better our own self-destructive tendencies, and release ourselves from anxiety and the suspicion that others are working against us.

Often the movement of planets through this house indicates a process of coming to terms with the meaning and implications of illness or misfortune in the person's life. The sign on the Twelfth House cusp indicates the approach taken. For instance, Aries on the Twelfth House cusp represents a battle with illness or suffering, courageous

or outraged. This could be a lifelong battle with a serious condition at one extreme, or a naively infuriated response to a bout of flu at the other. Through the Twelfth House we learn how to complete processes and to manage endings. This may be the end of a relationship, and the process of separation, or it may be letting go of life itself and the process of dying. For someone with Gemini on the Twelfth House the process of letting go might involve learning to stop busy mental activity and find her own inner stillness. It is part of the House's meaning that we find out how to integrate into our lives our mystical longings for unity with the whole of the cosmos.

Solitude and reflection are the key to the Twelfth House. Often a person goes through a long struggle with loneliness and finally discovers that this stems from her desire for the space to develop her inner life. Those who have many planets in the Twelfth House may take the path of the mystic.

We can explore the Twelfth House part of our lives by providing for our own solitude, retreating from the world intermittently, and by learning practices of meditation and contemplation.

8
Planetary Interrelationships
The geometry of the solar system

The ancient skywatcher noticed that when the Moon was half-full it was a quarter-circle away from the Sun (90° away). The planets, too, as they moved among the zodiacal constellations, could be measured to see the angle of their separation from each other. In astrology this angle is called an *aspect*. The aspects are the geometrical angles between planets, measured from our viewpoint on Earth (see Figures 8.1 and 8.2). (The word 'angle' is used as a technical term for the Ascendant, Midheaven, Imum Coeli and Descendant, as explained in Chapter 3.)

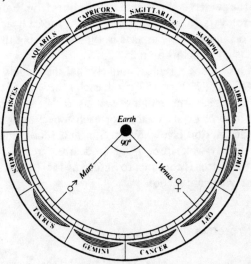

Figure 8.1 *The degrees between two planets measured from Earth.*

The aspects between planets show us how one planet relates to another, and so represents the way one part of the self relates to another. For instance, if, in a given horoscope, Venus is in Leo it would indicate that the person is warm-hearted and self-expressive in her affections. Mars in Taurus would show her hard-working, determined way of asserting herself. We see from Figure 8.1 that the two planets, Mars and Venus, make an aspect of exactly 90° because each is placed at 15° of its sign, showing there is confrontation and challenge between her fiery, outgoing affectionate nature and her more earthy, slow-moving, practical assertion of herself. The challenge between these two parts creates a tension. At times it feels like a block but the energy of the challenge is fuel for dynamic changes. In Figure 8.2 and Figure 8.3 the Moon is 60° away from Mars and we call this a *sextile* aspect. Mars is 90° from Saturn (called a *square*), Venus is 120° from the Moon (called a *trine*) and Venus is also 180° from Mars (called an *opposition*). The Moon and Uranus are close to each other; this is known as a *conjunction*. The Sun is 45° away from Venus (called a *semi-square*) and also semi-square to Saturn. Venus is also making a square aspect to Saturn, with the Sun midway between the two planets. When aspects are drawn into the horoscope, only the line *between* the planets is shown and not the lines from Earth (See Figure 8.3). Astrologers do not always mark in the aspect lines but provide a diagram detailing all the aspects in the chart, using the symbols for the aspects given below on p 252-255.

In one horoscope it is most unlikely that the planets will be placed exactly 45°, 60°, 120° or 180° from each other, but if the number of degrees is close to these figures we say they are *within orb* of an aspect. The *orbs* or allowances for each aspect are given with each aspect's description below. When Sun and Moon are involved, we allow a slightly wider orb, 1° or 2° degrees greater. For example, Mars at 8° Taurus is conjunct to Saturn at 15° Taurus and we would call this a wide conjunction.

The Interpretation of Aspects

In the past aspects were regarded as 'good' if they were trines and sextiles, and 'bad' if they were oppositions, squares and semi-squares. The interpretation of conjunctions has depended on the nature of the

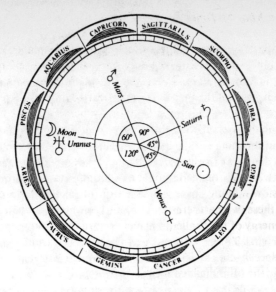

Figure 8.2 *Aspects measured from Earth*

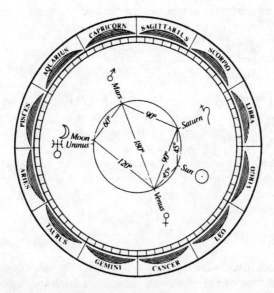

Figure 8.3 *The aspects drawn into the horoscope*

planets involved. Most contemporary astrologers have abandoned these 'good' and 'bad' categories and we now see aspects as difficult, challenging and formative, or easy, flowing and harmonious. The stressful aspects add strength to a chart; with too many easy aspects the person may lack depth and endurance.

It is very important to see that every aspect has the potential for growth and change within it, that the more difficult the aspect the greater strength it can give to the chart and the person. We need to feel the power of that challenge rather than only concentrating on the difficulty. We should also remember that the planets in the sky are in constant change, one with another; there is always a new pattern being woven. Through our lives the planets return to, and repeat, aspects they have made before; they move to a harmonious relationship where before there was a challenging one; they move into conflict from a harmonious beginning. Any aspect is one phase in the relationship between two planets. We are born with certain emphases but, as the planets move on, we also change and grow into new possibilities.

The Major Aspects

☌ *Conjunction* 0° apart, or nearly so. (An orb of 8° or 9° is allowed).

A conjunction is the coming together of the energies of two (or more) planets. Conjunctions in ancient times were the most noticed and regarded of all the aspects; they are often impressively visible in the sky. Modern astrologers also take great notice of a close conjunction in the chart; it means that those parts of the self the planets represent are intimately bound together. For instance, Mercury represents communication, mental processes and nerves, while Uranus represents individuality and uniqueness, and the desire for sudden change. A Mercury/Uranus conjunction might be expressed by abrupt speech, nervousness, a jumpy manner and a highly original and inventive way of thinking and communicating.

☍ *Opposition* 180° apart, or nearly so. (An orb of 8° or 9° is allowed).

An opposition occurs when two planets are opposite each other. It means that the planets work in very different ways from each other,

so differently in fact that there will be some similarities, as polar opposites are also alike. Oppositions are like a tug-of-war within us, pulling in two opposite directions, rather than clashing or colliding. The advantage of oppositions is that they provide us with a sense of greater perspective. If there are several planets in Cancer, for instance, another in Capricorn gives the opposite viewpoint. Planets in Cancer increase subjectivity and emotional responsiveness, while Capricorn is practical in pursuing objectives. The advantage of a Capricornian approach acting as a balance is obvious, even with the tug-of-war it brings. (There are also similarities between Cancer and Capricorn; though both like to take the initiative they are both somewhat introverted and private in expression.)

With many oppositions in the chart, the person tends to experience external difficulties in her life cycle rather than suffering from internal conflicts.

□ *Square* 90° apart, or nearly so. (An orb of 7° or 8° is allowed).

The 90° aspect is one quarter of a circle, and four of these aspects create a square inside the circle. Many cultures use a square symbol to show the foundations of the world and square aspects in the chart give us something solid to build on. They are tense but provide strength. Squares have the energy of collision; the two planets involved seem to be coming towards each other head on. For instance, the possessiveness a planet in Taurus may express meets head on with the detachment of a planet in Aquarius. There are also similarities in signs that square each other, in this example Taurus and Aquarius are both fixed signs and they share determination of purpose. Squares show a more internal conflict than oppositions and have a dynamic energy; the challenge within them animates the horoscope.

△ *Trine* 120° apart, or nearly so. (An orb of 7° or 8° is allowed).

A trine is an aspect of 120°, that is, one third of a circle. Trines are found between planets at similar degrees in signs of the same element (see Chapter 5).

The *trine* is one side of an equilateral *tri*angle, one of the most ancient symbols of abundance and of the Great Goddess in ancient times.

Trines express harmony, an easy flow. The elemental similarity means that the planets in question are 'on the same wavelength', and

tell of talents and blessings that the person has inherited at birth. When there are many easy aspects in the chart, and few challenges, trines may be expressed as self-indulgent patterns of behaviour. Moon in Scorpio trine to Mercury in Cancer in such a chart, for instance, could give an instinctive ease of communication covering a secretive and intense nature and sentimental attachment to the past. In most charts, however, such an aspect would be helpful and would ease other problems, offering a means of communicating some of the intense feelings of Moon in Scorpio.

✳ *Sextile* 60° apart, or nearly so. (An orb of 4° or 5° is allowed).

A sextile is an aspect of 60°, the angle used to draw up the hexagon and the six-pointed star, both of which have been recognised by many cultures to be symbols of harmony. The hexagon is the most economical way of joining together adjacent cells; if circles are squashed together they will tend to form hexagons, which is why the cells of a honeycomb are hexagonal. The sextile expresses openness to experience and the ability to take opportunity. It has not so much the perfected as the potential harmony of the trine. Two planets that are sextile will work well together and offer opportunities for growth.

For instance, Saturn at 27° Aries is sextile to Venus at 26° Gemini. The assertive determination to learn and achieve of Saturn in this sign can be activated by an open and friendly nature which Venus shows. The person makes many contacts and yet stays in touch with her acquaintances.

∟ *Semi-square* 45° apart, or nearly so. (An orb of 2° or 3° is allowed).

A semi-square, an aspect of 45°, is half a square aspect and has a similar energy of conflict and challenge, though somewhat weaker in effect.

⊼ *Quincunx or Inconjunct* 150° apart, or nearly so. (An orb of 2° or 3° is allowed).

A quincunx or inconjunct expresses a strain or unease between the planets, and seems to have a particular importance in medical astrology where it indicates stresses. Planets forming quincunxes are

totally different in their expression; their nature seems to be totally
'other'. There is not the same similarity in polarity that we find with
the opposition aspect. Yet a quincunx can also bring unexpected
benefits. Sun in Sagittarius quincunx Moon in Taurus shows strain
between such very different signs, but the person with this aspect is
likely to be surprising and stimulating.

The Minor Aspects

There are other, less influential, aspects that may be found in the
chart. The *Semi-sextile* (30°) ⊻ and *Sesquiquadrate* (135°) ⬚ suggest
strain. The *Quintile* (72°) Q and *Biquintile* (144°) BQ are two aspects
not yet well understood, but seem to relate to originality and
invention.

The Aspect Patterns

Every chart presents a particular pattern of aspects which is shared
only with those born on the same day. However, there are some general aspect patterns and shapes of chart which recur frequently.[1] Further reading and study is necessary to fully explore aspects. Useful
books are listed in the Astrology section of the Bibliography at the
end of this book. By understanding the patterns of the planets within
our own horoscopes we are able to form an overview of the interaction within ourselves of all the planetary parts of the psyche.

Reference

1   To find out more about aspect patterns we recommend *Alan
Oken's Complete Astrology*, Bantam Books, 1980.

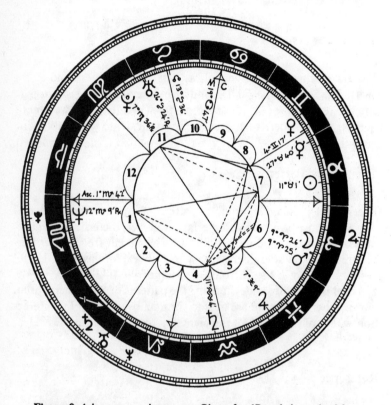

Figure 9 *A horoscope drawn up. Chart for 'Rosa', born 1st May 1962 at 5.31 p.m. in Santiago, Chile, with transits for 28th May 1987. The inner circle shows the pattern of the major aspects between the planets at birth (broken lines harmonious aspects, unbroken lines challenging aspects). The next wheel from the centre shows the positions of the planets at birth, with their exact degrees and minutes (subdivisions of a degree) of the zodiac signs, marked into the wheel of the houses (Placidus house system). The outer wheel shows the positions of transiting planets on 28.5.87.*

9
Integration
Understanding the Chart as a Whole

Once we have learned the separate components of astrology – the planets, signs, houses and aspects – and their unique interplay within each chart, we can gradually begin to develop an overview of a horoscope that combines all the necessary information for interpretation.

Sun, Moon, Ascendant and Strong Planets

On first looking at the horoscope we focus on the Moon, Sun and Ascendant, the strongest single factors in the personality. We cannot rigidly define parts of the psyche, for the unconscious self (Moon), conscious self (Sun) and the way we project ourselves when we meet people (Ascendant) all overlap and affect each other. However, it can be helpful to see the Ascendant as a window through which we see the world, and through which the world sees us. Behind that 'window' the person looking out can manifest strongly the energy not only of Moon and Sun but also of any other planet highlighted in her chart. This highlighting can be the result of strong aspects to the planet or by its placement in a sign in which its energy is expressed with ease.

The Pattern of the Whole Horoscope

All the planets, signs and houses, and the pattern they make by their interaction with each other, are important for interpretive purposes.
It would be useful here to remember the basic precepts outlined in

Chapter 3. The planets represent the basic energies universal to all of us; they are the subjects of the sentence, answering the question *what?* The signs describe *how* the planets manifest, the houses show *where*, while the aspects show the interrelationship between parts of the self.

Sometimes simple keywords help when combining the meaning of houses, signs and planets. Venus in Capricorn in the Twelfth House can be described as the instinct to relate (Venus) constructively (Capricorn) in the House of Seclusion (Twelfth House). One interpretation for this placement might be that the person concerned has a committed approach to relationships and is drawn to people who need a quiet and healing space for personal interaction. This Venus placement would be modified by other factors. If it occurred in the chart of someone with the Sun in Sagittarius, for instance, such an approach to relationships would give a more stable and introspective side to the personality (Capricorn is an earthsign) than is usually the case for fiery, restless Sagittarius. In the chart of someone with Sun in Pisces, the Piscean emphasis on healing would be echoed by Venus in the Twelfth House, and the person might work one-to-one with clients as a therapist or counsellor.

It is beyond the scope of this book to teach how to interpret a chart in detail. At the end of this chapter there is a reading list providing information for further study.

When learning astrology it is easy to become lost in detail, or to be too strongly influenced by one writer's analysis of a planetary placement or an aspect between planets in the chart. Readers are advised to maintain an open mind about alternative interpretations and to be particularly attentive to the more constructive meanings they read. Contemporary astrology leans more and more towards positive interpretation that can be of practical help in our lives.

As you learn more astrology you are likely to find that some of the most productive insights will come from your own thoughts of how the many factors of the individual chart will combine. The way the authors learned to interpret charts was by practising with friends, who helped by giving feedback. Any chart reading must be done with responsibility and care, as people can be badly affected by adverse comments and those who have just started to study astrology may not have the experience to see the positive potential in a difficult placement or aspect. Damage can also be done by imposing one's own

judgements on people. The main purpose of all chart interpretation is to validate the person's experience and provide helpful insights.

When first learning to read horoscopes the best information on the chart comes from its owner. (If you cannot imagine how her Venus-Jupiter opposition works, she can probably tell you!) Astrological information gained in this way stays with you far better than theories in books. The way a person manifests her chart is unique. We can learn about the psychology of the planets and signs, but their particular form of expression largely depends on the individual's experience and consciousness. The more you know of a person's circumstances and life choices, the better her horoscope can be understood. No two astrologers will ever give identical readings (although similar themes should emerge) for interpreting the chart is as much a creative as a learned process.

Moving Towards Wholeness

While the natal horoscope is a picture of one moment frozen in time – the solar system at the time of birth – we are not limited to this picture alone. As the planets move they make contrasts and echoes with the pattern of planetary placements at birth. It is by interpreting these annual or monthly movements (the transits) that we can forecast and explain trends in our lives. Many astrologers are moving away from prediction towards a counselling approach, which uses astrology to help us make sense of what is already happening. As a planet transits the natal chart (see Chap:er 3) a particular side of the individual is activated and comes to the fore. The future movements of the planets give us a context for the personal changes and struggles we experience in the present.

For instance, let us consider a woman who is, during a certain phase in her life, experiencing a great deal of confusion as Neptune in Capricorn opposes her Sun in Cancer. Neptune is not *causing* her feeling that she has no personal boundaries and is part of everything that is happening in the world around her. Rather, Neptune's movement in the heavens is a planetary signpost that can help her understand the process going on within her psyche. It is the Neptunian energy within herself, her own mystical instincts, that seem to overwhelm the sense of self-integration that her Sun represents.

As Neptune moves out of its transiting opposition to her Sun two years later it is likely that she will have reached a resolution in this crisis. She will have found a way to express the Neptunian part of herself which strengthens, rather than threatens, her sense of her own identity. As the Sun was in Cancer at birth, she will probably find that expressing herself in a Cancerian way, imaginatively and sensitively, provides scope to integrate her Neptunian empathy and compassion into her life more fully.

Astrology can best be used not to forecast events but to provide some knowledge of the pattern of a person's self-development. We can learn a great deal about ourselves from studying the cycles of planetary movement as the planets interrelate with our horoscopes.

Mind and Body

We cannot separate emotional self-development and healing on a more physical level.

Astrologers and natural healers are beginning to understand health in a new way. Health is increasingly understood to be a state of balance within the person, and disease – dis-ease – as a disturbance of that balance. Imbalances in the individual may manifest in emotional patterns, in disturbances in function, or in organic changes in the physical body. The horoscope gives a picture of wholeness (the entire circle of the zodiac and all ten planets that appear within it) and shows ways that the balance within that wholeness may be disturbed by over-emphasis or conflict in certain areas. Just as modern astrologers do not view the planets as malign influences attacking the individual, so the healer is evolving a new, and at the same time ancient, approach to disease. Natural healers do not focus on the 'attacking' germs or viruses but on the susceptibility of the individual to these agents.

It has also been suggested that the onset of disease or misfortune may be an unconscious attempt on the part of the individual to restore inner harmony on deeper levels. Just as difficult astrological transits and aspects may help us to grow, so the experience of physical illness may sometimes allow the individual to become healthier in the widest sense, once the mental, emotional and spiritual well-being of the person, as well as her physical health, has been taken into consideration.

For instance, a person who has felt a sense of isolation and loneliness over many years previously may never have been able to find a way to break out of this and make contact with others. When she develops health problems she may find that part of the process of coming to terms with their implications involves asking people for help and sharing feelings about her life as a whole. Many people in such a situation would say that their illness has led them to self-healing on a deeper emotional level. From the emotional level the healing process tends to move, often only gradually, on to the physical level.

The healing process is more than just the removal of symptoms or the passing of a challenging transit to the horoscope; it involves the rediscovery of a sense of wholeness.

In the past medical astrology has been greatly concerned with the identification of disease factors in a chart and the prediction of future illness based on these findings. We are doubtful of the usefulness of such predictions which often cause unnecessary alarm. (It requires an extremely proficient astrologer to be able to distinguish whether a tendency in the chart will manifest only emotionally or on the level of physical disease.)

Medical astrology, in fact, has a far more creative role to play. Using astrological correspondences the experienced astrologer can tell from a horoscope some of the factors in the chart involved in any existing health problems. The planets, signs, houses and aspects identified as relevant will tell of emotional and mental stresses as well as physical ill-health. By using astrological interpretation to better understand these conflicts we can discover ways to initiate changes in our lives. The increased sense of power this can give us is a major step on the way to self-healing.

Useful books for studying medical astrology are listed in the relevant section of the Bibliography at the end of this book.

The authors do not believe that all disease can be automatically controlled or arrested by changes in attitude or in emotional patterns, but they have found that emotional healing is the prerequisite for any lasting cure. Even if we have no health problems we can still turn our attention to difficult areas of the chart (which all of us have). Constructive consideration of the challenges presented is a form of preventive medicine. It can provide us with a framework for acceptance of the whole of the self, and guide us towards the choices we need to make the move towards wholeness.

Further Reading

Chart calculation, drawing-up and interpretation

Parker, Derek and Parker, Julia, *The Compleat Astrologer*, Mitchell Beazley, 1975.

Mayo, Jeff, *Astrology*, The English Universities Press, (Teach Yourself Series), 1964.

Oken, Alan, *Alan Oken's Complete Astrology: A Complete Guide to Astrological Awareness*, Bantam Books, 1980.

Hone, Margaret, *The Modern Textbook of Astrology*, L N Fowler, 1978.

Edmund Jones, March, *The Guide to Horoscope Interpretation*, Quest Books, 1974.

Meyer, Michael, *A Handbook for the Humanistic Astrologer*, Anchor Books, 1974.

Rose, Christina, *Astrological Counselling*, Aquarian Press, 1982.

Self-understanding through astrology

Arroyo, Stephen, *Astrology, Karma and Transformation*, CRCS Publications, 1978.

Greene, Liz, *Relating: An Astrological Guide to Living with Others on a Small Planet*, Coventure, 1978.

Ruperti, Alexander, *Cycles of Becoming – The Planetary Pattern of Growth*, CRCS Publications, 1978.

10
Into the Future

A Holistic View

When we come to understand all parts of the horoscope, and discover how they may be integrated into one complex picture, it becomes clear that every part is valuable.

Astrology teaches the same basic truths when it is used to understand human society on a global level. In the natal horoscope the positions of the planets show a picture of the energies available to the individual. The patterns in the heavens also manifest the spirit of the age. Astrology originally evolved as a means to understand the destiny of nations and people; it is only for a little over two thousand years that it has been used to provide personal information for individuals.

Astrology can help us to understand the destiny of all Earth-dwellers, rather than the fate of particular nations, if we take a holistic view, seeing all peoples as part of one human whole.

The Age of Aquarius

In the twentieth century many people have been inspired by a vision of a future without divisions between nations. Often this idealised vision has been hailed as the coming 'new age', a term which originates from the astrological cycle of Great Ages. Each age lasts between 2,000 and 2,200 years and is named after one of the twelve zodiac signs. Rather than following each other in the usual order, the cycle of ages moves *backwards* through the zodiac. The succession of Great Ages comes from the oscillation of the Earth's poles over a period of

around 26,000 years. Each year at the spring Equinox the Sun occupies a place in the heavens very slightly further backwards against the zodiacal constellations.

The beginning of the Age of Pisces was around 0 CE. We are now almost at the end of this age and about to enter the Age of Aquarius. Different traditions of astrology disagree about the date of the change-over of the ages, and it cannot in any case be confined to a single year. It seems likely that the Age of Aquarius is about one hundred or more years away. Many believe the new age will start in 2000 CE; certainly the concerns of each new age are relevant several hundred years before the approximate date of the changeover.

The Aquarian alternative is not yet established, but since a multiple conjunction of planets in Aquarius in 1962 many people have been inspired by visions of the group rather than the family as a social and emotional base, a group chosen rather than inherited. During a transitional period people tend to feel rootless and need the continuing inspiration of the idea of the coming new age.

The sign of Aquarius suggests the possibility of developing new ways of organising society, for Aquarius is a sign of revolutionary and evolutionary changes. Some writers have described the new age of Aquarius as 'The Age of Universal Brotherhood', and often illustrations depict a young Caucasian man as the image of the future. Such words and pictures are badly chosen. It would be far more appropriate to show those who have not been invited to the feast during the last two thousand years – women, the disabled, lesbians and homosexuals, and all the people whose cultures have been destroyed or fragmented by colonisation and invasion. The Aquarian impulse is towards equality, towards a recognition of humanity through the value of the individual, towards an awareness of our participation together on one planet. All that has been excluded has to be rediscovered to create a new wholeness.

Though the Aquarian vision is inspiring we cannot be certain the new age will manifest Aquarian energy in these most positive ways. We tend to believe so because we are part of the transition ourselves – the generations that straddle the passing age and the one oncoming.

It is important we understand the sign of Aquarius in order to bring about the most positive Aquarian expression, retaining some scepticism and full awareness of the faults, as well as the virtues, of the sign. One of the major failings of Aquarius is the tendency to arrogance

about one's own enlightenment or evolution. Though the message of Aquarius is one of equality, tolerance does not always extend to those who continue to practise traditional ways, even when they are not oppressing others by doing so. A truly evolutionary society needs to increase people's options rather than to replace them. The Aquarian Age, positively expressed, should bring about more choices in social organisation, in ways of living and in ways to meet emotional needs.

Millennial Anxiety

The changeover from one Great Age to another every 2000 years or so seems to be a time of flux and great anxiety. There have been many 'end of the world' scares throughout human history, and at the beginning of the Age of Pisces around 0 CE there was a particularly widespread belief that the world would be destroyed.

At the end of the second millennium since the Age of Pisces began, astrologers are often asked to comment on the years ahead. If we examine the planets' movements up until the year 2050 CE we find no special reason for panic. There are planetary conjunctions in Capricorn in the late 1980s and in the early 1990s which *are* very remarkable, and we can expect that world events will reflect their intensity. The millennial anxiety that accompanies the end of a Great Age makes many wary about the conjunctions to come. The massing of most of the planets in Capricorn precedes their movement into the sign of Aquarius at their differing paces during the last years of this century and the beginning of the next. This movement into Aquarius is a separate phenomenon from the arrival of the Age of Aquarius, but because of the time in which it occurs it would seem to be astrologically significant. It is as if the planets have to pass through the bottleneck of Capricorn before the dawning of the Aquarian age.

The over-emphasis on Capricorn shows us that humankind has become unbalanced and has unbalanced the world by systematised organisation and control. At the same time, the positive side of endurant Capricorn might indicate the gathering of all human resources to ensure the Earth's survival. Thankfully, at a time when hope is particularly needed, we find no evidence that the planets of the solar

system portend annihilation of life on their sister Earth, but rather a period of reassessment and reorganisation.

A Shift of Consciousness

It is the movements of the outermost planets, Pluto, Neptune and Uranus, which indicate changes in society on a very broad scale. Since the discovery of Pluto in the 1930s, we have been experiencing a profound change in the context of human fears of world destruction. In the past most cultures have interpreted natural disasters to be manifestations of the wrath of the gods, but now we ourselves have taken their place as potential destroyers of the Earth. Humankind has found its mass destructive power, symbolised by Pluto, and so needs to bring out from within the transformative and regenerative power of this same planet. As we have access to the negative Plutonian energy within ourselves, so we can also contact its positive expression. The message of Pluto is that *we* have the power – we can blow ourselves up, or not, as we choose. We can use the transformative Plutonian power to stop the destruction, once we fully realise that it is ourselves and neither the gods nor 'fate' which have determined our present situation.

Though we cannot rely on the arrival of the new age to solve our problems as we cross a mythical dateline, thinking optimistically of love and peace, the impetus for positive changes is stronger than the reactions against them.

To enter the Aquarian Age we must enter it first in mind and in spirit, though personal growth and healing can never be a substitute for work towards societal transformation. Work towards planetary healing has to proceed on all levels simultaneously.

A vivid understanding is required of the active role to be played in *making* a future. This cannot be done merely by believing in survival, but by actions in the present that are committed to the future. Our actions need to be informed by understanding that the world is in a perilous state, not only because of the possibility of ecological or nuclear disaster but also because of the imbalance in the sharing of resources and power.

The shift of consciousness must take place at many levels, in our

relationships with ourselves, with each other and with the Earth as a whole.

Beyond Pluto

As we consider the state of world crisis that has arisen since the discovery of Pluto in the 1930s it is helpful to learn there may be other planets to be found beyond Pluto. The discovery of a new planet seems to coincide with a collective shift of consciousness in the way the world is viewed.

Astronomers have calculated the likely orbit for a planet beyond Pluto and this planet is now being sought as the solar system is explored. The planet has been provisionally named Persephone, the first planet (rather than an asteroid or moon) to be named after a goddess in 3000 years. The authors of this book believe that the search for Persephone correlates with the growing awareness that women's vision and experience need to play a far greater part in the shaping of society than they do at the present time. The Persephone consciousness tells us that when the Earth has sorrowed long for her loss she will return.

Past, Present and Future

Newly identified planets are new only to us, their human discoverers; like all planets of the solar system they orbited the Sun long before the evolution of life on Earth. The planets interest us today in a new way but they, together with the Sun and Moon, have preoccupied human consciousness for as long as written records have existed. In the past the planets have provided themes for our mythology; in the present they allow us to explore the inner space of the psyche through their astrological interpretation. Through our desire to understand them better by the peaceful exploration of outer space they animate futuristic visions.

The archaeologist who translates an ancient manuscript of sky omens is considering the same Moon as the seven-year-old who takes a book out of the library on lunar exploration.

The discovery of the new is also the appreciation of the very ancient, for past, present and future are always woven together. To the wise-women of the ancient world the phases of the Moon represented the three strands in the knot of time. We are not usually aware of the darkened part of the Moon when we gaze at the growing crescent of the new lunar cycle, just as we often forget the past when we move on towards the future. But in certain atmospheric conditions we can see the dark part of the Moon faintly shining with a reflected glow from earth. In folklore this phenomenon has been described as 'the new Moon with the old Moon in her arms'.

We can take with us into the future the long tradition of the ancient sky-watchers and their awe and respect for the changing sky around them. The inheritance from our ancestors lives within us and gives us the images in our dreams, in our art and literature and in the stories we tell our children. The dark circle of the old Moon of the past is never lost, for the young Moon of the future cradles her grandmother in her luminous arms.

Epilogue

Time passed and the twelve sisters saw and heard that all was not well on the Earth. They discovered the existence of war, of torture, rape, imprisonment and slavery. They found out that riches piled up while people starved. They saw the beautiful Earth herself despoiled. They watched lives cramped and empty of the joy of self-expression.

It took time for them to take in their shock at this state of affairs. After many thousands of years grieving they held council together. At first they were seeking the culprits: some blamed their brothers, some blamed each other.

They said *Aries* had emphasised activity and courage so that humankind worshipped action and glorified war.

They said *Taurus* had over-emphasised the value of beautiful possessions so that everyone wanted the best for themselves.

They said *Gemini* taught people how to manipulate the truth and that she made them restless for novelty.

They said *Cancer* taught love of security so that people only cared about those closest to them, and held tightly to them even when they needed to leave.

They accused *Leo* of teaching people to crave importance and power. They said she ignored the humble.

They said *Virgo* had invented drudgery and that from her example people had lost the overall design by looking too much at detail.

They said *Libra* had made her Temple of Harmony so attractive that people wished to live in romantic illusions about love, avoiding all struggle.

They said *Scorpio* had fascinated people with dangerous ideas about death, sex and power, pulling them into morbid introspection.

They said *Sagittarius* wanted people to become fanatics. They

spoke of the arrogance of fervent belief, of explorers who trampled all over new found lands.

They said *Capricorn* encouraged people to repress the imagination in order to manage and control the environment.

They said *Aquarius* lived only in the future and ignored the present, and that life was becoming unbalanced by constant and dangerous invention.

They said *Pisces* led people to escape into meaningless dreams. They spoke of the excesses of martyrdom and self-sacrifice, of addiction to suffering.

They said bitter things to each other because they felt so much pain about the state of the Earth and her creatures. Then they sank into a long, brooding silence.

Time passed as despair enshrouded them; they started to lose memory of who they were and looked at each other with blank eyes.

Then, suddenly, out of the bottom of this abyss of despair rose a great cry of rage. They were terrified until they realised the cry came from *Aries*. As each one understood this she started to remember who she was.

They did not know what to do while this dangerous sound still reverberated through the valley. Eventually *Scorpio* rose.

'Sisters,' she said, 'I would like to take you somewhere where we have never been, where air explodes, where fire burns underground and earth runs like water, where all moisture is evaporated into air. Come with me if you will.'

Gradually each one got to her feet and followed *Scorpio*. They walked for days in unfamiliar terrain. They hardly talked, each one remembering the sound of *Aries*' rage and knowing it was her own rage, too, knowing that the cry had saved them from despair but that they had been changed utterly by it.

As *Pisces* walked she had a vision of her brothers. She saw that they, too, were journeying, to a place deep beneath the waves where the salt water eats away even the hardness of iron, where fishes bright as parrots swim through the hulls of wrecked boats. She saw the fear of the waters in their faces, and then sand swirled around them and her vision was gone.

The path the sisters walked led upwards and eventually they reached a mountain-top. There was a massive dark crater from which smoke escaped. The ground was hot.

Capricorn stood still near the rim of the crater. 'I can feel the earth moving deep beneath my feet. As I feel it I realise that this is our Mother, too, as much as the lovely valley.' It was not easy to recognise this truth, for they sensed that the mountain-top might blow apart at any moment.

Cancer said, 'As I stand here I am aware that we could call forth destruction, that from despair we could wish for it, and then everything we love would be destroyed.'

'We are all very frightened,' *Virgo* said clearly, 'and that is wise and justified. Yet we have come here for transformation.'

They were thrown into a long silence, for none knew how that was to be effected.

Eventually *Sagittarius* spoke. 'I believe that we *can* find a new way with our pain and our anger.'

Libra's words were quiet. 'It will mean going beyond blame to find true justice.'

They considered this in the stillness until *Aquarius* wondered aloud. 'How can we make a just world without guilt or blame? We can try to become different people but that will not work. Better for us to face and accept what we are. We each know one thing best; we should decide how we can use what we know for the healing of Earth.' The truth of this reached them all.

'That is right', said *Taurus*, 'But let us not forget our terror and respect for this place. You cannot patch together a volcano's crater, or cover it over, or ignore it,' and she laughed softly, for she would have liked to have ignored it. Her laugh hung on the sulphurous air; then *Leo* started to dance the dance of the laugh, of the child, of the innocence they had lost. She looked small and insignificant against the sides of the volcano but, as she danced higher, she was thrown into sharp silhouette against the yellow-brown sky. She danced around the rim of the crater, and her sisters followed her to stand around the edge in a wide circle and gaze into the smoky earth. They were just close enough to hear *Aries*' words as she shouted them into the smoke.

'I dedicate myself to righteous struggle. I shall be the Warrior until the Earth is healed.'

Taurus cried, 'I dedicate myself to knowing the Earth's needs, I shall be the Caretaker until the Earth is healed.'

Gemini cried, 'I dedicate myself to increasing understanding between people. I shall be the Interpreter.'

Cancer cried, 'I dedicate myself to recognising vulnerability. I shall

be the Protector.'

Leo cried, 'I dedicate myself to the celebration of life. I shall be the Playmaker.'

Virgo cried, 'I dedicate myself to Truth. I shall be its Servant.'

Libra cried, 'I shall be the Bringer of Peace, dedicated to Justice.'

Scorpio cried, 'I dedicate myself to the right use of power, I shall be the Transformer.'

Sagittarius cried, 'I dedicate myself to wisdom. I shall be the Believer.'

Capricorn cried, 'I shall be the Organiser dedicated to our survival.'

Aquarius cried, 'I shall be the Prophet dedicated to a future of equality.'

And *Pisces* cried, 'I am dedicated to the oneness of our experience, and I shall be the Dreamer of Dreams.'

The words of each rang out and reverberated around the rim before sinking into echoes within the crater. After each had told of her commitment they stood still in their circle, but they did not know why they waited.

Then *Gemini* spoke and they realised with surprise that she had been unusually silent except for her words of commitment.

'I am learning how to listen. I am the one who hears messages and I know that we are not alone in the healing.'

Then she whistled to all the birds that had followed her up the mountain, the birds whose language she had learned. They settled upon her arms and shoulders, birds of many shapes and colours.

'They have been watching the Earth,' she said, and released them one by one into the air above her. As they rose each bird sang of what it had seen.

They sang of those who would express their anger rather than give up, and of those who would hear it rather than run away. They sang of women who discovered their own strength at the bottom of a pit of oppression and despair.

They sang of people in pain who discovered kinship and respect for each other, of prisoners whose songs could not be kept behind bars, of soldiers who chose to desert or die rather than torture and kill. They sang of survivors.

The birds flew higher against the yellow sky. Their songs resolved into one great sound; strange and yet familiar.

It was the sound of the healing. It was beginning.

Bibliography

Astrology – General

Addey, John, *Harmonics in Astrology*, Cambridge Circle, 1976.

Arroyo, Stephen, *Astrology, Psychology and the Four Elements*, CRCS Publications, 1975.

Arroyo, Stephen, *Astrology, Karma and Transformation*, CRCS Publications, 1978.

Caine, Mary, *The Glastonbury Zodiac* (published privately), c/o 25 Kingston Hill, Kingston, Surrey, UK.

Caine, Mary, *The Kingston Zodiac* (published privately), c/o 25 Kingston Hill, Kingston, Surrey, UK.

Carter, Charles, *Astrological Aspects*, L N Fowler, 1930.

Collin-Smith, Joyce, *Astrology the Spiral of Life*, Astrological Association of Great Britain, 1980.

Cunningham, Donna, *An Astrological Guide to Self-Awareness*, CRCS Publications, 1978.

Cunningham, Donna, *Being a Lunar Type in a Solar World*, Samuel Weiser, 1982.

Davison, R, *The Technique of Prediction*, L N Fowler, 1955.

Dean, Geoffrey (ed), *Recent Advances in Natal Astrology*, Astrological Association of Great Britain, 1977.

Dobyns, Zipporah, *Expanding Astrology's Universe*, Astro-Computing Services, 1983.

Francia, Luisa, *Berühre Wega, Kehr'zur Erde Zurück – Trancen, Meditationen und Rituale mit Sternen*, Frauenoffensive, 1982.

Gauquelin, Michel, *Cosmic Influences on Human Behaviour*, Fortuna, 1976.

Gauquelin, Michel, *Cosmic Influences on Human Behaviour*, ASI Publications, 1978.

Gilchrist, Cherry, *Planetary Symbolism and Astrology*, Astrological Association of Great Britain, 1980.

Greene, Liz, *Relating: An Astrological Guide to Living with Others on a Small Planet*, Samuel Weiser, 1976.

Greene, Liz, *Saturn*, Samuel Weiser, 1976.

Press, 1977.

Greene, Liz, *Star Signs for Lovers*, Stein & Day, 1980.

Greene, Liz, *The Outer Planets and Their Cycles*, CRCS Publications, 1983.

Greene, Liz, *The Astrology of Fate*, Samuel Weiser, 1984.

Hamaker-Zondag, Karen, *Astro-Psychology – Astrological Symbolism and the Human Psyche*, Samuel Weiser, 1980.

Hand, Robert, *Planets in Transit*, Para Research, 1976.

Hand, Robert, *Horoscope Symbols*, Para Research, 1981.

Hand, Robert, *Planets in Youth*, Para Research, 1981.

Hickley, I, *Astrology, A Cosmic Science*, Fellowship House, 1970.

Holden, R W, *The Elements of House Division*, L N Fowler, 1977.

Hone, Margaret, *Applied Astrology*, L N Fowler, 1953.

Hone, Margaret, *Modern Textbook of Astrology*, L N Fowler, 1978.

Jacobson, Ivy Goldstein, *The Dark Moon Lilith in Astrology* (published privately), California, 1961.

Jansky, Robert, *Interpreting the Eclipses*, Astro Computing Services, 1979.

Jones, Marc Edmund, *The Guide to Horoscope Interpretation*, Quest Books, 1974.

Jones, Marc Edmund, *Sabian Symbols in Astrology*, Shambala Publications, 1978.

Lantero, Ermione, *The Continuing Discovery of Chiron*, Samuel Weiser, 1984.

Lionne, Crystal, *Feminist Astrology*, booklet distributed by Matriarchal Publishing Company, PO Box 113, Encinitas, California 92024, USA.

Lundsted, Betty, *Transits, the Time of Your Life*, Samuel Weiser, 1980.

Mann, Ted, *The Round Art*, Dragons World, 1979.

Marks, Tracy, *How to Handle Your T-Square*, Sagittarius Rising, 1979.

Marks, Tracy, *Principles of Depth Astrology*, Sagittarius Rising.

Mayo, Jeff, *Astrologers' Astronomical Handbook*, L N Fowler, 1965.

Mayo, Jeff, *Astrology*, The English Universities Press (*Teach Yourself Series*), 1964.

Mayo, Jeff, *The Planets and Human Behaviour*, CRCS Publications, 1986.

Messmer, Phoenix and Bärbel, *Venus Ist Noch Fern*, Come Out Lesbenverlag, Munich, 1979.

Meyer, Michael, *A Handbook for the Humanistic Astrologer*, Doubleday, 1974.

Moonfire, Blue, *The Matriarchal Zodiac*, available from Silver Moon, 68 Charing Cross Road, London WC2H 0BB.

Oken, Alan, *Alan Oken's Complete Astrology: A Modern Guide to Astrological Awareness*, Bantam Books, 1980.

Pagan, Isabel, *The Signs of the Zodiac Analysed: From Pioneer to Poet*, Theosophical Publishing House, 1978.

Parker, Derek and Parker, Julia, *The Compleat Astrologer*, Crown. 1984.

Pelletier, Robert, *Planets in Aspect*, Para Research, 1974.

Robson, Vivian, *The Fixed Stars and Constellations in Astrology*, Samuel Weiser, 1970.

Rudhyar, Dane, *Astrological Signs: The Pulse of Life*, Shambala Publications, 1970.

Rudhyar, Dane, *The Astrology of the Personality*, Doubleday, 1970.

Rudhyar, Dane, *The Lunation Cycle*, Aurora Press, 1986.

Rudhyar, Dane, *The Practice of Astrology*, 1968.

Ruperti, Alexander, *Cycles of Becoming: The Planetary Pattern of Growth*, CRCS Publications, 1978.

Sakoian, F, and Acker, L S, *The Astrologer's Handbook*, Harper & Row, 1973.

Schulman, Martin, *Karmic Astrology (Vol. 1): The Moon's Nodes and Reincarnation*, Samuel Weiser, 1978.

Thorsten, Geraldine, *God Herself: The Feminine Roots of Astrology*, Avon Books, 1981.

History of Astrology and Astronomy

Cornell, James, *The First Stargazers*, Scribner, 1981.

Kenton, Warren, *Astrology – The Celestial Mirror*, Avon, 1974.

Krupp, E C (ed), *In Search of Ancient Astronomies*, McGraw Hill, 1979.

Papon, D, *The Lure of the Heavens – A History of Astrology*, Samuel Weiser, 1972.

Parker, Derek, and Parker, Julia, *A History of Astrology*, Andre Deutsch, 1983.

Russell, Eric, *Astrology and Prediction*, Citadel Press, 1975.

Astrology Around the World

Burckhardt, Titus, *Mystical Astrology According to Ibn 'Arabi*, translated from the French by Bulent, Rauf, Beswara Publications, 1977.

Carus, Paul, *Chinese Astrology*, Open Court, 1974.

Dobbin, Rabbi Joel, *Astrological Secrets of the Hebrew Sages*, Inner Traditions International, 1977.

de Kermadec, J-M H, *The Way to Chinese Astrology*, Four Pillars of Destiny, George Allen & Unwin, 1983.

Sun Bear and Wabun, *The Medicine Wheel: Earth Astrology*, Prentice-Hall, 1980.

Tunnicliffe, K, *Aztec Astrology*, L N Fowler, 1979.

Volguine, Alexander, *Lunar Astrology*, ASI Publishers, 1974.

Astrological Tables

The Concise Planetary Ephemeris for 200 to 2050 AD at Midnight, The Hieratic Publishing Co., 1982.

Doane, Doris Chase, *Time Changes in Canada and Mexico*, American Federation of Astrologers, 1968.

Doane, Doris Chase, *Time Changes in the USA*, American Federation of Astrologers, 1968.

Doane, Doris Chase, *Time Changes in the World*, American Federation of Astrologers, 1968.

Michelsen, Neil, *American Book of Tables*, Astro Computing Services 1976.

Michelsen, Neil, *American Ephemeris for the 20th Century*, Astro Computing Services, 1983.

Michelsen, Neil, and Pottenger, Rique, *The Asteroid Ephemeris*, TIA Publications, 1977.

Women's Biography and Female Experience

Chicago, Judy, *The Dinner Party*, Anchor Press/Doubleday, NY, 1979.

Fernea, Elizabeth Warnock and Bezirgan, Basima Qattan (eds), *Middle Eastern Muslim Women Speak*, University of Texas Press, Austin and London, 1977.

Frank, Anne, *The Diary of Anne Frank*, Pan Books, 1954.

Frauen in der Kunst, *Kunstlerinnen International 1877-1977 – Catalogue of the Exhibition*, NGBK, Berlin, 1977.

Giffin, F C (ed) *Woman as Revolutionary*, (Mentor Books) New American Library, 1973.

Griffin, Susan, *Pornography and Silence*, The Women's Press, 1981.

Henry, Sandra and Taitz, Emily, *Written Out of History – Our Jewish Foremothers*, Biblio Press, 1983.

Hull, Gloria T, Scott, Patricia Bell, and Smith, Barbara (eds), *But Some of Us are Brave – Black Women's Studies*, The Feminist Press (US), 1982.

Hussain, Freda (ed), *Muslim Women,* St. Martin's Press, 1984.

Keller, Helen, *The Miracle of a Life,* Hodder & Stoughton (undated).

Lessing, Doris, *The Four-Gated City,* NAL, 1976.

Loewenberg, B J, and Bogin, Ruth, *Black Women in Nineteenth Century American Life*, Pennsylvania State University Press, 1976.

Merchant, Carolyn, *The Death of Nature – Women, Ecology and the Scientific Revolution*, Harper & Row, 1980.

Millay, Edna St Vincent, *Collected Lyrics,* Harper & Row, 1981.

Noble, Jeanne, *Beautiful, also, are the Souls of my Black Sisters,* Prentice-Hall, Englewood Cliffs, New Jersey, 1978.

Olschack, Blanche C (ed), *Lexicon der Frau*, Encyclios, Verlag A G, Zurich, 1953.

Rodden, Lois, *Profiles of Women – A Collection of Astrological Biographies*, American Federation of Astrologers, 1979.

Sicherman, Barbara and Green, Carol Hurd (eds), *Notable American Women – The Modern Period*, The Belknap Press; Harvard University Press, London, 1980.

Sterling, D, *Black Foremothers*, The Feminist Press (US), 1979.

Sweetman, James, *Women Leaders in African History*, Heinemann Educational Books, 1984.

Walker, Alice, *In Search of Our Mothers' Gardens*, Harcourt, Brace, Jovanovich, 1984.

The World Who's Who of Women, Melrose Press, 1982.

Mythology, Religion and History

Allen, R, *Star Names: Their Lore and Meaning*, Dover Publications Inc., 1963.

Alpers, A, *Maori Myths and Tribal Legends*, Murray, London, 1964.

Apuleius, *The Golden Ass*, translated by Robert Graves, Indiana University Press, 1962.

Ashe, Geoffrey, *King Arthur's Avalon*, Fontana, 1973.

Ashe, Geoffrey, *The Virgin*, Routledge & Kegan Paul, 1976.

Ayisi, Eric D, *An Introduction to the Study of African Culture*, Heinemann, 1979.

Bakhtiar, Laleh, *Sufi Expressions of the Mystic Quest*, Thames & Hudson, 1976.

Bates, Brian, *The Way of Wyrd – The Book of a Sorcerer's Apprentice*, Harper & Row, 1984.

Begg, Ean, *Myth and Today's Consciousness*, Coventure, 1984.

Blair, Lawrence, *Rhythms of Vision*, Croom Helm, 1975.

Branigan, Professor K (ed), *The Atlas of Archaeology*, St. Martin's Press, 1983.

Brunton, Paul, *A Search in Secret Egypt*, Samuel Weiser, 1984.

Campbell, Joseph, *The Masks of God – Oriental Mythology*, Souvenir Press, 1973.

Chambers's Encyclopaedia.

Christ and Plaskow (eds), *Womanspirit Rising – A Feminist Reader in Religion*, Harper & Row, 1979.

Cirlot, Juan, *A Dictionary of Symbols*, Routledge & Kegan Paul, 1972.

Colegrave, Sukie, *The Spirit of the Valley – Androgyny and Chinese Thought*, Virago, 1979.

Collier's Encyclopedia, Macmillan Educational Corporation, 1979.

Critchlow, Keith, *Islamic Patterns*, Thames & Hudson, 1976.

Critchlow, Keith, *Time Stands Still*, Gordon Fraser, 1979.

Cumont, Franz, *Astrology and Religion Among the Greeks and Romans*, Dover Publications Inc., NY, 1960.

Dames, Michael, *Avebury*, Thames & Hudson, 1977.

Despard, Charlotte, *Theosophy and the Woman's Movement*, Theosophical Publishing Society, 1913.

Diop, Cheikh Anta, *The African Origin of Civilisation – Myth or Reality*, translated from the French by Mercer Cook, Lawrence Hill & Company, 1974.

Douglas, Alfred, *The Oracle of Change – How to Consult the I Ching*, Penguin, 1972.

DuBois, W E B, *The World and Africa*, International Publishers Co. Inc, NY, 1965.

Durdin-Robertson, Lawrence, *Goddesses of Chaldea, Syria and Egypt*, Cesara Publications, Eire, 1975.

Easlea, Brian, *Magic, Witch Hunting and the New Philosophy*, Humanities Press, 1981.

Ehrenreich, Barbara and English, Dierdre, *Witches, Midwives and Nurses – A History of Women Healers*, The Feminist Press, SUNY/College, NY, 1973.

Ellis-Davidson, Hilda R, *Gods and Myths of Northern Europe*, Penguin, 1969.

Encyclopaedia Britannica.

Encyclopedia Judaica, Keter Publishing House, Jerusalem, 1971.

Everyman's Encyclopaedia.

Fagan, Cyril, *Zodiacs Old and New*, Anscombe, London, 1951.

Fagan, Cyril, *Astrological Origins*, Llewellyn, 1971.

Fainlight, Ruth, *Sibyls and Others (Poems)*, Hutchinson, 1980.

Ferguson, Marilyn, *The Aquarian Conspiracy*, J P Tarcher, 1981.

Ferm, V (ed), *Ancient Religions*, The Philosophical Library, NY, 1950.

Frazer, James, *The Golden Bough*, Macmillan, 1955.

Gimbutas, Marija, *The Gods and Goddesses of Old Europe, 7000-3500 BC*, University of California Press, 1982.

Gleadow, Rupert, *The Origin of the Zodiac*, Jonathan Cape, 1968.

Goldenberg, Naomi, *The Changing of the Gods*, Beacon Press, 1979.

Gordon, C, *Forgotten Scripts*, Basic Books, 1982.

Graves, Robert, *The Greek Myths (2 vols)*, Penguin, 1955.

Graves, Robert, *The White Goddess*, Farrar, Straus & Giroux, 1966.

Grian, Sinead Sula, *Brighde – Goddess of Fire*, available from Brighde's Fire, Glastonbury, Somerset, 1985.

Griffin, William, *Endtime – The Doomsday Catalogue*, Macmillan, 1979.

Hall, Nor, *The Moon and the Virgin*, Harper & Row, 1981.

Harding, M Esther, *Woman's Mysteries – Ancient and Modern*, Harper & Row, 1976.

Harrison, Jane, *Prolegomena to the Study of Greek Religion*, Humanities Press, 1981.

Harrison, Jane, *Themis – A Study of the Social Origins of Greek Religion*, Merlin Press, 1963.

Hastings, James (ed), *Encyclopedia of Religion and Ethics*, (Vol 12), 'Sun, Moon and Stars', Fortress, 1926.

Hinnells, John R (ed), *A Handbook of Living Religions*, Viking, Penguin Books, 1984.

Hope, Murry, *Practical Egyptian Magic*, The Aquarian Press, 1984.

Huxley, Francis, *The Way of the Sacred*, St. Martin's Press, 1986.

The Jewish Encyclopedia.

Jones, Gwyn and Jones, Thomas, *The Mabinogion*, E P Dutton, New York, 1978.

Lamy, L, *Egyptian Mysteries, New Light on Ancient Knowledge*, Crossroads Press, 1981.

Lao Tsu, *Tao Te Ching*, translated from the Chinese by Feng, Gia-fu and English, Jane, Random House, 1972.

The New Larousse Encyclopedia of Mythology, Paul Hamlyn, 1968.

Le Strange, Richard, *A History of Herbal Plants*, Arco Publishing Co., NY, 1977.

Lewis, H D and Slater, Robert Lawson, *The Study of Religions*, Pelican, 1969.

Lloyd-Jones, Hugh, *Myths of the Zodiac*, St. Martin's Press.

Mallowan, M E L, *Early Mesopotamia and Iran*, Thames & Hudson, London, 1965.

Matt, D C, *The Zohar*, Paulist Press, 1982.

Matthews, Caitlin and Matthews, John, *The Western Way (Vol 1)* – *A Practical Guide to the Mystery Tradition*, Methuen Inc., 1986.

Monaghan, Patricia, *The Book of Goddesses and Heroines*, E P Dutton, 1981.

Mozans, H J, *Women in Science*, MIT Press, 1974.

Murray, Alexander, *Manual of Mythology*, Charles Scribner's Sons, New York, 1887.

Murray, Margaret, *The God of the Witches*, OUP, 1970.

Mutwa, Credo, *My People – Writings of a Zulu Witch-Doctor*, Penguin, 1971.

National Geographic Magazine, article by Alexander Marshack, January 1975.

National Geographic Magazine, December 1975.

Neumann, Erich, *The Great Mother – An Analysis of the Archetype*, Princeton University Press, Bollinger Foundation, 1972.

The New Standard Jewish Encyclopedia.

Nicolson, Irene, *Mexican and Central American Mythology*, Newnes Books, 1967.

Noble, Vicki, *Motherpeace – A Way to the Goddess*, Harper & Row, 1983.

O'Flaherty, Wendy Doniger, *Hindu Myths*, Penguin, 1975.

Oliver, R and Fage, J D, *A Short History of Africa*, Pelican, 1962.

Pagels, Elaine, *The Gnostic Gospels*, Weidenfeld & Nicolson, 1980; Pelican, 1982.

Pagels, Elaine, *The Gnostic Gospels*, Random House, 1981.

Parker, Henry, *Stone Circles in Gambia*, The Journal of the Royal Anthropological Institute, Vol 53, 1923.

Parrinder, G, *African Traditional Religion*, Greenwood Press, 1976.

Parrinder, G, *Witchcraft*, Penguin, 1958.

Patai, Ralph, *The Hebrew Goddess*, Avon/Discus, 1967.

Poignant, Roslyn, *Myths and Legends of the South Seas*, Hamlyn, 1970.

Purce, Jill, *The Mystic Spiral*, Thames & Hudson, 1974.

Rola, S de, *Alchemy*, Thames & Hudson, 1973.

Ravenscroft, Trevor, *The Cup of Destiny*, Samuel Weiser, 1982.

Rawson, Philip, *The Art of Tantra*, Thames & Hudson, 1973.

Rees, Alwyn and Rees, Brinley, *Celtic Heritage*, Thames & Hudson, 1961.

Reynolds, Vernon and Tanner, Ralph, *The Biology of Religion*, Longman, 1983.

Roberts, J M, *The Pelican History of the World*, Penguin, 1976.

Robinson, H Wheeler, *The History of Israel*, Longwood Publishing Group, 1967.

Rothenberg, Jerome (ed), *Technicians of the Sacred*, University of California Press, 1985.

Schnapper, Edith, *The Inward Odyssey – The Concept of the Way in the Great Religions of the World*, George Allen & Unwin, 1965.

Seligmann, Kurt, *Magic, Supernaturalism and Religion*, Paladin, 1971.

Sen, K M, *Hinduism*, Penguin, 1961.

Sesti, G M, Mann IV, AT, Flanagan, M and Cowan, P, *The Phenomenon Book of Calendars 1979-80*, Phenomenon Publications, 1978.

Shah, Idries, *The Way of the Sufi*, E P Dutton, 1970.

Sharkey, John, *Celtic Mysteries – The Ancient Religion*, Avon Books, 1975.

Shuttle, Penelope and Redgrove, Peter, *The Wise Wound*, Gollancz, 1978.

Sieveking, Ann, *The Cave Artists*, Thames & Hudson, 1979.

Sjoo, Monica and Mor, Barbara, *The Ancient Religion of the Great Cosmic Mother of All*, Rainbow Press, 1981.

Spretnak, Charlene, *The Lost Goddesses of Early Greece*, Beacon Press, 1978.

Spretnak, Charlene (ed) *The Politics of Women's Spirituality*, Anchor/Doubleday, 1982.

Starhawk, *The Spiral Dance – A Rebirth of the Ancient Religion of the Great Goddess*, Harper & Row, 1981.

Stewart, Bob, *The Waters of the Gap – The Mythology of Aquae Sulis*, Bath City Council, 1981.

Stewart, R J, *The Prophetic Vision of Merlin*, Methuen Inc., 1986.

Stone, Merlin, *The Paradise Papers*, Virago, 1976.

Stone, Merlin, *Ancient Mirrors of Womanhood (2 vols)*, Beacon Press, 1987.

Suzuki, Shunryu, *Zen Mind, Beginner's Mind*, Weatherhill, NY and Tokyo, 1970.

Swiney, Frances, *The Ancient Road, or the Development of the Soul*, Bell, 1918.

Taylor, Henry Osborn, *The Classical Heritage of the Middle Ages*, Macmillan, NY, 1911.

Temple, R K G, *The Sirius Mystery*, St. Martin's Press, 1978.

Toulson, Shirley, *The Winter Solstice*, Jill Norman & Hobhouse, 1981.

Vajranatha and Klapecki, Lynne, *Tibetan Astrological Calendar and Almanac*, Kalachakra Publications, Kathmandu, 1978.

Velikovsky, Immanuel, *Worlds in Collision*, William Morrow, 1984.

Vogh, James, *Arachne Rising*, Dial Press, NY, 1977.

Walker, Barbara, *The Woman's Encyclopedia of Myths and Secrets*, Harper & Row, 1983.

Waters, Frank, *Book of the Hopi*, Penguin, 1977.

Wemoon Almanac 1986, c/o Musawa, La Serre Darre, Pouzac 65200, France.

Weston, Jessie L, *From Ritual to Romance*, Doubleday/Anchor, 1957.

Wex, Marianne, *Let's Take Back Our Space*, Frauenliteraturverlag, Hermine Fees, 1979.

Whitmont, Edward, *The Return of the Goddess – Femininity, Aggression and the Modern Grail Quest*, Routledge & Kegan Paul, 1982.

Wind, Edgar, *Pagan Mysteries in the Renaissance*, W W Norton & Co., 1969.

Witt, R E, *Isis in the Graeco-Roman World*, Thames & Hudson, 1971.

Wolkstein, Diane and Kramer, Samuel, *Inanna – Queen of Heaven and Earth*, Harper & Row, 1983.

Worsfold, Sir Cato T, *The History of the Vestal Virgins of Rome*, Rider & Co., 1934.

X, Malcolm, *On Afro-American History*, Pathfinder Press, NY, 1970.

Health, Healing, Counselling and Psychology

Cornell, H L, *Encyclopedia of Medical Astrology*, Samuel Weiser, 1972.

Ernst, Sheila and Goodison, Lucy, *In Our Own Hands – A Book of Self-Help Therapy*, The Women's Press, 1981.

Ferucci, Piero, *What We May Be – The Visions and Techniques of Psychosynthesis*, Turnstone Press, 1982.

von Franz, Marie-Louise, *Lectures on Jung's Typology*, Spring Publications, 1971.

Geddes, Sheila, *Astrology and Health*, Aquarian Press, 1981.

Harding, Esther, *The I and the Not I*, Princeton University Press, 1965.

Jansky, Robert, *Astrology, Nutrition and Health*, Para Research, 1977.

Jung, C G, *Synchronicity*, Princeton University Press, 1973.

Kübler-Ross, Elizabeth, *On Death and Dying*, Macmillan, 1969.

Millard, Margaret, *Casenotes of a Medical Astrologer*, Samuel Weiser, 1984.

Naumann, Eileen, *American Book of Nutrition and Medical Astrology*, Astro Computing Services, 1982.

Perera, Sylvia Brinton, *Descent to the Goddess – A Way of Initiation for Women*, Inner City Books, 1981.

Pottenger, Maritha, *Healing with the Horoscope: A Guide to Counselling*, Astro Computing Services, 1982.

Rose, Christina, *Astrological Counselling*, Newcastle Publishing Co., 1983.

Rosenblum, Bernard, *The Astrologer's Guide to Counselling*, CRCS Publications, 1983.

Tyl, Noel, *The Principles and Practice of Astrology, Vol 9: Special Horoscope Dimensions – Success, Sex and Illness*, Llewellyn, 1977.

Vithoulkas, George, *The Science of Homeopathy*, Grove Press, NY, 1980.

Vries, Marco de, *The Redemption of the Intangible in Medicine*, Institute of Psychosynthesis, London, 1981.

Whitmont, E, *Psyche and Substance*, North Atlantic Books, 1980.

Index

Lindsay River originally trained as a drama teacher after graduating in English from Cambridge. She has studied astrology and interpreted horoscopes since 'the disintegration of my rigid scepticism in 1973'.

She has been inspired by many ancient cultures, by the Women's Movement, the Welsh hills, the Arizona desert, and by the natural healing force of the body.

In 1984 she completed four years of training in holistic medicine. She has a practice in London, where she also teaches astrology, works as an astrological counsellor and continues her own research and writing.

Sally Gillespie is a New Zealand born astrologer currently running a holistic health practice in Sydney, Australia. Her work incorporates astrology, herbalism, massage and the insights of Jungian psychology. She has a firm belief that a connection with the creativity and wisdom of the unconscious is basic to well-being.

After studying in London she went to Sydney in 1982 to work at the Women's Healing Centre as a practitioner and a teacher. In 1984 she returned to London to co-write *The Knot of Time* at Lindsay's invitation.